CHRISTMAS IN CANADA

CHRISTMAS IN CANADA

Heartwarming Legends, Tales, and Traditions

HOLIDAY

PUBLISHED BY ALTITUDE PUBLISHING CANADA LTD.
1500 Railway Avenue, Canmore, Alberta T1W 1P6
www.altitudepublishing.com
1-800-957-6888

Extreme care has been taken to ensure that all information presented in
this book is accurate and up to date. Neither the author nor the
publisher can be held responsible for any errors.

Publisher	Stephen Hutchings
Associate Publisher	Kara Turner
Series Editor	Jill Foran

We acknowledge the financial support of the Government
of Canada through the Book Publishing Industry Development
Program (BPIDP) for our publishing activities.

Altitude GreenTree Program
Altitude Publishing will plant twice as many trees as were used
in the manufacturing of this product.

We acknowledge the support of the Canada Council for the Arts which
in 2003 invested $21.7 million in writing and publishing throughout Canada.

Canada Council   Conseil des Arts
for the Arts   du Canada

National Library of Canada Cataloguing in Publication Data

Christmas in Canada / edited by Jill Foran.

(Amazing stories)
Includes bibliographical references.
ISBN 1-55153-759-1

1. Christmas--Canada. I. Foran, Jill II. Series: Amazing stories
(Canmore, Alta.)

GT4987.15.C5636 2004   394.2663'0971   C2004-903755-2

An application for the trademark for Amazing Stories™
has been made and the registered trademark is pending.

Printed and bound in Canada by Friesens
2 4 6 8 9 7 5 3 1

Contents

Editor's Note

All of the tales featured in *Christmas in Canada* have been taken from the five books that make up Altitude Publishing's Amazing Stories Christmas series: *Christmas in Atlantic Canada*, by Joyce Glasner; *Christmas in Quebec*, by Megan Durnford; *Christmas in Ontario*, by Cheryl MacDonald; and *Christmas in the Prairies* and *Christmas in British Columbia*, by Rich Mole. Each of these books explores the same Christmas themes and topics, and it is fascinating to note the unique voices and perspectives that the authors have brought to their regional audiences. As you read through this collection of holiday stories, you may notice differences in writing style, in approach, and in regional material. However, you will also see many similarities in the ways that Canadians across the country celebrate the most festive of seasons. Organized by chapter and then region for easy navigation, the *Christmas in Canada* collection reflects our country's diversity and celebrates our shared Christmas traditions.

Introduction

anada is a land made for Christmas. Most areas in this country have snow in December, turning the drab, early-winter landscape into a dazzling whiteness worthy of a Christmas card. Most Canadians live within easy distance of vast stretches of open land, close to the pines, cedar, and spruce that epitomize the holiday season. And, despite urban sprawl and modernization, we have managed to preserve enough historic architecture to effortlessly re-create Christmas scenes that seem to have been lifted right out of the pages of Dickens.

At first glance, many of our Christmas traditions appear to have come from the same source, Victorian England. Cedar garlands strung along railings, holly arranged on mantelpieces, mistletoe dangling from doorways, caroling, and festive toasts — all are part of that legacy. Even the Christmas tree, which originated in Germany, comes to us in part because of Queen Victoria and Prince Albert's holiday celebration.

But Christmas was celebrated in Canada long before Victorian times. Well before roast turkey and goose graced festive tables, early settlers dined on local fare — fish caught in rushing streams, deer from the vast forests, beaver tail or moose nose. Tourtière, the savoury French-Canadian pie now made with pork or beef, was originally filled with the meat of passenger pigeons.

From the earliest time of European settlement, Canadians have adapted Old World Christmas traditions to New World conditions. The result has been a uniquely Canadian blend. For instance, when French priest Jean de Brébeuf wrote the first Canadian Christmas carol for the Huron of his Ontario mission in 1643, he combined a French folk tune, Christian traditions, and Native hunters in a lyrical ballad. *Jesous Ahatonhia*, familiar from coast to coast as the "Huron Carol," remains one of the most haunting and most *Canadian* sounds of the season.

Despite such shared traditions, it is difficult to define Christmas in Canada. Outside of Newfoundland, few Canadians engage in mumming, where men and women cross-dress, cover their faces, and visit their neighbours to enjoy food and drink. Many Canadians have never tasted *kolach*, the traditional bread served during Ukrainian Christmas festivities. If you are a Newfoundlander or a Ukrainian-Canadian, mummers and *kolach* are an integral part of seasonal celebrations. If you are not, both may seem interesting and exotic, but hardly necessary for a memorable Christmas.

One thing that is common across the country is the range of emotions the season evokes. When we celebrate the holiday, we are often caught in a kind of mental time warp. On the one hand, there is Christmas Present, the here-and-now occasion. On the other, there is Christmas Past, all the other Christmases we remember. Existing side by side in our hearts and minds, Christmas Past and Christmas Present colour our perceptions of the holiday, stirring up a gamut of emotions, ranging from overwhelming sadness to joy.

Generally thought of as one of the happiest days of the year, Christmas can be one of the most bittersweet. More than any other day, Christmas is when we want to reach out, to say or show how much we love the people who are important to us. When we cannot, we long for the faces and places we love. Immigrants to Canada, from the earliest settlers to recent arrivals, have felt this as they celebrate far from homelands and families they may never see again. So have other Canadians with loved ones far away. Perhaps the most bittersweet Christmases, though, were those experienced during wartime, when, in addition to the loneliness of separation, there was the gnawing anxiety that the empty chair at the table might never be filled again.

But Christmas is primarily a time of joy and thanksgiving. There is the exuberant excitement of children who cannot wait to see what Santa Claus has brought them, the quiet contentment of elders surrounded by beloved generations of family. There is the joy of reunion, especially after a long separation. And, ideally, there is also much gratitude, as people reflect on the richness that surrounds them: the loveliness of the land, the artistry of Christmas ornaments, the unique, irreplaceable beauty of cherished family and friends.

Charity toward others is one of the hallmarks of the season as well. Christmas is the season of light, not just the flickering of candlelight or the glow of electric decorations, but the spiritual light within each one of us. At this special time of year, that light shines a little more brightly, warming those around us through gestures of compassion, whether they are one person's spontaneous act of kindness or the carefully organized work of volunteer groups. Sometimes, those charitable acts send out ripples that continue to be felt decades after. For example, every year, the city of Halifax sends a Christmas tree to the people of Boston, Massachusetts, in gratitude for the assistance the American city provided after the Halifax Explosion of 1917.

Christmas in Canada includes stories of charity, inspiration, separation, reunion, and celebration. It looks at diverse regional events, harrowing holiday adventures, and heartwarming tales of inspiration. Each tale is as different and distinctive as a hand-carved Christmas ornament, conveying the details of how specific people celebrated specific Christmases in specific times and places.

Examine each story, savouring the individuality, the special characteristics that set it apart, that particular time and place. Then step back a little, just as you would after decorating your family Christmas tree. Look at the stories all together, how they sparkle and complement one another, how they show the spirit of Christmas transcending time and place. You'll come away with a deeper understanding of what Christmas means to all Canadians.

Cheryl MacDonald
Nanticoke, Ontario

Chapter 1
Christmas Traditions

Atlantic Canada

hristmas just wouldn't be Christmas without the myths, rituals, and traditions that give the holiday its special flavour. Throughout the centuries, some of the most colourful customs of the season, from mumming to hunting the wren, have been observed in Atlantic Canada.

The Twelve Days of Christmas

Although the Twelve Days of Christmas are all but obsolete today, they were once a vital and significant part of Atlantic Canada's Christmas season. In fact, just about every other tradition of the season is somehow connected to these twelve days. It was during the Twelve Days of Christmas, for example, that the tree was put up (and taken down again), the Yule log was lit, the mummers went mumming and the belsnicklers belsnickling.

The Twelve Days of Christmas, which fall between December 25 and January 6, were first instituted in the sixth century. In those early days of Christianity, Church leaders were eager to convert as many pagans as possible. One way of doing this, they reasoned, was to replace pagan festivals and feast days with Christian ones. For several centuries prior to the birth of Christ, the weeks between December 21 and January 6 had always been a time for celebration. From the commemoration of the rebirth of the sun during the winter solstice, to the Germanic festival of Yule (which marked the passing of the old year and beginning of the new), these two weeks were filled with great ritual and ceremony. So it was no small coincidence that church leaders chose December 25 as the date of the Nativity and January 6 as the Epiphany, with various saint's days filling up the calendar in between. By superimposing their own holidays on those of ancient pagan feast days, Church leaders not only eased the transition from paganism to Christianity, they also created the much-loved Twelve Days of Christmas.

During the Victorian era, the Twelve Days of Christmas were packed with solemn church services, festive parties, and lavish balls. And in Halifax in the 1850s, the biggest social event of the year was the Twelfth Night ball at Government House.

In 1853, an 18-year-old socialite named Sarah Clinch recorded the events leading up to that dazzling event in her diary. On December 24 she wrote: "We have received an invitation to the Uniacke's [Attorney General Richard John Uniacke] next Thursday and another to an 'At Home' at Government House on Twelfth Night. It is on Twelfth Night that the ring is drawn for. I wish I could get it. It is worth ten dollars and whoever draws it opens the ball with the Governor."

For the next twelve days, Sarah recorded all of her daily activities — the visiting, the dances, the church services, the shopping, and most importantly, the preparations for the ball on Twelfth Night. Her anticipation is palpable in the detailed descriptions of what she planned to wear and how she would do her hair for the event. On January 5 she wrote: "... I am to have my hair flattened tonight at Mrs. Moren's to try the effect and if it is good, I will wear it to Government House tomorrow." She also daydreamed about who would be there and, more importantly, with whom she would dance. "As it is to be the only 'At Home' at the house for the season, it will be very large and there will be no ring ... Charlie Almon is going to take a pencil to Government House tomorrow for me to write down the names of my dancing partners as I forgot this evening once I was engaged to him. He has engaged me for the second quadrille tomorrow evening."

Finally, the highly anticipated day arrived: "Jan. 6. Twelfth Night. I was so tired that I had to lie down this afternoon so as to be able to go to Government House tonight." That evening, Sarah would have been resplendent in her new gown, a gauzy, elaborate creation that she and the seamstress had worked on for hours that week. "My dress will be Indian muslin double skirt with three rows of narrow satin ribbon on each skirt, breadth of crepe and ribbon flowers in my bosom," she wrote. "And a very pretty wreath in my hair which will be braided behind and curled in front."

It was a fairytale evening, with Sarah and her cousin Miriam being escorted to the ball by "the Chipman's." Government House was undoubtedly decked out in garlands of greenery with a lavishly decorated Christmas tree in the main ballroom, but the 18-year-old was far too busy floating around the dance floor to pay much attention to the decorations. As she later wrote with satisfaction, "I danced every quadrille and was engaged for six more, when the ball broke up."

Mummers and Belsnicklers

Perhaps the most colourful tradition connected to the Twelve Days of Christmas is mumming. This ancient custom of dressing up in costumes and parading through the streets began in Europe in the Middle Ages. The tradition is believed to have sprung from the Romans' Saturnalia festival. Brought to Newfoundland with the first English and Irish settlers, mumming became a popular form of entertainment among the working class during the Christmas season. Members of the upper class, however, abhorred the practice. They felt mumming was a crass form of entertainment, and that mummers were no better than everyday hooligans.

There were two forms of mumming in Newfoundland. In the urban areas, mummers paraded through the streets, while those in the outlying areas usually went door to door like children at Halloween. By the mid-19th century, the rowdy antics of the mummers, or "Jannies" as they were known in some areas, had gotten completely out of hand. Throughout the Twelve Days of Christmas, large gangs of mummers would parade through the narrow streets of St. John's led by a hobbyhorse. Wearing masks, outrageous hats, and white shirts bedecked with hundreds of coloured ribbons, the mummers cavorted after the hobbyhorse, mocking and harassing those who gathered to watch the spectacle. Many mummers carried small bags of flour, or "bladders" filled with pebbles, which they pelted at the innocent bystanders. Some even carried whips, with which they threatened those not in costumes. Occasionally, the mummers performed a play involving characters such as Saint George, the Grand Turk, a doctor, and others. But more often than not they just acted up.

On December 28, 1861, the situation reached a breaking point in Bay Roberts. That day, Isaac Mercer and his two brothers-in-law were making their way home after a long day's work in the woods when they spied a group of men wearing grotesque masks heading in their direction. Before Mercer and his companions knew it, the mummers had surrounded them. The masked men drunkenly taunted Mercer and his companions, and a brawl broke out. Mercer was the first to hit the ground. In a frenzy, the masked men fell upon him, kicking and beating him until he stopped struggling. Fearing they may have killed him, the mummers staggered off into the darkness.

After picking Mercer up and carrying him home, his companions fetched the doctor. Once he had examined the victim, the doctor reluctantly informed Mercer's young wife that her husband's skull was fractured. There was little that could be done for him. Tragically, Isaac Mercer died early the following morning.

The vicious beating death of Isaac Mercer shocked the people of Newfoundland. The fact that the attackers had been disguised in their mumming costumes and couldn't be identified sent a chill through the population of Bay Roberts and beyond. The public outcry against mumming reached a fevered pitch. And on June 25, 1861, an act outlawing the tradition was passed. The act, "to Make Further Provision for the Prevention of Nuisances," declared that, "Any person who shall be found at any season of the year, in any Town or Settlement in this colony, without a written licence from the Magistrate, dressed as a Mummer, masked or otherwise disguised, shall be deemed to be guilty of a Public Nuisance, and may be arrested by any Peace Officer..." If found guilty of the crime, the offender would be "committed to Gaol for a Period not exceeding Seven Days" or fined up to 20 shillings, which was about a week's wages for the average person at the time.

Still, despite the ban, the custom lived on in rural communities. Today, "going out in the mummers" is still practised in many parts of Newfoundland during the Christmas season. Beginning on December 26, men and women dress up in costumes and travel from house to house knocking on doors. When the door is opened, the question, "Any mummers 'llowed in tonight?" is posed in "mummer talk," which consists of disguising the voice by using ingressive speech. Once inside, the mummers amuse their hosts by dancing, singing, and talking mummer talk. They remain in disguise until the hosts guess their identities. Then the masks come off and refreshments are served.

In Lunenburg County, Nova Scotia, the ritual of dressing in costumes and going door to door at Christmas is known as belsnickling. Like mummers, belsnicklers wear masks to disguise their identities. There are a few different theories about the origin of the word "belsnickling." One theory suggests that it sprang from the fact that the men used to dress up in ox hides and wear bells around their necks when they went out on their rounds. A more likely theory is that "belsnickles" was an abbreviation of "The Bells of Saint Nicholas." Belsnicklers frequently carry musical instruments on their rounds and entertain their hosts with a musical performance before being served refreshments.

Many in Lunenburg County feel that belsnickling is one of the best things about the holiday season. Ron Barkhouse of New Ross remembers the thrill of getting dressed up and going out belsnickling with his cousins back in the 1930s and 40s. "The main objective," he says, "was to disguise your identity."

The belsnicklers' costumes are usually quite simple. Often they consist of nothing more than a fisherman's scallop bag or a paper bag (with eyeholes cut out) covering the head, and some old clothes (usually those of the opposite sex). Some belsnicklers, however, are a little more creative in their costume designs. Barkhouse remembers a man coming to his door one year dressed as a house, his head concealed in a cardboard box painted up to look like a chimney!

Hunting the Wren

Like mumming, the hunting of the wren also came to Newfoundland with the early settlers. Until late in the 19th century in many parts of Newfoundland, packs of boys marched from house to house with a dead wren attached to a pole topped with greenery and ribbons on St. Stephen's Day (Boxing Day). As they paraded through the streets, the boys would sing, "The wren, the wren, / The king of all birds, / On St. Stephen's Day / Is caught in the furze."

This curious ritual is another example of the residual influence of ancient paganism on this holiday season. Pagans held the wren in high esteem, calling it the "King of all Birds." It was believed that since the wren was so mighty, its ritualistic sacrifice would appease the gods, guaranteeing good luck for the coming year. Though the Christian Church frowned upon it, the custom somehow survived into the 20th century. However, in later years, a facsimile often replaced the actual wren.

Talking Animals

In one way or another, animals have always been an important part of Christmas in Atlantic Canada. In the Eastern Passage area of Nova Scotia, folks tell the tale of the Christmas when one of the locals was frightened to death by his team of oxen. It was around midnight one Christmas Eve when the old man happened into the barn and overheard his oxen having a conversation. Word has it that one oxen said to the other: "This time tomorrow we'll be hauling wood for our master's coffin." Overcome with fright at this astonishing occurrence, the old man keeled over and died right on the spot.

The myth of animals miraculously being endowed with the gift of human speech at the stroke of midnight on Christmas Eve is still believed by many throughout the Maritime Provinces. It is said that at midnight, oxen and cows in the manger will sink to their knees and begin talking. But if a person should happen to overhear their conversation, he or she won't live to see the next Christmas. This myth, which has been passed on for centuries, has a number of variations. One version tells of people being struck blind when they attempt to witness the miraculous occurrence. Others suggest the cows don't actually speak, but sink to their knees and low in adoration, just as they did in Bethlehem the night that Christ was born.

The Yuletide Tree

One custom that was practiced in Halifax during the Victorian era included animals in the celebrations in an interesting manner. During the Christmas season in the late 1800s, a special "Yuletide tree" was erected at the foot of George Street in downtown Halifax. Rather than being decorated with the usual strings of cranberries, popcorn, and glass ornaments, however, this tree had apples and containers of oats dangling from its branches. The fruit and grain were special Christmas treats for the many cabbie horses that spent their days and nights hauling fares up and down the cobblestone streets of the city. On Christmas Eve, the cabbies would take their horses to the Yuletide tree for their Christmas treat. Once motorized vehicles replaced horses as the main mode of transportation, the custom died out. But in 1960, some 55 years after it had disappeared, the tradition was revived. This time, the treats on the Yuletide tree weren't for horses, but for the birds.

Like most things, Christmas customs and rituals are constantly changing to reflect society's values. Many traditions that were once a significant part of the holiday season have gradually died out, or have been replaced by new customs. For example, Atlantic Canadians no longer hunt the wren at Christmas; instead, they honour animals by featuring them in live nativity scenes and processions. Of course, there are some holiday traditions — such as mumming and bel-snickling — that have changed very little over the centuries, and these will likely remain a part of the Christmas season for many years to come.

Quebec

n Quebec, the Christmas holiday season is known as *Les Fêtes*. Today, there are many similarities between how Quebecers and other Canadians celebrate this season. However, for hundreds of years, up until the early part of the 20th century, *Les Fêtes* involved a unique set of religious and secular celebrations between Christmas Eve and Epiphany (January 6).

A Rural Christmas Scenario
In the 19th century, a typical family in Quebec would begin to prepare for Christmas weeks and weeks before the holiday arrived. The older children in the family spent countless hours rehearsing Christmas hymns for the midnight mass, Mother prepared special clothes for the sacred event, and all of the family members worked together to prepare festive

dishes for the *réveillon,* or wake-up meal.

Around the first week of December, Father butchered a fattened pig, some chickens, and a sheep. Then, Mother and the aunts spent long days preparing sausages, ham, blood pudding, and meat pies. The women also prepared a host of sweets, such as doughnuts and dessert pies. The summer kitchen (a small room attached to the house but not heated during the winter) was packed with delicacies.

By the time Christmas Eve finally arrived, the children could hardly contain their excitement. After devouring stacks of pancakes in the early evening, those who were over the age of 14 — and therefore entitled to go to midnight mass — took short naps. They knew that shortly after 10 p.m., while grand-mother and the young ones slept on, they would be awakened and readied for the Christmas celebration.

After what seemed like only a few moments of slumber, the children rubbed their eyes and looked outside to see Father harnessing the horses and preparing the *cariole,* the family's sleigh. They donned their long red choir robes and scampered quietly downstairs, where Mother was setting the table for the *réveillon* meal.

Snow began to fall gently as the family clambered into their *cariole.* With warm woolen clothing, bear skins on their laps, and hot bricks at their feet, they were hardly aware of the sub-zero temperature. Little bells on the horse's harness tinkled in response to the distant church bells, which were calling people to midnight mass. Sleighs began to arrive at the parish church, one after the other, for this special night of joy and mystery. The men hitched the horses to posts and then covered their animals with heavy blankets.

Hundreds of flickering candles cast a warm glow on the bundled-up villagers crowding into the church. Just before Christmas Eve, the *curé* (parish priest) had directed the community's young men to collect homemade tallow candles from all of the homes in the area. All the parishioners contributed generously to this Christmas ritual.

Suddenly, the best tenor soloist of the choir burst out triumphantly:

> *Minuit, Chrétiens,*
> *C'est l'heure solonelle*
> *Où l'homme Dieu descendit jusqu'à nous ...*

Midnight mass had commenced.

All of the participants of the mass were resplendent in their ceremonial clothes. The sacristan (keeper of religious articles) wore a long, red, embroidered coat, and the choirboys were debonair in their long red or black robes. Churchwardens (lay assistants to the priests) wore long coats with pointed collars. The *curé* also wore his finest garments for this holy night.

The midnight mass was entirely sung in Latin by the cantor. Although not everyone in the congregation could follow the exact meaning of the liturgy, the exhilaration of the cantor's voice proclaiming Christ's birth was clear. After midnight mass, the *curé* celebrated the *messe de l'aurore* (mass of the dawn).

This mass was not quite as solemn as the midnight mass and the villagers were welcome to join the choir in singing traditional Christmas carols such as *Il est né le divin enfant, Les anges dans nos campagne, Ça berger, assemblons nous,* and *Nouvelle agréable.* Singing these cherished melodies helped everyone to stave off fatigue a little bit longer.

When the worship came to a close, each family went up to the *crèche* by the side altar to visit the infant Jesus lying in his manger. The villagers gazed at the babe with the rosy cheeks, lovingly swaddled in lace and linen. Then they left the church in a state of serene joy.

Outside in the crisp night air, friends and neighbours shouted Christmas greetings to each other as they got into their respective sleighs. Then it was time to rush home (around 2 a.m.) for the highly anticipated *réveillon.*

This meal was the first meal of *Les Fêtes* — a series of special family occasions between Christmas Eve and *Le Jour des Rois* (Epiphany). The *réveillon* itself was an intimate family meal, so no guests were invited.

After a long, sleigh ride in the wee hours of the morning, the family was very happy to be back in their cozy home. Thick logs of maple wood crackled in the fireplace, and the rooms were filled with the delicious smell of festive dishes, which had been simmering patiently.

The family roused grandmother and then they all sat down to a groaning board of homemade food, including *cretons* (a form of pâté), *ragoût* (meatballs and pig's feet in a rich gravy), *tourtière* (a mildly spiced meat pie), mashed potatoes, pickled vegetables, doughnuts, and *tarte au sucre* (maple syrup pie). Not surprisingly, the family slept late on Christmas morning.

New Year's Traditions

New Year's was a great celebration in traditional French-Canadian society. It was a time to make merry with friends and family and give presents to loved ones. It was also a time to feast!

La Guignolée

On December 31, French Canadians participated in a very important charity collection called *La Guignolée*. The most popular explanation for the origin of this term involves a New Year's ritual performed in ancient Gaul. Apparently, Celtic priests collected *feuilles du gui* (mistletoe) from sacred oak trees to herald the arrival of the New Year and then they exclaimed "*Au gui, l'an neuf.*" The inhabitants of New France brought this term with them from their homeland.

Guignolée collections began in Quebec in the early 1800s. On December 31, all the households in rural Quebec began to anticipate the arrival of the *guignoleux*, a group of villagers who collected food and money for underprivileged people in the community.

The ragtag troupe of *guignoleux* arrived at each doorstep by horse and sleigh. The large sleigh — ready to be filled as a horn of plenty — was usually gaily decorated with evergreen boughs, and sometimes torches were affixed to it.

The leader, in a heavy fur coat with a red sash, announced their arrival with a trumpet call. Then both the homeowner and the *guignoleux* engaged in a special ritual. While tapping out the rhythm with long poles, the *guignoleux* began to sing a song of supplication, which everyone knew by heart.

Bonjour le maitre et la maitresse
(Hello to the master and the mistress)
Et tous les gens de la maison
(And all of the people in the household)
Nous avons fait une promesse
(We have made a promise)
De venir vous voir une fois l'an
(To come visit you once a year)
Une fois l'an, ce n'est pas grand'chose
(Once a year is not a lot)
Qu'un petit morceau de chignée
(Just a little piece of pork)
Un petit morceau de chignée si vous voulez.
(A little piece of pork if you like.)

Then, the master and mistress of the house would

perform their role in the ritual by inviting the *guignoleux* into the house to warm up and to have a little drink of whisky or *rhum*. Sometimes a snack, such as a doughnut or a piece of bread, was offered as well. After drinking to their host's good health, the *guignoleux* would pick up the family's donations — which consisted of choice cuts of meat, potatoes and other root vegetables, preserves, and sometimes even firewood and clothing — and then set off with great fanfare to the next household, bellowing, "*Qui donne aux pauvres, prête a Dieu*" (Those who give to the poor, will be recognized by God). Every house in the parish was visited; sometimes that meant that the *guignoleux* were still going in the wee hours of the morning.

Unfortunately, there were some disgraceful abuses of this tradition, especially in the growing towns and cities of Quebec, where several groups of *guignoleux* did the rounds simultaneously. On some occasions, the food and/or money never made it to the poor people for whom it was intended.

The 1857 *guignolée* in Montreal, however, was conducted with utmost honesty — a welcome surprise after years of unseemly behaviour. According to the *Dimanche-Matin* newspaper of January 2, 1857: "On the first night of the New Year, Montreal re-experienced a custom which we thought was gone. Groups of young men with drums and violin went out to collect the guignolée, they asked for money and a little food for the local poor ... we are happy to see that it did not cause any disorder, the guignoleux were content to laugh, sing and collect money for the underprivileged ... In the past there were many groups that became drunk, and got into fights with other groups. Also, too many young people forgot to give the fruits of their labour to the poor."

But then, three years later in 1860, there were so many incidents of drunk and rowdy *guignoleux* disturbing the peace (and sometimes even stealing the proceeds of the charity drive) that the mayor of Montreal decided to issue licences for the *guignolée* and policemen were ordered to supervise their activities.

Today, the term *guignolée* is still used in Quebec to describe charity collection during the holiday season. However, no colourful rituals are associated with the modern *guignolée*. It is simply another occasion to write a cheque for a charitable organization.

New Year's Day

New Year's Day was a time to visit with friends and family. In traditional French-Canadian society, the New Year started as soon as the children were able to wake up the patriarch of the family for the time-honoured New Year's blessing. Then the married children would arrive with their own families, and they, too, would ask for the father's blessing for the coming year.

With all of his children and grandchildren gathered around him on bended knee waiting for the blessing, the father of the family was usually overcome with emotion.

Naturally, most men responded with the words that their fathers had used before them. Some fathers simply made the sign of the cross with their hand and then uttered a simple phrase such as, "*Que le bon Dieu te bénisse comme je te bénis*" (May God give you his blessing as I have given you my blessing). Other fathers chose to list all of the family's blessings and wishes for the future and then end with, "*Et le paradis a la fin de tes jours*" (And paradise at the end of your days).

Once the blessing was bestowed it was gift time! Most children hung stockings at the end of their beds on December 31. When they woke up the next morning, they could usually count on receiving fruits, raisins, and candies such as barley sugar in animal forms. In some families, children also received practical gifts, such as clothing, on New Year's Day, as well as simple handmade toys, like wooden trucks and cloth dolls. The children did not necessarily think that Santa Claus had brought the gifts. Up until the mid-19th century, children were taught that the Infant Jesus had come during the night to deliver presents. Considering how influential the church was regarding every aspect of family life, children would have been easily convinced that it was the Baby Jesus bringing them gifts.

Then the family was off to the parish church for a special mass that included a New Year's blessing. This mass was as much a part of the day's celebrations as the gifts. Following church, the entire extended family gathered for a New Year's feast.

While the women of the family bustled around setting up tables and finishing the meal preparation, some of the men went out to offer New Year's wishes from their family to friends and neighbours and to catch up on the latest gossip. Naturally, it was *de rigueur* for the men to have a little drink at each home.

Serving New Year's dinner was a huge undertaking, as traditional French Canadian families had numerous children. It was not uncommon to seat 40 to 50 people! But it was yet another opportunity to enjoy the bounty of the family farm. Although this meal included many of the same dishes as the Christmas Eve *réveillon*, the New Year's meal was typically a grander meal, featuring a greater variety of dishes and a number of guests.

Most families enjoyed chicken and/or pork roasts (turkey was considered too expensive), *tourtière* and other meat pies, mashed potatoes, *boudin* (blood pudding), cooked vegetables, *ragoût*, and pickled vegetables. This would be followed by a vast array of desserts: *beignes* (doughnuts), *croquignoles* (slightly lighter dough than a *beigne* and prepared as round balls), *tarte au sucre*, and *tarte au ferlouche* (a molasses and raisin pie).

The main beverage during dinner was water, although the men sometimes started the meal with a glass of whiskey, and the women might have had a glass of homemade cherry or black currant wine.

After a washing-up marathon to clean hundreds of

dishes, the family settled into other diversions, such as card games, storytelling, and candy making. While the children ran wildly through their grandparents' house, some family members would bring out a violin and some spoons for percussion. Time to dance!

As the towns and cities of Quebec grew, New Year's traditions continued in a similar fashion. Ritual social visits on New Year's Day were also a Scottish tradition. So in the city of Montreal, which had a significant population of Scottish immigrants, both Anglophones and Francophones were earnest visitors.

These social visits were a serious duty to strengthen bonds of friendship and to smooth over the disagreements of the previous year. Each family would set out their best wines and cakes, specially made for the occasion. Then the women of the household, dressed in their finest gowns, would wait in the drawing room for their visitors.

In Montreal in the early 1800s, it was customary for small groups of men to spend most of New Year's Day visiting. They were entitled to stop at every house where any one of the men had even the most casual acquaintance. And, thanks to an old French custom, male visitors were allowed to kiss all the ladies of the house on New Year's Day. So it is not surprising that young, single men met with as many ladies as possible on that day.

Men who had numerous business and social acquaintances might have made as many as 80 social calls on New

Year's Day. Considering that they would have been expected to have a little drink at each house, it is almost amazing that they found their way home again!

Epiphany

Le Jour des Rois, or Epiphany, marked the end of the holiday season known as *Les Fêtes*. According to biblical lore, Epiphany was when the three kings — Melchior, Caspar, and Balthazar — arrived in Bethlehem bearing gifts of gold, frankincense, and myrrh for the baby Jesus. In traditional French-Canadian society, most people attended a special mass on the *Jour des Rois*.

On the day before the mass, the sacristan of the parish church would have located the plaster representations of the three kings and their camels and placed them in the *crèche* (nativity scene), which the parishioners had been enjoying since midnight mass on December 24.

The *Jour des Rois* was also a very exciting occasion for children. After the church service, the family would return home for *gâteau des rois*, a special cake in which a bean was hidden. Whoever found the bean in his or her serving had to make a speech and was then crowned king or queen for the day. This tradition dates back to pre-Christian times, when ancient Greeks and Romans entertained themselves by electing a king of the feast.

Ontario

t happens every year. The days get shorter; the temperature drops. The sun seems to disappear for days on end as Ontarians brace themselves for winter, which, even in the moderate south, brings considerable snow and ice. But even as the darkness and chill settle in, there is a glimmer of hope, a feeling of growing excitement. For the start of winter also means the beginning of the Christmas season, a time of celebration that goes back to the earliest days of Ontario settlement and far beyond.

Christmas has been observed in Ontario since the mid-1600s, when French missionaries brought their religious and festive traditions with them to remote mission outposts. Later, when Europeans settled permanently in the province, they introduced other holiday customs, which eventually took root in the new land.

Over time, Christmas celebrations changed. Some were abandoned as old-fashioned or barbaric. New ones developed, although it can probably be argued that Ontario has no truly unique Christmas traditions. At some level, nearly every aspect of Christmas can be traced back hundreds of years, sometimes thousands, to winter solstice celebrations of the distant past. In that respect, Christmas in Ontario is fundamentally no different from Christmas in Quebec, or British Columbia, or, for that matter, Australia.

Yet, on another level, every Christmas is unique, as is every individual's experience of Christmas. It is a magical, mystical time, sometimes fraught with anxiety, pain, and longing, but more often full of hope and joy and goodwill towards all. How it is celebrated depends on the time and place and circumstances, but for most Ontarians Christmas has been, and probably will always be, one of the most memorable times of the year.

Ontario's First Christmas Carol

On Christmas Eve 1668, a 14-year-old girl lay fighting for her life at La Jeune Lorette, near Quebec City. Thérèse was a member of the Huron, a nation that had been pushed out of their traditional homelands near eastern Georgian Bay by the Iroquois. To comfort herself, as well as to mark the approaching holiday, she sang *Jesous Ahatonhia*, a carol which described the birth of Christ in a setting that closely resembled the Ontario wilderness. Father Pierre-Joseph Chaumonot, the Jesuit who gave Thérèse the last rites, heard the song, which had been passed along among Christianized Hurons for many years. When Thérèse died on Christmas Day, he mentioned the song in passing. This was the first written reference to the "Huron Carol." Later transcribed and preserved for posterity, young Thérèse's favourite song was the first Canadian Christmas carol and probably the first carol written in North America.

While there is no definite proof, traditional accounts claim the carol was written by Father Jean de Brébeuf (1593–1649). A French missionary, Brébeuf was a skilled linguist who eventually wrote a Huron grammar and dictionary, so it is highly plausible that he translated the Christmas story into the Huron language. The words were set to the tune of an old French song, *La Jeune Pucelle* (The Young Maid).

Brébeuf first went to live among the Huron near Georgian Bay in 1626. In 1634, he was one of a group of Jesuit priests who revived a French mission at Sainte-Marie-Among-the-Hurons, near Midland. Located close to main canoe routes, Sainte Marie was designed to be a self-supporting European community, as well as a central mission for Christian Natives. For a time it flourished, and many of the Huron who visited learned the haunting song describing the birth of the Christ Child. But in 1648, the old enemies of the Huron, the Iroquois, began a series of attacks. The result was the martyrdom of several missionaries, including Brébeuf, who was killed on March 16, 1649. Two months later, the remaining missionaries abandoned Sainte Marie, burning what buildings remained.

Somehow, the song survived in the Huron language until it was written down by Father Étienne de Villeneuve. A Huron lawyer by the name of Paul Picard then translated it into French as *Jésus est né*. Finally, in 1926, poet Jesse Edgar Middleton provided English words:

'Twas in the moon of winter time
When all the birds had fled
That mighty Gitchi Manitou
Sent angel choirs instead
Before their light the stars grew dim
And wondering hunters heard the hymn:
"Jesus your King is born
Jesus is born: In excelsis gloria!"

Within a lodge of broken bark
The tender babe was found
A ragged robe of rabbit skin
Enwrapped his beauty 'round
And as the hunter braves drew nigh
The angel song rang loud and high:
"Jesus your King is born
Jesus is born: In excelsis gloria!"

The popularity of the song has grown tremendously since then, especially after Canada's centennial celebrations in 1967 awakened interest in Canadian history. *Jesous Ahatonhia*, the "Huron Carol," is now a Canadian Christmas tradition.

Pagan Roots

Although the "Huron Carol" was created specifically for Canada, it is part of a rich Christmas legacy stretching back to ancient times. While Christmas commemorates the birth of Jesus, many of our holiday customs are, in fact, pagan in origin. Since the sun was worshipped by most civilizations at one time or another, the winter solstice was an important date on most calendars. Starting in September, the sun's power gradually weakens until it reaches its lowest point in mid-December on the shortest day of the year. From then on, the days lengthen and the sun gains strength, a phenomenon that in ancient times was cause for celebration. So the Romans held Saturnalia, with gifts, revelry, and decorated homes.

As the Roman Empire and Christianity spread into Europe, other customs were blended with the traditions of Saturnalia, including those of the Germanic peoples in northern Europe and the Celtic Druids. Evergreens were highly prized as decorations — their ability to stay green while all other vegetation withered seemed magical. Ivy, used by the ancient Romans, was dedicated to the god Bacchus and was said to prevent drunkenness. Holly, also known in Roman times, was regarded by early Christians as the "holy tree." Some believed the wood had been used for Christ's cross, and the prickly leaves and red berries symbolized the crown of thorns. The Druids considered mistletoe a sacred plant, especially when it was found growing on oak trees, and harvested the leaves for use in ceremonies.

Although the mystical meanings of these plants were eventually forgotten, their presence remained essential at Christmastime, especially among homesick colonists.

Many early Ontario settlers were too busy with day-to-day survival to bother much with Christmas decorations. In 1828, describing workers on Ottawa's Rideau Canal, one anonymous pioneer wrote, "In Dow's great swamp, one of the most dismal places in the wilderness, did five Irishmen, two Englishmen, and one Scotchman hold their merry Christmas — or rather forgot to hold it at all." Some down-played Christmas celebrations because of religious reasons, a legacy from Puritan times when anything remotely resembling Catholic celebrations was banned. Yet others simply could not imagine Christmas without evergreens. Catharine Parr Traill was one of them.

Catharine was a genteel Englishwoman who, along with her husband and other relatives, including her sister, Susanna Moodie, immigrated to the Peterborough area in 1832. Catherine was 30 at the time, and Susanna was two years younger. Both wrote extensively of their experiences in the backwoods of Canada, including Catharine's nostalgia for the evergreens that decorated English homes and churches during the holidays. She and her husband had not yet settled into their own home, but that did not prevent her from wandering into the fields near the house where they were staying and gathering some wintergreen to hang on the mantel in their host's home. Although some laughed at her efforts, Catharine later wrote, "It seemed to me these green branches might be held as emblems to remind us that we should keep faith bright and green within our hearts."

By 1838, she was settled in her own house. In the previous 12 months, panic had swept through Upper Canada after rebellion broke out on December 5, 1837. The insurgents were quickly dispersed. Their leader, William Lyon Mackenzie, fled to the United States, but rumours of imminent violence put a damper on Christmas celebrations, as did the absence of many men on militia duty. Although rebels Samuel Lount and Peter Matthews were executed, and others were imprisoned or exiled to Australia, several additional attempts were made to overthrow the colonial government during 1838. In February, rebels attacked Pelee Island in western Lake Erie. In June, another force raided the Short Hills, south of St. Catharines. In November, rebels under Colonel Nils von Schoultz occupied a windmill and several houses near Prescott. The skirmishes that followed left 16 British-Canadian defenders dead and 60 wounded. A few weeks later, on December 4, Windsor was invaded.

Ontario

Across Upper Canada, able-bodied men were called to militia duty. Following the Prescott and Windsor raids, troops were stationed in Toronto, the provincial capital. Among them was Catharine's brother-in-law, John Moodie. Wanting to distract her worried sister Susanna and Susanna's young family, Catharine planned an English-style Christmas and sent her hired man, Malachi, and a young servant, Martin, to gather a sleigh-load of evergreens.

The boughs and branches cheered up the Traills' log cabin considerably, but, Catharine wrote, "when all our green garlands were put up, we missed the bright-varnished holly and its gay, joy-inspiring red berries." Hannah, Catharine's English maid, remembered that wintergreen and cranberries grew in a nearby swamp and suggested them as a substitute. Unfortunately, the wintergreen was buried under a couple of feet of snow, so they had to make do with "the red transparent berries of the cranberry" and a string of coral beads belonging to Catharine's young daughter, Katie. These were woven among the hemlock boughs with satisfactory results.

Then Catharine sent an ox-drawn sleigh off to fetch Susanna and her family. Years later, she described the vehicle as humble and rude, but noted how pleasant a ride in one could be, especially through a snow-laden evergreen forest: "Reposing on a bed of hay, covered with buffalo or bear skins, or good wool coverlets, and wrapped in plaids, with well-wadded hoods, we were not a whit less happy than if we had been rolling along in a gay carriage, drawn by splendid horses."

Catharine's description of that pioneer Christmas was published in 1860 in *The Canadian Settler's Guide*, one of many books written in the 19th century to help prospective immigrants adjust to their new life in Canada.

Lighting Up

Spectacle of some kind has always been part of Christmas, and lights are particularly important. Long ago, at the darkest season of the year, lighted candles created a kind of imitative magic, replacing the light of the waning sun. In Christian symbolism, lights were reminders of the Christ Child — the "Light of the World" — as well as the Star of Bethlehem, which pointed out his location to the Magi.

Today, almost every community in Ontario has some kind of decorative Christmas lights, which are often turned on with a formal light-up ceremony. London, Sarnia, Burlington, St. Thomas, and Owen Sound are among the many places that have established Christmas light festivals over the years. Probably the most spectacular, in terms of setting and sheer size, is the Niagara Falls Winter Festival of Lights. Billed as Canada's largest light festival, the event has been running since 1983. Concentrating on the falls, the Niagara River, and adjacent parkland, the award-winning two-month festival features more than 100 animated light displays and more than five kilometres of lights strung on trees. Many local homeowners and businesses also participate — at the Skylon Tower, some 5000 lightbulbs are arranged to turn the

160-metre (520-foot) structure into a giant Christmas tree. Set against the backdrop of the falls, with ice, snow, and mist adding extra sparkle, the Winter Festival of Lights has become one of Ontario's top Christmas attractions.

Because private businesses are also involved, no one is quite sure how many lights illuminate the festival, but estimates suggest there are close to a million. That is more than enough to dazzle the most jaded tourist. Yet, for many, one of the truly memorable features of the festival is the candlelight procession. Originally held in Queen Victoria Park, the event moved in 1997 to the outdoor Oakes Garden Theatre. Typically, around 2000 people turn out to light candles, walk through the park, sing carols, and watch a live nativity scene enacted by members of the Queensway Free Methodist Church. In the midst of blazing, state-of-the-art electrical displays, the candlelight and living tableau are poignant reminders of the origins of Christmas.

Compared to the Winter Festival of Lights, Simcoe's Panorama of Lights is a more modest event. But like the Niagara festival, it takes advantage of a lovely natural setting. And it claims to be the very first festival of lights in Ontario.

The light festival in this small town southeast of London began as a Santa Claus parade, an annual event meant to draw crowds to the town's downtown core and inspire them to start their Christmas shopping. By the late 1950s, there were concerns about the hazards of staging a single, short-run event so late in the year. One year, the temperatures were so frigid that the band's instruments froze. In 1957, the parade was delayed because of rain. The following year, cold, snowy weather threatened to keep the crowds away.

There was also some dissatisfaction about the amount of effort that went into preparing for an event that was over in a matter of minutes. Joan Daley, secretary of the Chamber of Commerce in the late 1950s, told writer Cheryl Bauslaugh, "We'd spend two weeks in the armouries building displays, and it was all over in about an hour."

Thinking that something more permanent might be the solution, organizers left two fairy tale floats in Wellington Park after the 1958 parade. There were immediate complaints from some residents who thought the Old Woman in the Shoe and Four-and-Twenty Blackbirds were ruining the town's charming riverside park. When the time to plan the next parade rolled around, the town's Retail Merchants' Association considered the possibility of establishing some kind of long-term Christmas attraction. Joan Daley and her husband Don presented a number of slides showing individual displays in other Ontario towns, including London and Dresden. There was some debate, but finally the association voted by a narrow margin to try a lighted display in Wellington Park.

From the outset, Joan was determined that Simcoe's festival of light would stand out. Although other communities had various lighted displays, Simcoe's would be different because the exhibits would be linked by themes, with similar themes located close together in the park. There were plans to recycle the best floats from the Santa Claus parade, but the group also decided to build three new displays. However, it was already October, so a lot of work had to be accomplished if the exhibits were going to be ready for Christmas.

Joan Daley took the lead by drafting a flyer to ask local businesses for financial support. Realizing she needed a name to make her pitch, she came up with Panorama of Christmas. Volunteers were recruited, and the group quickly raised nearly $2000. They also persuaded the town to pay for the cost of electricity needed to run the lights.

Right from the start, the exhibits focused on two main themes, faith and fantasy. For the first year, Panorama organizers moved four floats to the park: Santa and his reindeer, the Old Woman in the Shoe, Four-and-Twenty Blackbirds, and a giant poinsettia. To impart a religious element, three new exhibits were constructed: a giant open Bible telling the story of Christ's birth, a manger scene, and a church steeple.

In a few short weeks, three new exhibits were ready. To provide a touch of Christmas music, parks manager Grant Anderson, who lived next to Wellington Park, had a loudspeaker hooked up to his record player and persuaded his wife to keep the long-playing records going when the exhibit was lighted up.

The official opening was scheduled for November 27, 1959. As night fell, crowds of local residents, from babes-in-arms to senior citizens, gathered in the park. One by one, each of the exhibits lighted up. The very last was the church steeple, and just as the lights winked on, the strains of *Silent Night* floated into the darkness. "There wasn't a dry eye in the park," Joan Daley later recalled. "It was magical."

Since then, Simcoe's Panorama has drawn thousands of visitors each year. It has expanded from seven exhibits to more than 70, and is illuminated by more than 65,000 lights. It is not the biggest, nor the most ambitious light festival in Ontario, but the lighted scenes, surrounded by trees and reflected in the Lynn River, are right in the middle of the town's main thoroughfare, and anyone who travels through Simcoe on Highway 24 after dark is immediately drawn into the magic spell of Christmas light.

The Prairies

ree land! This startling offer from Canada
captured the imaginations and fired the
hopes of people from all over Europe,
Britain, and the United States. And so, in tens of thousands,
they journeyed across oceans and strange lands to begin their
lives again on the Canadian Prairies. Most of the newcomers
who heeded that call brought little more than their memories, keepsakes, and traditions. These traditions — especially the traditions of Christmas — are still cherished in the
great expanse of land now called Manitoba, Saskatchewan,
and Alberta.

Music and Meals of Home

The soaring sound slows pedestrians hurrying through their
last-minute shopping on Christmas Eve. On the corner of

a Winnipeg street, a young girl loading a disc into her CD player pauses, pulls the earphones from her ears, and looks up. Voices lifted in song float through an open window of an apartment above the storefronts. Few listeners can understand the words, but there is no mistaking the pure emotion in the lyrics.

It's the sound of a place that the singers' grandparents called home — a place where most of the singers themselves have never been. It's the sound of a *koleda*, a Christmas carol, whose evocative words and haunting tunes first floated over the snow-swept Manitoba prairie from thick earthen-walled soddies 90 years ago.

In the singers' modern apartment, there is an old sideboard. On the top shelf, in a space usually reserved for teacups, a traditional *szopka*, or manger scene, is displayed. In this apartment, and in the homes of other Polish descendants all over the Prairies, many other old-country traditions will be observed during the holidays.

Later on Christmas Eve — after the first star has appeared in the night sky — young and old will stand around the dinner table to say grace. The *oplatek*, an unleavened wafer stamped with the figures of the Christ child, the Blessed Mary, and the holy angels, will be shared amongst the group. The first *oplatek* will be offered by wife to husband. This is the "bread of love," so husband and wife will embrace and kiss. Everyone else will then do the same.

Glasses of *krupnik* (alcohol and honey), will be raised in

a celebration toast. Then hosts and guests pass among them the dozen meatless dishes that represent the 12 apostles. First there is *barszcz* (beet soup) and *uszka* (dumplings and mushrooms), followed by jellied fish and some *golabki* (cabbage rolls stuffed with rice or buckwheat). Then it is on to fried carp, *pierogi* (dumplings stuffed with cheese or potatoes), and finally, fruit compote and baked sweets, such as poppy seed rolls or apple strudel.

Often, the meal is eaten by the light of two candles, each bedecked with blue ribbons. In some rural homes, hay will be strewn under the tablecloth to symbolize Christ's birth in a manger, and a sheaf of wheat will be placed on the floor near a window. In years gone by, that wheat would then be tied around the fruit trees to ensure a better crop the next summer.

Similar in many ways to the Polish traditions are the customs still observed by the descendants of Ukrainian immigrants. No time of the year is more festive than the Ukrainian Christmas season, which, when New Year and Epiphany are included, encompasses two weeks of feasts, carols, and special religious services.

Because the Ukrainian Orthodox Church still uses the Julian calendar, instead of the Gregorian calendar, Christmas Eve and Christmas Day fall on January 6 and 7. Although most modern-day families of Ukrainian descent observe Christmas at the same time as other Canadians, the older generation still celebrates on January 6.

At the Christmas Eve supper, two *kolachi*, circular braided loaves, create a traditional table centrepiece, complete with a central candle anchored in a glass of salt. As in the Polish tradition, the twinkling of the first star on Christmas Eve is the signal for the feast of 12 meatless dishes to begin. But farming families don't eat until the livestock have been fed! This is not the night to skimp when feeding the animals. Legend has it that animals are granted the gift of speech on this special day. That means they might complain to God if they feel slighted by owners.

The feast begins with Christmas *kutia*, a special sweet dish of boiled wheat, poppy seeds, and honey. The first spoonful is thrown at the ceiling for good luck, but the rest is kept for the diners. *Borsch* (cabbage and beet soup), *pryohy* (dumplings with various fillings), *holubtsi* (rice wrapped in cabbage leaves), as well as fish, cornmeal, sweet buns, and more fruit and vegetable dishes, ensure nobody goes hungry.

Christmas Eve is but the first of three days of the Ukrainian Christmas. After an early service on Christmas Day, feasting, carolling, and visiting continue for two days. There is more fun and celebration on *Malanka*, New Year's Eve.

The third major holiday is Epiphany (January 19), also known as the Feast of the River Jordan, to celebrate Christ's baptism. The night before Epiphany is called Generous Eve and is celebrated as a second Christmas Eve with its own traditional festive meal and the singing of *shchedrivky*, special Epiphany carols.

The Prairies

The traditional water-blessing ceremony, conducted on January 19 — often in bone-chilling temperatures — includes a solemn procession of singers making their way to a riverbank. Here, the priest blesses the water, and members of the congregation take jars of the blessed water home as protection against evil or to give to sick relatives or friends.

In the prairie homes of German descendants, as well as in Mennonite and some Hutterite colonies, an evergreen Advent wreath graces the middle of the table for a month before Christmas. The wreath encircles four tall candles, three pink and one white. Every Sunday, another candle is lit — the first by the youngest child — until Christmas, when all the candles are replaced with white candles. Croatians place three candles in a bowl of four-inch-high grass; the candles represent the three wise men.

For Norwegians, Christmas culinary dishes include flatbread, *lutefisk* (dry cod soaked in lye), and tasty bakery delicacies such as *fattigmand* and *julekake*. For the descendents of Icelandic immigrants, it is the succulent taste of *hangikjot* (smoked mutton) and perhaps the sweet indulgence of the prune-filled *vinar-terta* (Vienna tart) or *ponnukokur* (thin pancakes spread with brown sugar).

For the English, it is goose or turkey, plum pudding and mincemeat, followed by port and cheese. After the heavy meal, rounds of favourite carols such as "God Rest Ye Merry Gentlemen" are sung beneath garlands of holly and clusters of mistletoe.

These, then, are just a few of the many old-country Christmas traditions and treats. Thousands of kilometres, and more than 100 years distant from their origins, they are still enjoyed and cherished by thousands of Canadians.

Loneliness and Longing

Between the late 1890s and 1913, three million immigrants flooded into the Canadian Prairies. About two-thirds were from Europe and Britain, and a third from the United States. In spite of religious, linguistic, and cultural differences, almost all shared one common trait — loneliness. This was never felt more keenly than at Christmastime.

Harry and Kathleen Strange first experienced loneliness at Christmas in London, long before the couple left England to come to Canada. It so happened that during the Christmas holidays of 1918, both Harry and Kathleen's families had left London. The young couple prepared themselves for a dismal, depressing Christmas Day. Depression turned to delight as they received a Christmas morning invitation to attend a reception, concert, and dance at the Royal Albert Hall.

As wonderful as the event was, it was the experience of turning a dismal day into something special that made an impression on them. When they immigrated and settled on a farm near Stettler, Alberta, the couple vowed to extend their own hospitality each Christmas to others who were far from home and family.

Many of the guests invited to their farmhouse

provided unexpected surprises. Among the "succession of interesting, delightful and amusing strangers," Kathleen later recalled, was the grain elevator worker who turned out to be a Cambridge fellow and mathematician. Another guest, a lonely, disheartened, unemployed bachelor, turned out to be the scion of one of England's oldest families. Unfortunately, this blue-blooded fellow had trouble holding a job. Inspired by his place and time in his adopted country, he kept putting down his tools and picking up a pencil to immortalize his observations in verse.

Kathleen had some misgivings about another guest, a taciturn individual regarded by many as a severe and unapproachable fellow. In retrospect, it is easy to understand the man's demeanor. Life was tough; you had to be tough to survive. Yet, this grouch "was transformed by two glasses of port, into a most delightful dinner table companion and an intimate of the very best literature."

Sometimes, the hospitality unexpectedly revealed just how destitute the visitors really were. Imagine the shame and wretchedness of the young man who fell violently ill immediately after dinner. A doctor was summoned and the boy was bedridden for days. His malady was easily diagnosed. He had not had a real meal for weeks. Finally given the opportunity to eat his fill, his digestive system simply rebelled.

In an article for the *Lethbridge Herald*, Kathleen Strange confessed that, as appreciative as her guests might have been for the opportunity for good cheer and companionship, it was she and her husband who "probably had most of the pleasure."

A decade before Kathleen and Harry settled in northern Alberta, another English immigrant, Monica Hopkins, joined her husband, Billie, at their newly established ranch in Priddis, near Calgary. It was just a few months before Christmas and this would be her first Christmas away from home. Now that thousands of kilometres separated her from parents and siblings, she longed for a parcel from them — something she could open on Christmas Day — something that would make her feel they were not quite so far away. Much to her disappointment, her family's parcel didn't arrive in time.

"We had quite a lot of English parcels from friends, but they were not quite the same ..." Monica wrote to a friend. Happily, the parcels were at the Priddis Post Office when Billie went to look for them on Boxing Day.

"My parcels from home were lovely," she wrote. "Mother and Father still think that we are more or less on the verge of starvation and that we can only get the absolute essentials ... and I have no intention of disillusioning them at present."

The Words of Charles Dickens

Bob Cratchet, Ebenezer Scrooge, Tiny Tim — the names, and the characteristics they represent, are as familiar today as they were when Charles Dickens created them more than 150 years ago. When British immigrants packed their belongings to come to Canada, many tucked in a copy of Dickens'

A Christmas Carol among the Christmas ornaments and keepsakes. The classic story was, and still is, a cherished part of the British celebration of Christmas, even though families today are more likely to watch the film version on television than dig out the book to read.

However, those hardy souls who settled the Prairies were without the easy entertainment of television, so they relished the tradition of a formal reading of Dickens' Christmas classic. Occasionally, though, the festivities themselves thwarted theatrical and oratory efforts.

Dickens' own son, Francis, was among the many men who endured the tedious, and sometimes tempestuous, ocean voyage to call the Canadian West his home. In 1876, while serving as a North-West Mounted Police inspector, Dickens was invited to Christmas dinner at Fort MacLeod, south of the area now known as Calgary.

Before dinner was served, Inspector Dickens sampled — liberally — the potent "Milk Punch." As dinner and drinking progressed, the good inspector began to feel the effects of the punch bowl. Having advance knowledge of Francis's attendance, a somewhat presumptuous guest produced a copy of the famous book and asked the inspector if he would read a passage or two.

It was probably not the first request of its kind. There is no way to know for sure, but by this time it is likely that Inspector Dickens was heartily sick of his father's tale, and his association with it. Dickens rose unsteadily to his feet, looked balefully about the room, mumbled the immortal line, "God bless us everyone," and then collapsed back in his chair — much to the consternation of those who expected more from the son of the father.

Nellie McClung, the famous author who advocated for women's rights during the early and mid-1900s, told a story about a Dickens' reading that got an even chillier reception. In wind-swept Manitou, Manitoba, in December 1901, a well-educated English immigrant, a certain Frederick Vander, decided to offer "An Evening With Dickens —The Christmas Carol" in the Manitou Town Hall.

The draughty wooden building was heated — but scarcely so, on this particularly blustery night — by a solitary stove in the middle of the floor. The small audience huddled around the stove, and out strode Mr. Vander in formal evening attire. In true Dickensian fashion (for, in his later years, the famous author himself gave spirited readings throughout much of Europe and North America), Mr. Vander played all the characters of the story, and did so with enthusiasm. However, his challenging task was made even more difficult because he was in competition with the elements outside the hall, and with a diligent caretaker inside the hall.

This caretaker periodically upstaged the reader with a performance of his own, as he set about noisily feeding the fire with more fuel from the woodpile. Outside, the wind howled and the tin roof rattled. Inside, the fire crackled and the caretaker clanked and clanged. The hour grew late and the temperature dropped, but the performance went on and on. Finally, unable to endure the cold any longer, some members of the audience tip-toed out of the hall to make their way home. As they opened the door, an icy blast sent the rest of the audience shivering deeper into coats and mufflers. At this point, even the star of the show had shrugged on his coat and gloves.

That was when Mr. Vander realized he was no longer in competition with the caretaker. It seemed he had left also, taking the last of the firewood with him! The persistent performer picked up the pace of the story and released the remaining faithful patrons before they all perished. Those who endured the ordeal felt they had truly "entered the magic circle of the Dickens' fellowship."

Fellowship may have also been the sentiment behind the decision of two young men to read the seasonal classic to the celebrating patrons of Edmonton's Alberta Bar. Or perhaps it was simply the Christmas cheer the place afforded. In any case, on this Christmas Eve, in the early 1960s, future publisher, journalist, and poet Jon Whyte decided that he and a friend would perform a two-man Dickens reading at the watering hole. Would the bar's habitués appreciate young University of Alberta students actually reading *A Christmas Carol*? Could the two compete with — perhaps even contribute to — the friendly laughter and happy conversation of the bar's Christmas Eve patrons? They were keen to find out.

Stuffing his copy of *A Christmas Carol* into his coat

pocket, Jon set off on that bitterly cold night with his friend, eager for a comfortable, warm-hearted evening of drinks and Dickens. It would have been better, he and his friend agreed, if they both had copies of the book. What were the chances of finding another copy, at this hour, on this night? As they hurried along 100th Street, they came across a newsstand. Miraculously, there it was: a paperback copy of *A Christmas Carol!* A propitious sign: obviously, this special event was meant to be.

However, on that fateful Christmas Eve, the two would-be readers never discovered if the patrons were Dickens fans. They never had the opportunity to savour the applause — and perhaps the free round of drinks — their performance might have earned. They never even managed to step across the bar's threshold.

As the two young men headed towards the bar, they heard the loud wail of fire engine sirens. Within minutes, the bar patrons had tumbled out into the cold to follow the chilling sound. The two university students did likewise. Before long, they could see the glow of the fire. The large Sterling Furniture Warehouse was an inferno.

Jon, his companion, and hundreds of other Edmonton residents braved the cold that Christmas Eve to witness one of the largest, most destructive fires in the city's history. Dickens might have brought a halt to talk and laughter inside the warm intimacy of the Alberta, but out here on the street, firefighters — and the blaze they were battling — were the showstoppers. Sadly, this particular Christmas Eve, Bob Cratchet, Ebenezer Scrooge, and even Tiny Tim were all forgotten in the tangle of hoses, the pall of smoke, and the heat of the flames.

British Columbia

f you were to ask a handful of Canadians to think of a classic Christmas scene, it is very likely that most would describe a scene from a Victorian Christmas. Idyllic images of well-dressed Victorian families trimming their Christmas trees, caroling out in the snow, or visiting with loved ones in gaily decorated drawing rooms are often foremost on our minds when we think of Christmas. Indeed, many of our most cherished holiday traditions either emerged from or were popularized during Victorian times. Of course, not all Victorian Christmases were pleasant and idyllic. For the men, women, and children who came to British Columbia in the mid- to late-19th century, these Christmases were often filled with the hardships and challenges of trying to settle in a new land.

Furs and Farms

About 150 years ago, Victoria was merely a rude and rustic outpost of the British Empire. If it weren't for the fickle dictates of British fashion, the fur-trading colony at the tip of Vancouver Island would not have existed at all. As it was, Fort Victoria was nothing terribly special, merely one of a number of the Hudson's Bay Company (HBC) trading posts hewn out of the wilderness.

Ironically, it wasn't the fur trade with the Native peoples who lived around Victoria Harbour that helped expand the settlement beyond the wooden stockade. It was meat and vegetables. While people in the United Kingdom wanted furs, people who lived much closer needed something much more basic — food. In the early 1850s, the HBC founded Puget's Sound Agricultural Company and established four farms within a comfortable ride from the fort. One of the closest was called Craigflower.

Kenneth McKenzie, from East Lothian, Scotland, was the manager of the Craigflower farm. In 1852, he and 20 farm hands (many with wives and children) left their homes in Scotland to start their lives anew on Vancouver Island. The group celebrated their first Christmas away from home on the open seas. They had already rounded the dreaded Cape Horn and were plying their way up the Pacific coast when December 25 found them opposite Mexico.

"Christmas kept. Grog for all hands," McKenzie noted tersely in his Royal Emigrants Almanack. Then he added thoughtfully: "Riot with Mate and Seamen." The riot was probably caused by over-imbibing, just as likely to have been brought on by boredom as by Christmas merry-making. After all, it had been almost five months since they had left British soil.

What the weary seafarers would discover the next time Christmas came around was that they would celebrate fairly riotously at their final destination as well. By all accounts, the settlers were prepared to get into the "spirit" of the season, much to the chagrin of a few.

"What are we to expect of this young, but desperate Colony of ours?" Scottish settler Robert Melrose sniffed. "Dissipation is carried on to such extremities my readers will be expecting to find nothing in my Almanack, from Christmas till past the New Year, but such a one drunk, and another drunk, and so on ... The grog-shops were drained of every sort of liquor, not a drop to be got for either love or money."

Life on the island was difficult, and the work was back-breaking as McKenzie's farm hands hacked out their homes from the forests and wrested stubborn stumps from future farm fields. Little wonder the first Christmas at Craigflower was a time for "fiddling, dancing, singing, eating and drinking," as Melrose reported. He added that New Year's was celebrated "in a glorious Bacchanalian manner."

Glorious? Perhaps Melrose enjoyed the festivities after all. The almanac writer then borrowed a term his fellow Scots often used to describe the season's craziness, labelling it, "the daft days."

It is likely that Christmas provided a very legitimate excuse for the depletion of grog-shop stocks. Given the hardship and loneliness endured by the province's earliest settlers, drunkenness may have been inspired as much by the sweet oblivion that followed the emptying of so many bottles as by the actual celebration of the holiday season.

A Little Bit of England

Victoria has always had the reputation of clinging tenaciously to its British heritage. That heritage and its Christmas customs were never celebrated more obviously than during the late 1800s. Holiday rituals among Victoria's "upper crust" were models of Victorian-era culture.

"Talking of Victoria today, which likes to advertise itself as 'A little big of England', I myself think it's a little farfetched."

The speaker was Major Roger Monteith. The "today" he was referring to was 1962, when he recorded his reminiscences. The major remembered a very different kind of Victoria. Born in 1885, he grew up in an earlier era of transplanted Englishness — real Englishness. "The population of Victoria today is totally different to what it was in the early days that I remember," he continued. "In those days, you had genuine English people, born in England, brought up and educated in England — English ways, English ideas, and possibly, I might say, English accents." And, of course, English Christmases.

Among the many homes in late 19th century Victoria that hosted old-fashioned English Christmases was *Pentrelew*, which meant "The House on the Hill." Pentrelew was built by Henry Pering Pellew Crease, one of Victoria's leading barristers and British Columbia's first attorney general. A mansion in the true sense of the word, Pentrelew's 33 rooms featured expansive windows and floors covered with thick, colourful Turkish carpets. Many were heated by large open fireplaces. Dinner was announced by a drumstick-wielding servant who rang an immense Chinese gong in the main hall. There was no mistaking when dinner was served, even for those in the rooms at the far end of the enormous house. Madge Musket, Crease's granddaughter, was a small girl at the time, but Christmases in the baronial home made a lasting impression.

"We used to have the real old English Christmas dinner with a huge, enormous turkey. Being a child, of course, at the time, I remember it was about 30 pounds. We thought it was just terrific. We used to have the turkey and the roast beef and the plum pudding — a huge plum pudding — brought in by the servant, flaming most wonderfully."

Traditional rounds of visits were another of the season's cherished rituals. For Helen Hood, the daughter of BC premier and lieutenant governor E.G. Prior, English-style Christmases were usually celebrated at the 1000-acre farm of her uncle, Dr. William Tolmie. From there, they would set out to see family friends, including Roderick Findlayson, the HBC chief factor. "We'd have another lovely Christmas there and play ring-around-the-rosie and kiss-in-the-ring and blindman's buff and musical chairs. They were real old-fashion Christmases, you know, there were huge, big turkeys and huge plum puddings and umpteen things to drink — the table loaded down!"

At the home of Dr. John Sebastian Helmcken, the colony's first physician, Christmas dinner was always a family affair. Among those at the table was the doctor's granddaughter, later Mrs. Cecilia Bullen. "It was a family dinner always, you see — always 20 or more sat down to this enormous great table," she later recalled. "The dinner was simply — I don't know — I think you'd call it, *prodigious.* How we ever got through it I don't know, but we always started off with oyster patties." Soup followed, and then an enormous roast turkey and a goose. Rounding out the sumptuous dinner were chicken, ham, mountains of vegetables, plum pudding, enormous mince tarts, and fruit of all sorts — mostly dried.

After the dinner and its obligatory toasts, the entire family sang around the piano in the Helmcken drawing room. Then they were called back into the dining room where a colossal Christmas tree stood. The tree was pushed into another room so everyone could dance. "I tell you, it was quite a night," Cecelia said. "How the mothers survived, I don't know."

The door of the doctor's old wooden house — still preserved, on the grounds of the Royal British Columbia Museum — was thrown open to the public at large every New Year's. This tradition began soon after the doctor arrived at the fort, in 1850, and it lasted for decades.

"Grandfather held open house and anyone who wanted to come was very welcome," Cecilia remembered. "The dining room had an enormous long table. You never would have what people nowadays call a buffet supper. Everyone had to be seated every time, and we very often had to set the table about four or five times for all the people. Then, when it actually came to midnight, we were all expected to gather in the dining room — and really, there was never enough room, some had to be outside — and then we all had to sing Auld Lang Syne."

An HMS Christmas

Then, as now, Victoria was a navy town. In this bygone era, however, it was the Royal Navy. Christmas was a particularly important time for the ratings and officers "serving of her majesty" in one of the empire's far-flung ports. The men who served were on the West Coast for so long — four years — that they were allowed to bring their families out from England. Accommodation was provided for them in Esquimalt's rows of naval housing.

The navy was a great asset to the city financially. The supply of necessary provisions for the seamen generated income for local merchants. And the sailors, naturally, spent their pay at various local establishments.

"My Dad, he catered to the ships, supplied them with hardtack," remembered Hamilton Smith, whose father owned both a bakery and a hardtack factory. "He took me down in a two-wheeled cart. The road to Esquimalt was only a trail in those days and it was pretty tough going for a horse and cart."

Christmas was a busy time for the Smiths, with ships such as HMS *Royal Arthur* and HMS *Imperieuse* stationed on the West Coast. At Christmastime, every sailor would receive a fruitcake, courtesy of the Royal Navy. Sometimes the Smiths had to supply five ships — a lot of fruitcake for one Christmas.

During Yuletide, the Royal Navy made more than an economic contribution to the city, it made a cultural and entertainment splash, as well. "Oh yes," Madge Muskett recalled. "They used to put on the most wonderful shows in what was called the 'sail loft' out in Esquimalt. The sailors would put on one show one night — oh, frightfully amusing — and then the officers would also put one on another time ... songs, dances and plays ..."

At this time, these were the real thing — genuine English people. With as much style and energy as possible, in what those back home in Britain would have called an outpost of the empire upon which the sun never set, they created for themselves a very English Christmas.

Yuletide Courtship

In the late 1800s, a happy group of BC residents was celebrating the newly laid tracks of the Shuswap & Okanagan Railway. Compared to the mammoth Canadian Pacific Railway, the Shuswap & Okanagan Railway was a tiny operation, but no less important to the people in the north end of the Okanagan Valley, where stagecoaches still bounced over the dusty, rutted roads until winter snows made them impassable, and stern-wheelers churned the lake between Vernon and Penticton. The new railway, along with the stagecoaches and stern-wheelers, helped to banish the isolation of the Okanagan Valley, but travel was still a tedious endurance test.

Alice Barrett passed that endurance test in the spring of 1891, when, after an uncomfortable five-day train trip from Ontario, she stepped onto the station platform in Sicamous, BC, and into the arms of her brother, Harry. A confirmed spinster at the age of 29, Alice had left the comfortable home of her large and affluent family at Harry's urgings. He and their Uncle Henry were working hard to establish the 320-acre Mountain Meadow Ranch, north of Otter Lake in the Spallumcheen. Taking care of the ranch left the two bachelors with little time, energy, or inclination to care for the house. Much to Alice's surprise, "the house," turned out to be a very simple three-room cabin. For the better part of the next two years, Alice would "rough it."

Four days before her first Christmas at Mountain

Meadow, Alice's uncle was "up at the shop all day ... making a sleigh," while she was busy making plans and extending invitations for a Christmas party. However, arduous winter travel made those plans tenuous, at best.

"My Xmas party is rather uncertain, no-one but the Hardings and Mr. Parke having accepted positively," Alice wrote in her journal. "It is a little provoking — I'd like to know, but it can't be helped. It has been snowing all day today — the roads are good now — but no mail has come up again tonight — the track is too heavy from Sicamous for the hand-car to run. I suppose they will send an engine ..."

Mr. Parke's acceptance for a stay-over at Christmas was no surprise — at least, not to Harry. Freight-handler Harold Randolph Parke had first met Alice a month after she arrived and had cunningly arranged with her brother to make the ranch an overnight wagon stop. His long, slow courtship of Miss Barrett had begun. Alice confessed to her journal that she "did not care for his appearance — a short, fair man, partly bald and evidently over forty." He was 45, actually, but, as Alice was soon to discover, Hal's age and physical appearance concealed an adventurous spirit.

A student of Upper Canada College in the 1860s, Hal Parke had run away to join the Confederate forces in the American Civil War. During the war, he was wounded and later brought back home by his infuriated father. But a university degree and a comfortable position at his older brother's London, Ontario, law firm weren't going to quench

Hal's thirst for adventure. The West beckoned. Hal packed up again and became the 100th member of the newly formed North-West Mounted Police. Sometime later, he witnessed an historic meeting with Sitting Bull. Now, he was one of the many enthusiastic, hard-working optimists who were making a future for themselves in the rapidly developing Okanagan Valley.

As Alice prepared her first Christmas dinner in the Okanagan, her brother, Harry, was more of a help than she expected. "Dear old Harry! He has been so good to me today, baked a splendid lot of bread today — twelve loaves! — and picked the chickens, for our turkey has proved a vain illusion — fancy a Christmas without a turkey.

"We are going to try and have a jolly one, though."

And jolly it was! Just in time, at midnight on Christmas Eve, Harry arrived back with "letters and parcels from home." The stage had got through! The household awoke early on Christmas Day, and they all opened their presents to and from each other — Harold Parke presenting Alice with a pair of embroidered, buckskin gloves — and from those far away in Dover, Ontario. Dinner was splendid for the seven who eventually sat down at the table that afternoon. Afterwards, Alice would recall, "We had quite a gay time in the evening playing games and acting as if we were young and jolly. Uncle actually joined in, though he pretended he would rather read."

Hal missed no opportunities. On Boxing Day, Alice

wrote, "Harold and I took a little drive to Armstrong. It was a beautiful morning — sleighing perfect — the trees bending over with snow wreaths hanging from every twig, even the ugly barbed wire fences beautified by their festoons of snow."

When Alice returned to Ontario to be with her family, Harold followed. Finally, after many refusals, Alice said yes to Harold Parke's persistent proposals and in 1893, the couple was married.

Chapter 2
Celebrating the Season

Atlantic Canada

rom the first Christmas celebrated by Europeans in a permanent settlement in Canada, to the great Christmas blizzard of 1970, Atlantic Canada's past is filled with historic events, large and small, which have occurred during the holiday season.

The First Noel

One of the first Christmases celebrated by Europeans in Canada took place in 1604 on Isle Ste. Croix on the border between New Brunswick and Maine. There, French fur trader Pierre du Gua de Monts, explorer Samuel de Champlain, and 120 men — including skilled labourers, a priest, and a minister — set up the first French colony in Acadia, the region extending from Pennsylvania to Cape Breton, Nova Scotia. Compared to the lavish celebrations they were used to back in France, that first Christmas in the New World must have seemed dismal to the settlers.

After searching for a suitable location for several weeks, Champlain and his companions finally settled on the island in June of 1604. At first it seemed the ideal place for the settlement. Its location made it easy to defend and its beauty made it a pleasant haven in the foreign wilderness. The group spent the summer clearing the land, building houses, and planting gardens. By the time winter set in, they felt they were quite prepared for it. But the severity of that first winter exceeded all expectations.

"Winter came upon us sooner than expected, and prevented us from doing many things which we had proposed," Champlain later recorded in his journal. It began to snow early in October and continued almost non-stop for the rest of the winter. By early December, the river was choked with ice, making it all but impossible to leave the island. Since the men had stripped the island of most of the trees in order to build their settlement, they had little fuel left for heating. In addition, there was a serious shortage of clean drinking water. As Champlain wrote: "We were obliged to use very bad water, and drink melted snow, as there were no springs nor brooks." Worse still, with the exception of some Spanish wine and cider, their entire supply of liquors froze.

The place that had seemed so idyllic in summer had become a frigid, inhospitable prison by Christmastime. And although the men had plenty of salted meat and fish to eat, they had little in the way of fruits and vegetables. Malnourished and freezing, many of the settlers began to come down with what Champlain called the "mal de terre," or scurvy. At one point, 59 of the men suffered from the dreaded disease. By spring, 35 had succumbed to it.

Although there is no record of how Champlain and his companions spent Christmas that first year, undoubtedly it would have been a highlight in that otherwise miserable winter on Isle Ste. Croix. The colony's priest and minister would have performed Christmas services in the little chapel. Special dishes such as pigeon pie, stew, and baked squash may have been prepared for the Christmas dinner. And no doubt some of the precious Spanish wine would have been used to toast their first Christmas in the new world.

Somehow, the colonists managed to survive that inaugural winter, and in the spring they set out in search of a more suitable location for the settlement. Two years later, Champlain, de Monts, and the others were settled into the first permanent colony in North America at Port Royal, in what is now Nova Scotia. Although conditions had improved dramatically from those endured that first winter, there was little to keep the men entertained during the long, dark winter evenings. Morale began to lag.

In order to alleviate the tedium of the winter months, Champlain came up with the notion of a social club of sorts, which he named *L'Ordre de Bon Temps*, or the "Order of Good Cheer." The idea was that each day a different chief steward was appointed to oversee the evening's meal and entertainment. The Order of Good Cheer was an instant success. Shortly after its inception, the men began competing to see who could provide the best meat, game, fish, and other delicacies for the feasts. In his *History of New France*, poet and historian Marc Lescarbot described the pomp and circumstance involved in these nightly feasts: "The ruler of the feast or chief butler ... marched in, napkin on shoulder, wand of office in hand, and around his neck the collar of the Order, which was worth more than four crowns; after him all the members of the Order, carrying each a dish. The same was repeated at dessert, though not always with so much pomp." After the meal was over, the collar of the Order was passed to the next day's chief steward. And the evening ended with the outgoing and incoming stewards drinking a toast to one another.

Christmas at Port Royal that year would have been a festive affair. The long, low-ceilinged dining room may have been festooned with evergreen boughs and filled with firelight and music. Special dishes such as roast venison, rabbit stew, squash, and bread would have been washed down with copious amounts of wine and spirits. And guests, such as Mi'kmaw Chief Henry Membertou and others, may have been invited to join the colonists for the Christmas feast that year. The French held Chief Membertou in high regard. They were indebted to the Mi'kmaq, who not only supplied the settlers with fresh meat, but also taught them how to survive in the hostile environment. So, inviting them to this special celebration would have been an appropriate way for the French to show their gratitude.

Acadian Christmas

A little over a century after Samuel de Champlain and Pierre du Gua de Monts started the first permanent settlement in Acadia, the British overthrew the French to become the reigning power throughout much of the Maritime region. However, France still had a toehold in the area at Fortress Louisbourg, in what is now Cape Breton. That, combined with the fact that the Acadian population remaining in the region after the takeover outnumbered the English three to one, made the British nervous. Fearing an uprising, they demanded that all Acadians swear an oath of allegiance to the British Crown. The Acadians feared that signing the oath would mean they'd be forced to take up arms against their own people in the event of war with France. As a result of this concern, most refused to sign. They were a peaceful, agricultural society and wanted to remain neutral.

In 1755, the Acadians were again pressed to sign an oath of allegiance to the British. This time when they refused, the British decided once and for all to rid themselves of these "bad subjects." The expulsion of the Acadians began in September of 1755. Acadians throughout the region were rounded up, their property and livestock were confiscated, and their homes, churches, and schools were torched. The

British planned to force the Acadians onto ships and transport them to various points all down the eastern seaboard. The idea, no doubt, was to scatter them in small pockets so they would be less likely to reunite and return en masse. The embarkation began the following month. Men, women, and children were herded like cattle onto dozens of overcrowded ships. Many were separated from families and loved ones, some never to see each other again.

The gruelling journey south took up to three months, and conditions aboard the ships were appalling. Overcrowding, scant provisions, and bad water caused illness among the passengers. Many died before reaching their destination. Those who survived the journey found themselves destitute and thousands of miles from home that December. Christmas must have been a miserable affair for all Acadians that year. Being thrust into foreign surroundings without family or friends would have been the worst situation imaginable for this close-knit, family oriented community.

The British thought the expulsion would rid them of the Acadians once and for all. However, they underestimated the spirit of the Acadian people and their attachment to the land they had lovingly farmed for generations. Many made the long trek back to Acadia, the place they would always consider home.

Today, Acadians throughout New Brunswick, Nova Scotia, and Prince Edward Island celebrate Christmas like no other culture in Canada. The festive season, with its rich foods, joyous music, and, most importantly, visits with family and friends, is a time many look forward to all year long. For most Acadians, midnight mass on Christmas Eve marks the beginning of the holiday season, and is an occasion not to be missed. After mass, families gather together for a *réveillon* with plenty of music and singing, as well as the traditional feast. Tables groan beneath the weight of *poutines, râpées,* and *tourtière* laid out for these late night feasts.

In addition to the sumptuous array of food, no Acadian get-together would be complete without music. At Christmas, the spoons, fiddles, accordions, mandolins, and pianos are tuned up, and the distinctive sounds of lively jigs, reels, and, of course, carols, keep toes tapping into the wee hours of the morning. While most Anglo families are crawling out of bed early on Christmas Day, Acadians are just tucking in for a few hours' sleep before the next round of visiting and feasting begins.

White Christmas

On December 24, 1970, Fredericton's daily newspaper reported that a "rare celestial event" was to take place early the following morning. Astronomers had predicted that the planets Venus, Jupiter, and Mars would cluster together near the crescent moon on Christmas morning. This phenomenon, which only occurs once every 800 years, was believed to have been the same one that appeared in the heavens during Christmas in 7 BC — the year of Christ's birth. In fact, astronomers speculated that this conjunction of the planets may very well have been the miraculous phenomenon known as the "Star of Bethlehem," which led the Three Wise Men to the baby Jesus. For those who follow the stars, a significant celestial event such as this would have seemed an appropriate omen in the early 1970s, a time of global turbulence and transition. And in retrospect, in the Maritime Provinces at least, the phenomenon must have seemed quite ominous.

A snowstorm had been forecast for the Maritime Provinces on December 23, 1970. Fredericton's *Daily Gleaner* predicted eight inches would fall that day. The storm would be over by Christmas Eve, they said, leaving the area cloaked in a fluffy layer of fresh white snow for Christmas Day. The prediction was not quite accurate though. The snow didn't *start* to fall until the afternoon of the 24th. And when it finally came to an end late the next day, the Maritimes were buried beneath drifts the likes of which had rarely been seen before.

Mabel Groom peered anxiously out her living room window as the snow began falling early in the afternoon on Christmas Eve. It was coming down much faster than she'd expected. She and her husband, Wesley, had planned on driving over to pick up her parents a little later that afternoon. Ever since Mabel and Wesley had started a family of their own, her parents had been coming to spend Christmas Eve with them. The suddenness and severity of this storm made Mabel nervous. She decided they should leave for her parents' place early.

As the Grooms pulled out of their driveway in Pennfield, New Brunswick, and crept along Route 1, visibility was so poor they could barely make out anything beyond their car's engine bonnet. The highway was filled with holiday travellers heading home for Christmas. The heavy traffic, poor visibility, and slippery conditions made driving treacherous. Mabel and Wesley had only gone about 10 kilometres when they rounded a corner and went into a skid. Wesley managed to pull out of it in time, but the incident frightened Mabel. She thought of the children back home with the babysitter. If something should happen to her and Wesley out there, the children would be all alone on Christmas Eve. The couple decided they'd better turn around and get home while they still could. Wesley took a back road home to avoid the heavy traffic, a move they were both thankful for later that day.

The Grooms owned and operated McKay's Motel and Restaurant, which was located right next to their house on Pennfield Ridge. When they finally arrived home after their aborted attempt to pick up Mabel's parents, Wesley headed over to the restaurant. Since it was Christmas Eve, he had intended to close early that day so the staff could get home to their own families at a decent hour. In the meantime, Mabel began preparing for a cozy Christmas Eve with just the six of them. Although she was disappointed her parents wouldn't be there for their traditional family Christmas, she was tremendously relieved that she and Wesley had made it home safely and wouldn't be separated from their own children that night. After all, with a new baby in the house, this would be a very special Christmas for the Grooms.

Shortly after he returned to the restaurant, Wesley called over to the house to tell Mabel that he'd probably be late getting home. "You had better prepare for company tonight after all," he added. A nine-vehicle pile-up had occurred just up the road, and the RCMP had blocked off the highway, leaving hundreds of motorists stranded in the small community.

Once the residents of Pennfield found out about the accident and roadblock, they forgot all about their own plans for the evening and went to work helping out those who were stranded in their community. In the spirit of the season, they generously opened their homes and businesses to the storm-stayed travellers. Phones rang all along the line as neighbours called one another to find out who had room for another guest or two. Dinners were organized, supplies and bedding were scavenged from wherever they could be found, and makeshift accommodations were set up.

At least 80 people crowded into McKay's Motel and Restaurant. Many were families with young children on their way home for Christmas. They all looked a little shell-shocked as they ducked in out of the storm, brushing thick layers of snow from their hats and coats. While the waitresses rushed around taking orders and trying to make their guests as comfortable as possible, Wesley sorted out the accommodations. Once all 12 units of the motel were filled to capacity, he offered shelter in the basement to any who wanted it. One family was sent over to the house to stay with Mabel and the children, others curled up anywhere they could find a spot in the restaurant.

The mood among the people at McKay's became a little emotional when darkness fell and it became clear that, like it or not, this was where they were going to spend Christmas Eve, and possibly Christmas Day. For some, the thought of being separated from their loved ones that night was devastating. Others found the situation amusing. The majority, however, were just glad to be in out of the storm. As the evening wore on, the mood grew more festive. Among those stranded at McKay's that night was a band from Boston. Finding themselves with a captive audience, the band members decided to put on an impromptu performance. They set up their instruments beside the Christmas tree and before long everyone was singing along.

Many wayfarers throughout the Maritimes were not as lucky as those stranded in Pennfield that night. Hundreds spent the night trapped in frigid vehicles. For one family of seven, that Christmas Eve blizzard turned into a nightmarish ordeal. Fred Kelly, his wife, and their five children spent 14 hours stuck in a drift on the Trans-Canada Highway just beyond the town of Sackville, New Brunswick.

At about 9:30 on Christmas morning, the snow was still accumulating at an alarming rate. Nothing in the area was moving but snowploughs and snowmobiles. Unable to get out and patrol their territory, the Sackville detachment of the RCMP decided to turn to local snowmobilers for assistance. They asked that the snowmobilers form search parties to help find stranded motorists in the area. The snowmobilers responded immediately. Not long after they began combing the area, one search party discovered the Kelly family. Their car was almost completely buried beneath mountainous drifts. And after spending the night in their vehicle with the motor running, all seven were suffering from carbon monoxide poisoning. Once the rescuers had dug them out, they were rushed to the hospital, where they spent the next few days recovering from their ordeal.

For another group travelling by bus from Moncton to Fredericton, Christmas Eve of 1970 was one they would not soon forget. The bus, carrying 24 passengers from the Moncton airport to Fredericton, departed at about 5 p.m. that day. Under normal conditions, the trip would have taken about two hours. However, conditions were anything but normal that day. By the time the driver ground the bus into gear and pulled away from the terminal, the storm was in full fury. As the bus slipped and skidded along the highway, ploughing through drifts almost as high as the windshield, the passengers grew nervous. From time to time, gasps and squeals were heard above the droning of the engine. After a tense five-hour drive, the bus finally spun out of control. White knuckles clutched the backs of seats as the bulky vehicle skidded sideways. The bus finally lurched to a halt in the ditch near Lakeville Corner, where it would remain for the rest of the night.

Although the passengers were a little shaken up by their ordeal, no one was hurt. Once they realized they were destined to spend Christmas Eve on the bus, everyone onboard tried to make the best of the situation. Still, most of them would have preferred to be home with family and friends rather than stuck in a ditch with 23 strangers on Christmas Eve. It wasn't until late the next morning that the passengers managed to burrow through the drifts surrounding the bus and board another that had arrived to carry them on to their destination.

In addition to those stuck in snowdrifts, hundreds of holiday travellers spent most of that Christmas stranded in train stations and airports across the region. The CN Railway station in Moncton was filled to capacity on Christmas Eve. Approximately 73 passengers spent the night on hard benches in the drafty building, singing carols and swapping stories to pass the time.

Although the great Christmas blizzard of 1970 pounded all three Maritime Provinces, Saint John and Moncton took the brunt of the storm. As the snow continued to pile up, both cities were forced to declare a state of emergency. Meanwhile, crews in all urban centres struggled to keep main arteries open for emergency vehicles throughout the holiday. In the besieged province of New Brunswick, one catastrophe followed close on the heels of the last. During the height of the storm, on Christmas Eve, an explosion rocked the chemistry building on the University of New Brunswick campus in Fredericton. It took firefighters several hours to extinguish the resulting blaze, which destroyed two floors of the building. The following day, the roof of Moncton Stadium collapsed under the crushing accumulation of snow. In addition, multi-car pile-ups and house and business fires kept emergency workers in the province rushing from one scene to the next. Tragically, at least five people in the region died as a result of the blizzard. Among the casualties was a pair of young cousins who were struck and killed by a careening taxi while walking along the side of the road near their home in New Brunswick.

On Prince Edward Island, snow began falling in the Summerside area at about 4 p.m. on Christmas Eve. By the next afternoon, 47 centimetres had buried the town, bringing everything to a halt. Midnight masses and traditional Christmas Day services were cancelled. Three- to four-metre drifts prevented everything but snowmobiles and snowplows from moving, and even the plods had to work hard to break through some of the more massive drifts. Electricity and telephone lines were knocked out on many parts of the Island. So, not only were Islanders left shivering in the dark on Christmas Day, most couldn't even enjoy their traditional turkey dinner — they had no way to cook it.

All in all it was a truly memorable Christmas for most Maritimers.

Quebec

hristmas has always been a special time of year. Even in contemporary society, people are more generous towards each other, children are on their best behaviour, and the poor and the sick among us regain a sense of hope — all because it is Christmastime!

In traditional French-Canadian society there were a number of wondrous and supernatural events associated with the celebration of Christmas. One common belief was that on Christmas night the dead could rise from their graves. According to old Quebec storytellers, the dead would leave their coffins and kneel together next to a cross in the cemetery. Then a priest in a white surplice with a golden stole would arrive and recite the prayers of the nativity. The congregation of deceased men and women would respond to the religious worship with great fervour. Then they would leave the cemetery to go look around their village and their old homes one last time, before quietly filing back into their coffins.

Another wondrous tale from Quebec folklore described how farm animals magically gained the power of speech at the stroke of midnight on Christmas Eve. However, farmers who wanted to eavesdrop on the animals' conversations might have been disappointed, as the animals were not necessarily rejoicing on that night. In fact, more often than not they were complaining about their living conditions. The cows, horses, and sheep in the barn could be heard talking in a plaintive tone about how their hay was dry and there were hardly ever any oats to eat. Some of the animals bemoaned their lack of freedom. They remembered how they used to frolic gaily in the meadows in the days before they had harnesses and chains about their necks.

Finally, French-Canadian storytellers sometimes told the men, women, and children huddled around the fireplace that untold riches were revealed at Christmastime. Apparently, on Christmas night, the sands on the shore, the rocky hillsides, and the deep valleys would all split open, and anyone who dared to go and look could see amazing treasures shining in the moonlight.

After imparting these tidbits of Christmas lore, the storytellers would launch into the creative retelling of a holiday legend. "The Legend of Tom Caribou" and "The Legend of the

Chasse-Galerie" have been passed down to successive generations of Quebecers by the oral tradition. Both legends take place at logging camps. This is not pure coincidence. Dozens of Quebec legends are set in logging camps because the men who worked in these camps were passionate storytellers.

The Legend of Tom Caribou

There were 15 men working at a small logging camp near Ottawa: the boss, the clerk, the cook, and 12 labourers. They were all great guys — they didn't argue, they didn't curse. Of course, they all had a little drink of whiskey from time to time, but they never got too drunk.

There was one fellow from Trois-Rivières, however, who really liked to drink. When he had a bottle in front of him, he just became a funnel. Tom Baribeau was his name. The Irish foreman couldn't pronounce the "Baribeau" part very well, so the men gave him a nickname — Tom Caribou.

He was a scoundrel; that was for sure. And he was a lazy bum. He talked to the devil, blasphemed the good Lord, renounced his parents five times a day, and hardly said any prayers. He sure didn't look like the kind of fellow who would go straight to heaven.

Some of the men at the camp claimed they had seen him roaming around like a *loup-garou* (a man who has turned into a beast because he's neglected his religious duties or has openly communed with the devil). Indeed, Caribou was often seen on all fours, but he never ran like the *loup-*

garou. He was always too drunk for that.

Once, one of the loggers, Titoine, saw Tom climbing out of a tree. Upon reaching the ground, Tom grabbed Titoine and threatened to rip out his guts if he ever told anyone at the camp about the tree. Titoine told the other loggers what happened anyway, but the men kept it a big secret.

Every night after dinner, Tom went off on his own. He always turned his back as he was walking away to see if anyone was following him. After he was out of sight, everyone would try to guess where the rascal had gone. The men knew that he hadn't gone off on a *chasse-galerie* (a flying canoe driven by the devil), and he certainly hadn't gone to say his prayers. Strangely, Tom reeked of *rhum* every morning, even though there wasn't a drop of alcohol in the camp.

One day, shortly before Christmas, a group of neighbouring lumberjacks heard there was going to be a midnight mass somewhere in the woods. Apparently a missionary who was in the area to help the Nipissing peoples was prepared to sing the Christmas mass.

A group of loggers from Tom Caribou's camp really wanted to attend. They hadn't seen the baby Jesus or angels or any of those things for months! Of course, they weren't as bad as Tom — they didn't blaspheme the saints and insult the scriptures. But living in the woods six months of the year made it pretty hard to attend mass regularly.

On Christmas Eve, there was a full moon and the snow was just right for snowshoeing through the woods. A group of men decided that if they left right after dinner they would probably arrive in time for the mass. Then they would return to camp in time for breakfast the next morning.

Tom had no intention of going to midnight mass. When some of the men asked him about it, he slammed down his fist, said that he couldn't care less, and then unleashed a torrent of swear words. There was no way anyone was going to try to convince him to go.

The foreman told Tom that he could stay behind and watch over the camp. Then he added, "You may not want to see the good Lord tonight, but I hope you don't see the devil instead!"

The men set off into the woods on snowshoes, each of them carrying little bags with tobacco and dry biscuits. It was an excellent nighttime adventure — walking alongside the river on fresh, light snow with the stars above. One logger began to sing his favourite Christmas hymn, *Nouvelle Agréable*, and he imagined that the bells of his own parish church were ringing and calling him to worship.

He had this strange sense that he was back home, and that his father's horses were right behind him with their manes flying freely in the wind and the little bells on their harnesses tinkling gently. But then, when the men arrived at the midnight mass in the woods, he remembered where he was.

That impromptu midnight mass was really not an elaborate affair. The missionary was not well set up for a proper mass like the kind everyone was used to back home. The altar dishes were not highly polished, the cantors did not sing like proverbial nightingales, and the assistant who helped with the mass really looked like he would be more comfortable swinging a pickaxe than handling an incense burner. And there wasn't even a little wax baby Jesus. Without baby Jesus, what kind of midnight mass can you have, anyway?

The men had tears in their eyes. Even though it was the most rustic set-up they had ever seen for a mass, it was so beautiful just to hear those Christmas songs that most of the men had to look away so that they wouldn't cry.

Right after the mass was over, the men began the return trip to the logging camp. It was a long journey, and by the time they spotted the cabin in the distance, it was already daybreak.

The men were a little surprised to see that there was no smoke coming out of the chimney. Then they noticed that the cabin door was wide open. They went inside and discovered that the wood stove was cold and that Tom Caribou was nowhere to be found. Their first thought was that the devil had finally taken him.

The men decided that they should at least look around for the scoundrel. The search, however, would be difficult because it hadn't snowed for a while and there were dozens of tracks all around the cabin — finding Tom's tracks among them would be nearly impossible.

The boss suggested that the men take his dog, *Polisson.*

So off they went into the woods with a loaded gun and the dog sniffing the ground, wagging his tail wildly. They had barely been walking two minutes when the dog suddenly stopped and began to tremble like a leaf. One of the men raised his gun and walked in the direction the dog was pointing.

Soon he spotted Tom Caribou, stuck in the fork of a wild cherry tree. Tom was as white as a sheet and his eyes were practically jumping out of his head. A mother bear was holding on to the tree, two feet below him. The loggers were not scaredy-cats, but when they saw that bear, the blood nearly froze in their veins!

The men knew this was no time to hesitate — it was the bear or them. And no one wanted to get massacred by a bear. So one of them picked up the rifle and shot two bullets into the bear's chest. The animal groaned, let go of the tree, and fell on its back, dead.

The men then saw another creature tumble out of the tree — Tom Caribou, senseless, with a massive scratch mark on his face and a chunk of flesh missing from his bottom. His hair was completely white. Fright had aged him in an instant. He was barely recognizable.

The loggers made a stretcher out of sticks, picked up Tom, and carried him back to the camp. Next, they hauled away the bear. The men noticed that the bear smelled so strongly of alcohol that some were even tempted to lick the dead animal. Tom, the rascal, had never had sweeter breath!

When Tom regained consciousness, he told the others

what happened. On Christmas Eve, while most of the men were at midnight mass, Tom Caribou had had some kind of private party. He had hidden a bottle of whiskey in the fork of a wild cherry tree. At one point, he'd tried to pour himself more whiskey, but was already so drunk that the spirits just spilled all over the place — and onto the sleeping mother bear.

The bear had licked its chops sleepily, wondering why the rain had such a curious smell. But when the animal blinked, the whiskey poured right into its eyes. It yelped from the stinging sensation, and from being so rudely awakened from hibernation.

With a raging mother bear on his tail, Tom had leapt into the fork of the tree. Slowly, the whiskey had taken effect on the angry bruin, and she'd hung onto the tree in a mild stupor. Tom, trembling in fright, had crouched in the fork.

Poor Tom Caribou. It took about three weeks to get him back on his feet because he had so many wounds. He was convinced that the devil himself had inflicted the injuries.

Tom looked pitiful, sitting there covered in white plasters — like a doughnut rolled in white sugar — asking everyone, including the dog, to forgive all of his tomfoolery and his swearing.

Anyway, the men knew, and Tom Caribou knew, that his meeting with the bear was his punishment for not celebrating Christmas with a pure heart, for not joining his fellows at midnight mass in the woods.

Quebec

Cric! crac! cra!
Sacatabi, Sac-à-tabac!
That's the end of the story!

The Legend of the Chasse-Galerie
Joseph Ferrand worked at a logging camp on the Gatineau River one winter and he worked non-stop — felling trees, loading the logs onto sleighs, and then helping the horses get the wood out along the icy logging roads. Every night was pretty much the same as the night before. He had a simple dinner of beans and pork with the boys and then, exhausted, fell asleep as soon as he landed on his hard wooden bed.

But New Year's Eve was different; Joseph and his friends had a real party. The foreman had bought a barrel of *rhum* for everyone, and some of the boys got out the fiddles and spoons. They really made merry that night. Joseph soon lost track of how many glasses of *rhum* he had drunk!

He lay down on his bed to make the room stop spinning. Then Baptiste Durand asked him if he would like to see his girl. Would he like to see Lise? Of course! All night long, Joseph had been imagining how Lise was celebrating New Year's Eve. He had imagined the fiddle music, the square dances, the steaming tourtières, but most of all, holding his girl next to him.

"Of course I want to see Lise," said Joseph. "But she lives in Lavaltrie, more than a hundred leagues away. It would take weeks to walk there."

Baptiste Durand assured Joseph that they could travel to Lavaltrie in a couple of hours and that they would be back by six o'clock the next morning. Then Baptiste mumbled something about taking a canoe.

"You mean a *chasse-galerie*?" Joseph asked nervously. Other loggers had told him about this enchanted canoe operated by the devil. He wanted to see Lise — his beautiful, angelic Lise — but was he crazy enough to risk his eternal soul?

Baptiste didn't seem concerned. He was too busy chatting up other loggers who were willing to take a chance in order to be home for the New Year's Eve parties. Apparently, there had to be an even number in the canoe, so when there were seven interested men, Baptiste looked at Joseph and said, "Okay. You are number eight. Now let's go!"

Just before the loggers left the cabin, Baptiste asked Joseph to "jump in the New Year" by leaping over a barrel of lard (this was the ritual for the youngest man at camp). Joseph tried to jump over the barrel, just so the other guys wouldn't notice that something strange was going on. But he couldn't do it; he just couldn't concentrate.

Baptiste, Joseph, and two other loggers stepped outside into the freezing night. The clear, bright sky crackled with stars. There were four men from another logging camp waiting for them with long, slim canoe paddles. A birchbark canoe lay in a clearing, well lit by the full moon.

Someone shouted, "Baptiste, you steer because you know the canoe." Baptiste took the stern, and everyone piled in and took up their positions in the enchanted canoe. Baptiste stood up and looked the men straight in the eyes. He told them that they were about to take an oath to the devil and that they had better not joke. If everyone followed the strict instructions, there would not be any problems. The conditions of the trip were that the men had to abstain from swearing, drinking, and speaking the name of God. Also, they had to avoid touching a cross on a church steeple during the trip. The penalty for breaking any of these rules was almost too awful to think about.

All of the men repeated after Baptiste: "Satan, ruler of hell, we will surrender our souls to you if, during the next six hours, we pronounce the name of God or touch a cross. As long as we respect these conditions, you will transport us through the air to wherever we want tonight and then back to camp first thing in the morning."

Baptiste shouted, "Acabris! Acabras! Acabram!" Suddenly, the canoe began to float up into the night sky. It soared over the camp and across the forests of southern Quebec. It flew so fast that the frosty air felt like hundreds of tiny icicles jabbing at their faces. The men looked down in amazement at the broad mirrored surface of the mighty Gatineau River and the endless stretch of dense forest. Then they started to see clusters of little lights marking villages below. The men grew so excited thinking about the festivities there that they could practically smell the *tourtières* in the ovens!

They followed the Gatineau River all the way to Deux-Montagnes. Then Baptiste told the men that they were going to fly over Montreal and he suggested that they sing a song to pass the time. They narrowly missed hitting dozens of church steeples in Montreal as they careened through the air, belting out "*Mon pere n'avait fille que moi, Canot d'écorce qui va vole, et dessus la mer il m'envoie...*"

Finally, Baptiste announced that they were coming into Lavaltrie. He decided to land the *chasse-galerie* in his godfather's field. As soon as Baptiste said, "Bramaca, Irbaca," the canoe made a sharp turn and headed down towards a snowbank in the field. The men traipsed to the village in single file. The snowdrifts were up to their hips in some places, but they didn't care because they were already so close to their goal. They went straight to Baptiste Durand's godfather's house because Jean-Jean Gabriel usually knew if there was any dance or feast going on in the village. Unfortunately, the whole Gabriel family was out, but the hired girl who had been left in charge told the loggers that there was some kind of party going on at Batisette Augé's house on the other side of the river.

Without question, the loggers wanted to join that party. So they got back into the canoe and flew up over the river. Moments later, they saw Batisette's house all aglow. The party was in full swing, and they could even hear the fiddle music from outside the house. They hid the canoe and rushed in, seeking warmth and merriment, but most of all, the girls.

Baptiste reminded everyone again not to touch a drop of spirits and not to mention the Lord's name.

Batisette threw open the door and welcomed the loggers to join the party. Everyone was happy to see them, and they pestered the men to explain how they managed to make it to Lavaltrie for New Year's Eve. Baptiste said to them, "Come on, give us a chance to take off our coats and dance. There will plenty of time to explain everything in the morning."

Joseph pushed through the crowd, looking for Lise. Finally, he spotted her dancing with another man. He couldn't blame Lise. After all, Joseph had been gone for months. He went up to her casually, as if they saw each other every day, and asked for the next dance. Lise was amazed to see Joseph, but she didn't ask any questions. She just stared at him with her gorgeous blue eyes and said that of course she would dance with him. Joseph was so content to be in her arms that he completely forgot he was risking his eternal soul just to be with her for one night. They danced for hours, lost to the world. Lise and Joseph were so enamoured of each other that they did not even notice when the fiddlers stopped playing briefly to get some refreshments.

The other boys were having a ball, too. They were happy to see women again — it had been months since they'd seen any! At one point during the evening, Joseph was sure he saw Baptiste drinking whiskey. That seemed strange, considering how many times Baptiste had warned the others not to touch spirits. But Joseph was so happy to be with Lise, he didn't really think about it.

Baptiste came around at about four in the morning and said, "We have to leave now, and don't bother with good-byes or we will attract too much attention."

The thought of leaving Lise again made Joseph feel all weak and queasy. He took a chance and told Baptiste that he was going to stay in Lavaltrie. Baptiste reminded him that if they didn't all return together, there would be trouble. Of course, he couldn't jeopardize his mates' souls. So he grabbed his coat and fled the party.

The men could all see that Baptiste was drunk. They didn't want him to steer the canoe, but Baptiste was the only one who knew the way back.

The return trip to the logging camp was hair-raising. Baptiste did daredevil acrobatics with the canoe, and a couple of times they came very close to brushing up against a cross on a church steeple. Thankfully, they never actually did. It was almost as if someone was watching out for them. Either that, or the devil didn't find their souls very attractive.

The weather had changed overnight. Now the sky was dense with cloud and the loggers could not even see the moon. Baptiste worried that he might not be able to follow the Gatineau back up to the camp. Joseph became impatient, concerned that they wouldn't be able to return before their six o'clock curfew.

Then Baptiste shouted out, "Here we are boys — home again!" They landed unceremoniously in a clump of low trees. Half of the men were upside-down in the snow, and all of them were swearing a blue streak. At first, Joseph panicked because all night long they had been told to avoid swearing. But then he realized that it was okay, because they were safely back at the camp.

The next morning, Baptiste Durand was gone. Joseph asked two fellow loggers who had travelled with him the previous night where Baptiste had gone. The boys told Joseph that they didn't know whom he was talking about.

Ontario

usic is a part of most festivities, and Christmas is no exception. For centuries, special songs have been associated with the holidays. Frequently, the songs were sung by groups of revellers who travelled from house to house, both to bring Christmas cheer to the inhabitants and to collect treats or gifts for themselves or others.

When Georgina and Frederick Hyde celebrated their Christmas at Port Maitland in 1841, the evening ended with Georgina pulling her harp from the corner of the parlour and the family singing carols. Whether pioneer settlers had the inclination to go carolling door to door probably depended on the time, how well established a community was, and the fashion. Carolling apparently went in and out of fashion, as a writer for the *Niagara Mail* suggested in 1853: "For our part, we should be glad to see the revival of carol-singing that is, in a properly decorous spirit. There is something solemn and touching even now in listening to the chant of the street minstrels ... as it rises through the silence of the night, making one feel that peace and goodwill may become something more than sound."

Among the songs the anonymous writer may have heard were "The First Nowell" (the archaic spelling of Noel) and "God Rest Ye Merry Gentlemen," which had been brought to Canada by British immigrants in the early years of settlement. As the years passed, other carols arrived. In time, many became so well known that they were parodied. One parody with an Ontario connection is the "Twelve Days of Christmas" as sung by the McKenzie brothers, a.k.a. Rick Moranis and Dave Thomas. Moranis, who was born in Toronto, and Thomas, originally from St. Catharines, were well known for their portrayal of two "stupid hosers." In 1981, the brothers recorded an album of humorous songs, including their version of the traditional Christmas carol, in which the usual gifts from their true love were replaced with beer, two turtlenecks, three French toasts, four pounds of back bacon, five golden tuques and other odd items.

While a dash of humour or a modern version of a carol can be welcome, most Ontarians prefer to hear and sing well-loved traditional carols at Christmastime. And sometimes, the music can be put to work for a good cause. In 1924, hundreds of residents of Windsor designated Christmas Eve as the night to make music and raise money for charity. As members of the Border Cities Carolers society, they were divided into various teams, each with its own captain, who set out the areas they were to cover. Windsor residents had been told in advance that the carollers would be collecting for various charities and were reminded to give generously. In addition, just prior to Christmas Eve, society president J.R. Hewer requested that all city clergymen ask members of their congregations to think about opening their homes to the carollers, especially if the weather was extra cold. Meanwhile, various restaurants in the town offered free lunches to the singers.

The singing started at 6 p.m., with about 800 people participating. A local newspaper commented enthusiastically on how quickly the membership had increased in just a few short years. "The Border Cities Carolers have grown to a truly great organization composed of self-sacrificing men and women who will spend Christmas Eve bringing joy to the hearts of Border Cities' residents, with their Yuletide songs of cheer."

Over the years, other Ontario communities have made Christmas music in other ways. In 2001, more than 200 people poured into St. Mary's Church in Fort Frances on the Sunday before Christmas to hear "Hope was Born", the story of the birth of Jesus. Music and narration was provided by the Choraliers, a 72-member community choir. The cantata, part of a Fort Frances Christmas tradition dating back to 1990, thrilled both listeners and participants, who agreed the music was just perfect for putting people in the Christmas spirit.

In 2002, the cathedral choir of St. Paul's Church in London, Ontario, travelled to St. Paul's Cathedral in London, England, to replace the English choir for a few days. Among the songs the 34-member choir performed was the "Huron Carol." Although it added a distinctivly Canadian touch to the performance, it was especially appropriate for the cathedral — like the carol, St. Paul's dates from the 17th century.

While listening to carollers or choirs perform can be very enjoyable, for many people much of the fun in Christmas music is in singing along. Certainly this was the case one morning in 1945 when Christmas shopping came to a standstill for 20 minutes in the Toronto Simpson's store. As the 200-member staff choir lined up on the escalator and sang to the accompaniment of the Harmony Brass Quartet and the 48th Highlanders regimental band, customers, including harried mothers with young children, joined in. The choir had been conducted by 82-year-old A.P. Howells since 1921, and by this time its ability to soothe pre-Christmas nerves was legendary. According to the *Toronto Daily Star*, in the early 1940s one of the choir's brief concerts was broadcast over the radio. In New York, a harried cab company manager was struggling to find transportation for time-pressed customers. Partly to drown out their demands, he turned up the volume on his radio as the Simpson choir was singing. In a few minutes, the angry demands stopped. Everyone was too busy singing along to worry about getting a taxi, and for several years after that customers made a point of coming to the cab company for the week before Christmas just for the fun of singing Christmas carols.

Christmas Weather

Although many Ontarians may not realize it, dreaming of a white Christmas has as much to do with folk beliefs about health and luck as it does with picture-perfect holiday scenery. British and European folklore suggest that a green Christmas is a bad omen, as a St. Catharines newspaper reminded readers in 1865: "If the old saw be true that 'A green Christmas makes a fat churchyard,' then will the undertakers and grave-diggers of this section of Canada be the most prosperous and happy individuals found hereabouts next spring and summer, for the snow is all or nearly gone — and there was very little of it to go — and the weather is as mild and as entertaining as a young miss of sixteen with her first beau."

While it is fairly unusual, Christmas has occasionally coincided with unseasonably warm temperatures in Ontario. In 1893, Lady Aberdeen, wife of Canada's governor-general, described her first Christmas in Canada as a "horrible muggy day." Although the weather had been chilly earlier in the month, just before Christmas the temperature had suddenly soared. There were some very disappointed youngsters in the Aberdeen household. "Great lamentations over no skating or snow sports for to-day," Lady Aberdeen wrote. To make matters worse, it started to rain when the family was out visiting. "It was ridiculous to see the rain freezing as it fell & making it quite difficult to shut one's umbrella."

In 1923, Christmas in the Bay of Quinte area was so warm that many residents went for a sail on Lake Ontario. Meanwhile, in Stratford, F. Crocker found strawberries ready for picking in his garden. The following year, the *London Free Press* reported roses and primroses blooming a few days before Christmas. In 1994, when the temperature in Sault Ste. Marie climbed to eight degrees Celsius on Christmas Day, people put on bathing suits, sat outdoors on lawn chairs, or washed their cars.

Warm Christmas temperatures might be welcome as a respite from an Ontario winter, but they can also create additional hazards. In 1973, warmer temperatures in southern Ontario created serious, prolonged fog over several days, stranding thousands of holiday travellers. Six years later, five days of heavy rain dumped 100 millimetres of water on Toronto just before Christmas. Rivers rose to record heights, storm sewers overflowed and basements flooded — but at least no one had to shovel the water. If the temperature had been a bit lower, it was estimated, the rain would have been transformed into 100 centimetres of snow, about the equivalent of a typical year's snowfall.

Despite the occasional December heat waves, most Ontarians do get their share of white Christmases. Catharine

Parr Traill described a fairly typical one in the Peterborough area in the 1830s and how much her children enjoyed it: "A merry day it was to them, for our boy Martin had made them a little sledge, and there was a famous snowdrift against the garden fence, which was hard packed and frozen smooth and glare. Up and down this frozen heap did James and Kate with their playmates glide and roll. It was a Christmas treat to watch those joyous faces, buoyant with mirth, and brightened by the keen air, through the frosty panes; and often was the graver converse of the parents interrupted by the merry shout and gleesome voices of their little ones; and if a sadder train of thought brought back the memory of former days, and home, country, and friends, from whom we were for ever parted, such sadness was not without its benefit, linking us in spirit to that home, and all that made it precious to our hearts."

The day was so enjoyable that when it was over, Catharine was reluctant to part with her sister Susanna, and so she accompanied her to her home. They weren't the only revellers on the road: "Just as we were issuing forth for our moonlight drive through the woods, our ears were saluted by a merry peal of sleigh bells, and a loud hurrah greeted our homely turn-out, as a party of lively boys and girls, crammed into a smart painted cutter, rushed past at full speed. They were returning from a Christmas merry-making at a neighbour's house, where they too had been enjoying a happy Christmas, and long the still woods echoed with the gay tones of their voices, and the clear jingle of their merry bells, as a bend in the river-road, brought them back on the night breeze to our ears."

While cold weather and snow could bring Christmas fun, sometimes it caused problems on Christmas Day. In 1872, the Marchioness of Dufferin and Ava was in Ottawa with her husband, the governor general. Christmas morning was extremely chilly, with temperatures reading 28 degrees Celsius below zero. "Proprieties out of the question," Lady Dufferin wrote in her diary, then continued, "Must go to church in sealskin turbans, and must undress when we get there, as we sit near the stove; so that when we leave, the amount of things to be put on is frightful. There are my cloak, and my cloud, [a long scarf, wound several times around the neck] fur gauntlets, and woolen cuffs."

There were also several children to dress, including her son Fred, who was extremely nervous about the possibility of freezing his ears. "He is always feeling them and inquiring from passers-by whether they are frozen," she wrote. Fortunately for the Dufferins, just about everyone in church was busy putting on their own outer garments, so any commotion they made was lost in the general rush to get dressed and hurry home for Christmas celebrations. And given the heat in the building, Fred apparently did not have to worry about the state of his ears.

Christmas Amusements

From about the middle of the 1800s, school concerts and festivals were an important part of holiday festivities. In 1862, the *St. Catharines Journal* described a Sunday school festival for children of the St. James Church congregation, Port Dalhousie. It was held on Christmas Eve at the village schoolhouse. About 60 children attended, along with their parents, other relatives, and friends, so the one-room school was packed to overflowing. The children sat in the front seats, close enough to get a good look at a Christmas tree that had been decorated specially for them. "Brilliantly lit up," the tree held "a splendid crop of all sorts of juvenile attractions" including books, dolls, trumpets, baskets, and other items.

In small rural communities, the school Christmas concert was one of the social highlights of the year. In fact, many teachers' reputations and continued employment depended on how good their Christmas concert was. In *I Remember the One-Room School*, a Guelph area teacher, Myrtle Fair, tells the story of one school inspector who felt a teacher should be fired because her pupils were so far behind with their work. The school trustees, however, insisted on keeping her because she staged the best Christmas concerts.

Staging a good Christmas concert took a lot of hard work. Typically, there were weeks of rehearsals and preparation, sometimes including time spent placating parents who felt their sons or daughters deserved a better part in the presentation. Despite all the planning, when the big night arrived, there was usually a problem or two. Students forgot their lines or fell off the low platform at the front of the classroom that usually served as a stage. Most of the time, teachers were able to take these minor mishaps in stride, which occasionally even provided a bit of amusement. One rural Ontario teacher told how Santa arrived by sleigh for a 1938 Christmas concert. Everyone inside the school heard the jingle of bells, but when several minutes passed and Santa had still not entered the classroom, someone was sent out to check on him. A short time later, Santa made his appearance. His cap was crooked and it was apparent to most adults in the room that he was "high as a kite." He had obviously swallowed a little too much Christmas cheer, but was still very amusing as he spoke to the group and handed out gifts to the children. Nevertheless, the teacher was extremely relieved when Santa — actually a member of the school board — got back into his sleigh and drove away.

Another teacher recalled asking her brother to play Santa for her school concert. When he reached the schoolhouse, he found the front entrance so jammed with spectators that he couldn't get in. Instead, he grabbed a ladder, took it around to the side of the schoolhouse, and climbed in the window. The unorthodox entrance got plenty of attention, but nothing compared to the polka that Santa insisted on dancing with the teacher. While the pianist played mightily, Santa and the teacher danced around the platform at the front of the classroom. But the mask Santa was wearing kept slipping, blocking his vision. At one point, he danced the teacher right off the platform and the young woman found herself dangling in mid-air. Fortunately, Santa kept his grip, pulled her back to safety, and the crowd cheered.

The Prairies

owhere else but the rural Prairies, it seems, has the tradition of the Christmas concert become such a critical thread in the social fabric. Today, sitting comfortably in our split-level suburban homes a few short minutes from the mall, or standing on the balcony of our high-rise condo, gazing down at the city's Christmas lights, we might pause for a moment and wonder why that is.

A Tradition Begins

The "concert" was, in the beginning, a Christmas religious service. Travelling missionaries held their first services in houses on isolated ranches and farms. With the formation of school districts, services were held inside the small rural schools, simply because these were the only structures capable of holding more than a few people. In this classroom environment, it was only natural that, over time, children became active participants rather than passive spectators.

Later, with the construction of churches, the children's Christmas concert continued as a separate entity, still usually staged in the schoolhouse. The concert's religious anteced-ent was acknowledged by the centrepiece recitation and re-enactment of that long-ago eve in Bethlehem — a tableau complete with bed-sheeted worshippers, animals (some-times props, sometimes real), and a Mary, Joseph, and baby Jesus. However, it would take a unique combination of fac-tors to turn that special entity into a yuletide tradition.

Chief among those factors was rural prairie isolation. While the husband might have grumbled at having to hitch the horse to the cutter and drive "all that way" to the school on a chilly night, the wife likely considered it the special occasion it truly was. At last, a chance to get out of the house! At last, a chance to meet and talk with other women! The Christmas concert brought people together in a way that few other occasions did.

The Christmas concert was, then, both a social occa-sion and a rare evening's entertainment. In the early years between World Wars I and II, radio was still in its infancy. Like the phonograph and a stack of scratchy records, it was wonderful, but it still was not enough. The movies were a big treat, but the movie house was miles away "in town" — a twice-monthly destination to buy supplies. People craved live entertainment, but most rural families went years without hearing a live orchestra or watching actors on a stage. The concert provided that "live" entertainment. Better still, entertainment that starred their own children.

One of the most challenging tasks that befell a rural prairie schoolteacher every year was presenting some form of pageant or play that somehow ensured every student was given an opportunity to contribute. Nothing — neither costumes, songs, nor clever skits — mattered as much as that single fact. And parents? Parents represented much more than an audience.

The teacher needed help and parents were happy to provide it. Fathers hammered together stages, painted scenery, rigged special lights, and cut down and put up Christmas trees. One of the men was given the honour of playing Santa. Mothers stitched amazingly imaginative costumes: military uniforms, fairy gowns with gossamer wings, and outfits that turned children into Christmas candles. The thrifty and enterprising women fashioned some of the costumes so they could be utilized as "Sunday best" long after the concert.

These same moms then baked cakes, tarts, and other treats and either served them or packaged them up for the children in homemade bags. Usually, one of the mothers or grandmothers could be counted on to play the piano. Some families who had organs or pianos in their front rooms invited teacher and students to home-style rehearsals. These cooperative efforts of people living in far-flung farms and homesteads staved off the isolation, the loneliness, the sheer monotonous predictability of seemingly endless winter days and nights.

"Tell us about your Christmas concerts ..."
So great was the importance of the Christmas concert that the production was specifically referred to in the teachers' contracts. As many teachers realized, their ability to produce a truly special concert could be almost as influential in gaining and retaining employment as their formal education. The yuletide equation appeared to be: well-organized, imaginative program, plus well-disciplined performers equals good teacher. A teacher, therefore, became a combination of playwright, director, composer, and musical conductor — and, in some cases, musician.

The provincial government of Alberta and its educational leaders not only acknowledged the popularity of the concert, but also recognized it as a particularly powerful "teachable moment." By 1936, in its *Programme of Studies for the Elementary School*, the government was offering this guidance to teachers: "It is advisable that the Christmas concert, which is one of the important enterprises of the year, should grow out of schoolwork. Thus, the practicing of music, verse speaking and plays, will be carried on during school hours; for these activities are a legitimate part of school life, having a satisfying culmination in the concert itself."

Teachers obliged by creating plays and pageants that

reflected rural history, such as Chinook, Alberta's *In the Days of Grandma and Grandpa*, and 1951's Depression-era saga, *Sod*. They also created plays from stories in readers, such as Manitoba's Hodgson School's Shoe Maker and the Elves, and stoked the fires of patriotism with stories and songs about war heroes — Blindloss, Alberta's *Crippled Soldier* and Chinook's 1942 duet, *Big Ben*. The productions provided countless musical opportunities for students. In places like Biggar and Admiral, Saskatchewan, lucky students got the chance to play in school bands and orchestras.

All over the Prairies — in overheated, crowded one-room schoolhouses, and, later, inside cavernous gymnasiums of larger city schools — the Christmas concert was unsurpassed as a social, cultural, educational, and spiritual phenomenon. Despite the squalls of infants, clank and scrape of chairs, flickering lights, forgotten lines, miscued action, and other catastrophes, it was an event that provoked reminiscences — fond memories that often became the stuff of legend.

Dedicated and Talented Teachers
Teachers began planning their Christmas concerts early by "brainstorming" with other teachers at summer conventions and workshops. By the fall, pouring over catalogues, they were making notes in five-cent scribblers about costumes and props. The task of planning the concert was so challenging that teachers who moved from school to school soon learned to take their best props and costumes with them.

They read plays, poems, and short stories with a new purpose and saw them in an entirely new light. Would this make a good presentation?

Teachers became masters in the art of motivation. They knew their students' attentiveness, if not learning, improved when concert practice was promised at the end of the day's lessons. Hilda Adock, who taught at Coronation, Alberta, went one step further. In September, she entered into agreements with her students: rehearsals wouldn't begin unless every student was at a certain place in their textbooks by that crucial time before Christmas.

Teachers often had to cajole, scold, or nag to get good performances out of the kids. But, knowing that parents prized the children's happiness and sense of achievement far more than artistic perfection, they didn't push their charges too hard.

As well as pulling the concert together, teachers had to raise funds. They not only needed money for the production, they were expected to buy supplies to make decorations for the classrooms and treats and gifts for the students. Sometimes, with the help of parents, teachers organized raffles and called on area businesses and service clubs for donations. The lengths some teachers went to in carrying out these duties went down in local history.

In the days leading up to Christmas 1936, teacher Alice Moore had finally collected enough money to buy presents for her students. After the kids had agonized over department store catalogues and made their wish lists, Alice completed the order forms. A certain Monday was the deadline for mailing the order. That Monday night, Alice borrowed a pony and set out, bareback, in sub-zero temperatures, on the 20-kilometre ride to the town of Athabasca, Alberta.

Presumably, she found bareback riding was not to her liking, so she stopped at a farm and asked for a saddle. The farmer kindly gave her one, but was not gallant enough to put it on for her. To her consternation, she found the saddle was far too big for the dainty pony. After getting the oversized saddle on, she set out — a little more comfortably — in the pitch black. How many times she had to stop to re-cinch the saddle is not recorded, but it's safe to say she became very accomplished at the task. Finally, the lights of the town came into view. All she had to do now was cross the frozen Athabasca River.

She tied her pony to some bushes and stood on the riverbank, summoning her courage to walk on the ice. Luckily, there were other travellers crossing the river on foot. After watching one after another get across safely, she finally stepped out onto the frozen expanse and slowly made her way across.

Once on the other side, relieved and happy, she walked into the light and warmth of the post office. She picked up her mail, then tried to send her precious order. To her dismay, she was informed that the post-office was closed for business. She knew the kids wouldn't get their gifts in time for Christmas unless she mailed the order that night. With a sinking heart, she rushed outside, where the darkness hid her tears of "frustration, anger and weariness." Determined not to disappoint the children, she vowed not to give up.

The plucky teacher located the home of a storekeeper she had done business with and asked for his help. Fortunately, he was able to use his influence to bend the post office rules. The order got away in time. Many years later, Alice summed up her adventure: "Santa Claus did come to Big Coulee School that year!" she said with a triumphant smile.

Anything That Can Go Wrong...

The weeks and days leading up to the big show were always tense. Often, at the very last moment, catastrophe struck. Students and teachers, in true "show biz" tradition, redoubled their efforts. Such was the case in Drumheller, Alberta, the afternoon before the Christmas concert of 1934.

The school's lights were flicked off, and the door securely locked. Teacher and students had every reason to feel a sense of satisfaction as they headed home from school that December afternoon. The decorations were terrific and the play was great. All they had to do now was run through the dress rehearsal the next day, and then it would be "Show Time."

The next morning when they opened the door to the school, they stood in stunned dismay: the potbellied stove had belched smoke all night long. The once-white walls were black. The windows were completely blanked out. The big, bright silver bell positioned in the centre of the ceiling — the focal point — was a dull, dirty brown. The would-be thespians became a desperate cleaning crew as teacher and students frantically scrubbed, wiped, and polished as best they could. There was no dress rehearsal, but the show went on as planned!

Another Christmas concert was almost derailed in Vauxhall, Alberta, in 1947. Not by soot, but by snow. Students and teacher woke on the morning of the big show to find that nature had "upstaged" them with one of the biggest blizzards of the season.

Ploughing their way to school and up the steps was one thing — having to plough their way to the desks was another! Part of the roof had collapsed under the snow's weight and everything — table and desktops, decorations, and even the stovepipe — was buried. Snow removal took precedence over the final rehearsal, but students hit the stage on time that night.

A third story about how young Albertans rose to the occasion comes from Hanna. The class of 1939 was small; only 18 students sat behind the classroom's desks. But this was more than enough to put on what promised to be a wonderful Christmas concert. Then, in the final days before the show, students began waking up with spots. Chicken pox had come to town.

By the eve of the big day, the already-modest enrolment was reduced by 12. Should the concert be cancelled? Not a chance! Six children soldiered on and gave a shorter — but courageous — performance.

These three concerts were all memorable — and successful. But other concerts that delighted audiences, the ones remembered a century later, were those where the unexpected and unpredictable reigned supreme.

Consider the poor teacher in Fiske, Saskatchewan, who inadvertently provided an insightful and hilarious "shadow" drama throughout the concert. Although "hidden" behind a sheet, light from an unwisely positioned lantern made her frantic actions visible to the audience. The cajoling, threatening, exasperated director easily upstaged her young charges that night.

Pity the one frantically scratching youngster in Red Deer, Alberta, who discovered, to his mortification — and his parents' disbelief — that he had an allergic reaction to tension and excitement. The malady remained undiscovered until he twitched onto the stage.

Take a moment to puzzle at the 1926 concert in Craigmyle, Alberta, where a mysterious ailment struck down players in the middle of the performance! So determined were the youngsters that, in spite of their wooziness, they tried to go on with the show. But, after a third young performer collapsed onstage, moms and dads in the audience became alarmed. Attending school trustees wanted the show stopped. The teacher adamantly refused. However, the concert soon ground to a halt as child after child was bundled up in the sleigh and driven home by worried parents. Thankfully, all the children had recovered by the next morning, and the source of the contagion was discovered. A new electric light generator had recently been installed. Unfortunately, no one had thought to make a vent. So the generator that should have enhanced the performance by casting light on the players, felled them by spewing its carbon monoxide exhaust directly under the stage.

Jim Storey, of Dundurn, has another tale to share about Christmas concerts. This one involved a truly spectacular show. A few days before Christmas some time in the 1930s, the Storey family set off to see Jim's sister perform at her school, about two and a half miles away. During the concert, someone went outside, perhaps for a trip to the outhouse, perhaps to check the horses. Within minutes, he dashed back inside and spread the word: somebody's house was on fire! It turned out to be the Storeys' place.

By the time the family and most of the concert-goers arrived at the farm, the flaming wreckage of the house had fallen into the cellar. Jim's dad was mortified. He knew only too well what had happened. In the frantic last minutes before they set out for the concert, he had filled the small stove with coal, but neglected to do one small, crucial task.

"What you had to do was burn the gas off with the draughts open," Jim explains. "I guess they were in a hurry to get to the school. He shut down the draughts instead of leaving them open." The gas inside built up to a critical level and then, "the stove just exploded."

The farm Jim's parents worked on was actually owned by the operator of the lumberyard in the nearby town of Hanley, so the operator quickly moved a ready-made house to the same location and put it over the same cellar. Much to the Storeys' delight, they had a roof over their heads that Christmas, after all.

This next story took place "somewhere in southern Saskatchewan, sometime in the 1900s." Small town citizens are, as a rule, not quite as quick to change the prevailing mores as the folks in big cities. However, they are far more likely to notice these changes in mores — and to talk about them — as one discomfited teacher discovered.

The young teacher, Sarah Scott, unwisely decided to use the school Christmas concert to answer her detractors. She wrote a song, creatively skewering the gossips, then coached the kids to perform it. Imagine the shocked silence when parents heard their own children sing the following ditty:

Merry Christmas Mrs. Jonathan, Merry Christmas!
Mrs. Rip Van Winkle's sharp tongue made her
Husband blue,
But Dame Winkle had nothing on you.
Merry Christmas, Mrs. Jonathan, Merry Christmas!

The Prairies

Merry Christmas, Mrs. Brown, Merry Christmas!
Everyone knows where you go night after night,
Do you think at your age it is right?
Merry Christmas Mrs. Brown, Merry Christmas!

There were other verses — many others. The teacher's number-one target happened to be the person behind the curtain accompanying the students on the piano. Someone, most likely one of the conscience-stricken children, had tipped her off before the performance. To the teacher's sudden consternation, the vengeful accompanist kept playing at the end of the teacher's song, and the kids kept singing:

Merry Christmas, Miss Sarah Scott, Merry Christmas!
Wearing short dresses to flash your lacy pink panties,
Tells us your lifestyle is full of frailties.
Merry Christmas, Miss Sarah Scott, Merry Christmas!

The applause was thunderous.

British Columbia

**s** the saying goes, there's no place like home for the holidays. In the late 19th century and early 20th century, "home" in British Columbia meant very different things to different people. For some of the province's early settlers, home was a bunkhouse in a coastal logging camp or on a Cariboo ranch. For others, it was a stately mansion on the slopes above bustling New Westminster or a small room in a modest working-class house in Victoria's James Bay. Regardless of where these early settlers were living, it seems most of them did what they could to ensure that the holidays were celebrated in some way.

Christmas On Burrard Inlet
By the 1880s, grand, granite-faced homes were being con-

structed not far from the brick hotels, bars, warehouses, and chandleries that now ringed Victoria's harbour. Across the Strait of Juan de Fuca, New Westminster's Columbia Street wharves and buildings hugged the Fraser River, and homes dotted the hills above the water's edge.

Things were very different on the heavily wooded shores of Burrard Inlet to the north. There was no rosy glow from gas lamps to light the way for a weary party of CPR surveyors. There were no comfortable carriages waiting to roll revellers down broad streets cobbled with wooden "bricks." No cheerful greetings shouted in the warm, congenial atmosphere of the bar on the corner for the numb, exhausted men who had been laying out the route of the transcontinental railway from Port Moody to Coal Harbour, at the edge of what is now Stanley Park. On Christmas Day 1884, there was merely the moan of the wind and the soft swish of snow pushed aside by stumbling feet, as the 15 men trudged through two-foot drifts.

Goaded on by the crusty, white-whiskered Major A.B. Rogers, the group pushed its way through stands of giant fir and cedar toward the tiny inlet mill settlement of Hastings, not far from today's Second Narrows Bridge.

For Major Rogers, this final part of his work for the new railroad was likely anti-climactic. He had risked life and limb in the Rockies in search of the best route — perhaps *any* route — to the coast. Given the nature of the day, it was likely that the men needed none of Rogers's usual blasphemous tirades to wrap up their work quickly and head for the warmth of what passed for civilization. Otway Wilkie was one of those men. Years later, he remembered that particular December 25.

"At the conclusion of the day's labour, just as it was getting dark, we reached a bluff of land about half a mile or more east of George Black's Brighton Hotel ... we all got into our boat, a large clinker-built boat about twenty feet long and capable of carrying twelve or fourteen men; no masts, just oars, which was on the beach, and made our way to Black's at Hastings where we celebrated Christmas dinner."

It was, as Wilkie described it, a "jolly party." Lonely loggers and mill-workers from Hastings and the neighbouring settlement of Moodyville had left their shacks to join the visiting surveyors. The men's revelry continued into the next cold, gray dawn.

Two years later, Christmas was celebrated in brand new hotels and buildings of what would become the city of Vancouver. A disastrous fire had levelled much of the town, but Granville, as it was then called, had "risen from the ashes." That was reason enough for celebration, but there was another reason for merriment that Christmas of 1886. The chief incentive for the rebuilding was the coming of the railroad. The burning question of which settlement — Port Moody or Granville — would be the terminus of the railroad had been settled by none other than the railroad's architect, William Van Horne. Van Horne had journeyed to the West

Coast during the summer of 1884. Now, two years later, a newly constructed CPR wharf waited for the first trains. First, however, a very special free Christmas dinner awaited the CPR workers who had just finished the rail-line from Port Moody.

The city's future mayor, William Templeton, had ordered a ton of turkeys from Peterborough, Ontario, in honour of the occasion and as the community's expression of thanks for the hard-working railroad crews. The Methodist Church sponsored the free Christmas feast for the "navvies." Dan Campbell, Grandville's baker, slid 65 birds into his huge ovens for the Water Street banquet. A new city. A new railroad. They could see it coming, at last — urban civilization to rival Victoria and New Westminster.

A Christmas Comedy

Smithers, British Columbia, was by no means a large community in the early 1900s, but it offered its residents all the amenities. The town had three or four paved streets and a few real electric streetlights, courtesy of local entrepreneur W. J. "Wiggs" O'Neil, who operated a small electrical plant. It also had brick-fronted specialty shops — men's wear, ladies' wear, hardware, barbershops, a restaurant or two, a bank, and a drugstore. Indeed, it seemed that by 1913, Smithers had it all. It was enough to make people think carefully before making that long trip to Prince George to do their Christmas shopping.

As Christmas Day approached, the enterprising Wiggs O'Neil worked hard at putting the finishing touches on an attraction that he — and others — were sure would put Smithers on the map. There, on the corner of Main Street and Fourth Avenue, stood O'Neil's brand new movie house, the only one around for hundreds of kilometres. Crossing his fingers, he set the date of the grand opening for Christmas Eve.

On the appointed day, an eager crowd gathered out front, then filed inside and waited in anticipation for the lights to dim and the silent, black and white images to hit the screen. A few minutes later, the audience was sitting patiently in the dark, but no images lit up the screen. For some reason, the projector simply wouldn't project.

Frustrated and embarrassed, O'Neil gave his patrons back their tickets and asked them to return after Christmas dinner the following night, and they would "give it another try." The next night, after turkey and dressing, the people of Smithers dutifully did exactly that.

"People were really tolerant, in those days," O'Neil remembered. Most likely, the real incentive to return was the opportunity for a novel Christmas experience which was, most certainly, a first-time experience for many of those who bought tickets the night before. Besides, what was there to do back home? A card game or singing around the piano — you could do that any time — paled in comparison to the chance to experience this new marvel of the modern age. The equipment worked wonderfully. However, by the following holiday season, nothing in the theatre was working at all. It was dark and empty, its doors locked.

It seemed that Christmas 1914 would be a bleak one. There was a war on. And, as Wiggs recalled, "everyone was broke, or close to it." Business was bad. The movie theatre closed. Yet, more than ever, people needed a reason to laugh. Someone suggested to O'Neil that he send out for a film and run a show at Christmas, just to cheer the townspeople up. O'Neil got on the phone and ordered a two-reel comedy and a feature comedy. He didn't care what it was, as long as it was funny.

Other plans were underway. One of the few couples who had enjoyed a decent business that year were the Fatherbys. Hudson was a blacksmith, and his wife ran a boarding house and restaurant. The couple, O'Neil said, "decided to put on a swank Christmas turkey dinner. Invitations were sent out and it was the talk of the town for a week." Not all the talk was likely positive. "For some reason, he invited no one that didn't belong to the top crust of the town. The druggist and his lady, the Union Bank manager, the Buckley Hotel manager and his lady, the Grand Trunk Pacific superintendent and some others whom one might call our elite set." It is easy to guess the motivation for the inclusion of those on the guest list. Hudson and his wife had a lot to be thankful for, and undoubtedly knew who it would be most advantageous to thank.

As the night proceeded, flushed with the success of the

dinner, Hudson Fatherby, no doubt stroking his large black moustache, expansively invited all his diners to the picture show — on him!

Inside the theatre, everything was going off without a hitch. Everyone was having a wonderful time — upper crust and lower class alike. The lights came on as the reels were changed. Now, it was time for the feature. O'Neil had promised a "comedy" — he didn't specify what movie it was. Nobody did. This was long before "movie stars" or revered film directors. "Christmas Day movies" was all the towns-people needed to know. Or so they thought.

The lights went down, the projector whirred, and there, on the screen, was the title of the feature: *Blacksmith Breaks Into Society.*

Wiggs was mortified.

"I was nearly floored when I saw it, but what could one do?" Laugh, most likely, as people in the audience were already starting to do. It got worse — or better, depending on your point of view and status within the community.

"As the picture unfolded, it showed the blacksmith with a huge black moustache, very much resembling Hudson," O'Neil recounted 40 years later. "He tucked his napkin into his shirt collar, shovelled the food in with his knife, tried to balance peas on his knife and wound up by drinking the finger-bowl dry, lemon and all."

Any movie was bound to be a welcome attraction, but this one was an unqualified hit. O'Neil was relieved to learn that among those who laughed the loudest, "until the tears ran down his cheeks" was the Smithers blacksmith himself.

When the movie ended, the laughter continued out in the lobby.

"Some called me the incorrigible Wiggs, and accused me of pulling a put-up job because I had not been invited to dinner," O'Neil recalled. "But all I can say is, it was one of those rare things that just happened. I was as innocent as a babe."

Maybe.

Bulkley Valley Christmas Party

Christmas has always been a time for gathering together with friends and family. Like many British Columbians today, those who populated the province in the past often travelled out of their way to be with others. It often took them days to reach the homes of far-flung neighbours or family members, people they saw very rarely the rest of the year.

Somehow, despite the distances that separated the province's early settlers from one another, word would get out — by dogsled, stagecoach, telegraph, bicycle, or word-of-mouth — when a Christmas gathering was planned.

In 1915, Sarah "Nan" Bourgon and her friends began to organize a Christmas party for the growing community of Bulkley Valley. They sat and planned who to invite. "We've quite a few people in [the area] now," commented one of Nan's friends, thinking about people scattered over the countryside. "There's a couple up there, they have two little children. They look so lonesome ..."

As the party preparations continued, the friends settled on a place to hold their festive gathering. "Now, a French-Canadian named Billy Fidel put up a hotel," Nan remembered years later, "and I believe if you had gone and pushed against it, you'd push the damn thing over. It was that ramshackle ... So we went over and we looked at Billy Fidel's place. Well, the cracks in it were like all the rest of the places. You could shoot peas through the cracks."

In spite of its ramshackle condition, Billy's hotel was voted the designated party place. Further plans were made. Chickens were substituted for hard-to-find turkeys, and the women prepared mouth-watering mince pieces, plum puddings, and cakes. "They brought in the most gorgeous cakes," Nan recalled. "One of them was a huge chocolate cake, oh, about a four layer ... we stuck it in the centre of the big table in the kitchen."

Meanwhile, the men brought the small church organ into the hotel, and soon the hotel was filled with music and singing. The party went on and on. When the Fidel children grew tired, their mother put them to bed upstairs.

Then, in the wee hours, the revellers decided to raid the leftovers before starting for home. Into the kitchen they trooped. "When we got in there," Nan recounted, "these kids — there were no rubber pants in those days — these two darn kids had wet [the bed upstairs] and it had gone all through the middle of the chocolate cake! Then all of a sudden I laughed, and we all laughed. The part that amused me was all us women, when we saw these drips still dripping, you know, picking things up and running around — we had no place to put them. The only place we could put them was on the stairs. Then we all had one good big laugh ... That was our Christmas. It was the first one that we ever had in the Bulkley Valley. And I venture to say it was the best one, too."

Chapter 3
Christmas Trees and Christmas Treats

Atlantic Canada

For many of us, the Christmas tree is one of the nicest things about the holiday season. Going out on the annual tree hunting expedition — whether it be to a pastoral, snow-covered wood lot or a supermarket parking lot — is often an adventure in itself. And as the first waft of balsam fir or white spruce drifts through the house, and cherished ornaments are lifted from their storage boxes and hung on the boughs, memories of Christmases past come rushing back in a flood of nostalgia.

The Christmas tree has become such an essential element of Christmas over the past century that we tend to forget it hasn't always been a part of the season. Like so many other Christmas traditions, the custom of bringing an evergreen tree indoors and decorating it has its roots in ancient pagan rituals. The evergreen tree was a symbol of life in ancient times, and during the winter solstice the aromatic green boughs were brought indoors and hung over the lintel.

It wasn't until sometime in the 16th century, however, that the first evergreen tree was brought indoors and decorated. Some credit German theologian Martin Luther with being the first person to bring a tree indoors at Christmastime. Legend has it that one Christmas Eve he was so enchanted by the sight of a small, snow-covered evergreen glimmering in the moonlight, he decided to take the tree home to show his children.

The earliest Christmas trees were actually miniature versions of those we erect today. Often, in wealthier homes, each family member had his or her own little tabletop-sized tree. These little trees were trimmed with fruits, nuts, and paper ornaments, and gifts and sweets were laid out beneath their branches.

The tradition of the Christmas tree gradually spread throughout Germany and the rest of Europe. But it wasn't until 1848, when the *Illustrated London News* featured an image of Queen Victoria and Prince Albert and their children gathered around an elaborately decorated Christmas tree, that the custom really took off. By that time, however, German and Dutch settlers had already introduced the tradition to North America.

Two years before Victoria and Albert's tree made the news, a wealthy Halifax merchant erected one of the first Christmas trees in Canada. In 1846, William Pryor had the tree put up in his Coburg Road home. Pryor's wife, Barbara, was originally from Germany, and had grown up with the tradition. The Pryors' tree would have been attractively adorned with glass ornaments imported from Germany, cornucopias of candies, cranberry garlands, strands of popcorn, and dozens of candles. No doubt, the Pryors' tree was the talk of the town that season. And it wasn't long before the tradition caught on and spread throughout Nova Scotia and the rest of the Maritime Provinces.

In those early days, Christmas trees, with their dozens of burning candles clipped precariously to tinder branches, were extreme fire hazards. It wasn't long before people caught on to the fact that illuminating the tree with fire wasn't such a bright idea. Eventually, shiny tinsel and reflective glass balls replaced the candles. Then electricity came along and revolutionized the decorating of the tree. The strands of multi-coloured bulbs were much safer than candles for lighting up the tree. But in spite of this advance in technology, trees are still known to burst into flames every now and then.

Such was the case on December 23, 1964. That morning, the office workers at the Nova Scotia Department of Motor Vehicles in Halifax were busy finishing up paperwork before the Christmas holiday. Everyone was looking forward to Christmas Eve, when they would exchange gifts, have a few eggnogs, and go home to their families for the holiday. The office tree, a small tabletop balsam fir, had been trimmed with lights and ornaments the week before. All week long the pile of gifts beneath it had been growing steadily. Everyone agreed it was one of the prettiest trees they'd had at the DMV.

But just before noon that day, the quiet in the office was shattered when the little tree suddenly burst into flames with an audible "pouf!" A great commotion ensued as everyone scrambled to find a fire extinguisher. But there was no extinguisher to be found. Finally, someone ran to the janitor's closet and returned with a bucket of water, which they tossed on the blazing tree. By the time the flames were finally extinguished, the pretty little tree was nothing more than a blackened, smouldering skeleton, and the gifts beneath its branches a soggy ruin.

The Boston Tree

Standing among the thousands of spectators crowding the Boston Common, Janette Snooks felt a surge of pride as the master of ceremonies announced her mother's name and the trim 72-year-old Aileen Dixon strode on to the stage and took her place next to the premier of Nova Scotia. It was December 4, 1988, and Aileen and Janette had been invited as special guests of McDonald's Restaurants to participate in the annual Boston tree lighting ceremony. As Aileen and Premier John Buchanan walked over and flicked the switch that lit up the 18,000 bulbs on the magnificent tree, the crowd roared. It was a moment Janette would never forget.

The Halifax to Boston Christmas tree is an annual tradition that began in 1971, but its roots go back to 1917, the year of the Halifax Explosion. Aileen Dixon (nee Coleman) was only five months old on that fateful December 6, when the Belgian relief steamer *Imo* collided with the French munitions ship *Mont Blanc* in the Halifax Harbour. The resulting explosion levelled a large part of the city, killing and injuring thousands and leaving thousands more homeless. Although Aileen had not been injured, her father, Vincent Coleman, was one of those killed in the blast. A train dispatcher with the Canadian Government Railway, Coleman had sacrificed his own life in an effort to save hundreds of others that day.

The city of Boston was one of the first to respond to Halifax's plea for help in the wake of the Explosion. Their outpouring of generosity following that tragic event is something the people of Halifax have never forgotten. The Boston tree is a small token of Nova Scotia's appreciation for that aid.

When McDonald's Restaurants learned that Aileen was the daughter of Vincent Coleman, who happened to be featured on the restaurant's tray-liners at the time, the company invited her to the tree-lighting ceremony. Aileen was honoured by the invitation and by the opportunity to commemorate her father's heroic deed.

The Halifax to Boston Christmas tree is no ordinary conifer. In fact, it's arguably one of the largest, most impressive Christmas trees anywhere. The search for this perfect tree begins up to six months before Christmas. Representatives from the Department of Natural Resources comb the entire province for a balsam fir, white spruce, or red spruce that stands at least 13.5 metres tall and is perfectly symmetrical. Once found, the tree is carefully prepared for cutting. Bringing down a 13-metre conifer safely is no simple task. It takes up to four days and 25 workers just to prepare the site and the tree. First, the area around the base of the tree is cleared so that workers and equipment can get at it. Next, each branch on the tree is bound to the trunk to prevent damage. After the tree is felled it is loaded onto a flatbed truck and taken to the marine terminal, where it begins its three-day voyage to the Port of Boston. There, it is loaded onto another flatbed truck and driven through the streets of Boston, accompanied by a motorcade befitting a head of state. Once the tree arrives at the Boston Common, it is set up and trimmed in time for the tree-lighting ceremony. This joyous event, featuring performances by entertainers from both sides of the border, marks the beginning of the Christmas season for the people of both Boston and Halifax.

The Quest for the Perfect Tree
Some families are not fussy when it comes to choosing a Christmas tree — as long as it isn't too scrawny and will fit into the space available, with the angel on top, that's all that matters. Others, however, are a wee bit more particular. The Murdock clan from Rothsay, New Brunswick, definitely falls into the latter category. Year after year, the Murdocks would spend hours searching for the perfect tree. Because their

Christmas tree always stood in the hall at the bottom of the stairwell in the family's "old barn of a place," it had to be about six to seven meters tall — a criterion that excluded all "tree lot" trees right off the bat. In addition, it had to be bushy and as symmetrical as possible — no Charlie Brown trees permitted. The best trees, they discovered over the years, grew along the power lines.

It was a Murdock family tradition that in mid-December, Anne, Hamish, and their four children would all head out on their annual quest for the "perfect tree." So, in December of 1983, once all the children had arrived home from university for the holidays, the family piled into the Toyota station wagon and drove up to the power lines. Since it was the first time they'd all been together in a while, everyone was in high spirits as they started out. It was a bitterly cold day, however, and as they tramped over hill and dale for what seemed like hours, fingers and toes grew numb and spirits began to flag.

Finally, after what had begun to feel like a futile search, they came upon *the* tree. It was easily six meters tall, with a hefty trunk. The whole family agreed that its size and shape were *just right*. Hamish, who was just getting over a bad flu-bug, set right to work chopping down the tree. Anne and the children cheered him on from the sidelines, while stomping feet and blowing on fingers. It was growing late and they were all looking forward to getting home to a hot drink by a roaring fire.

As dusk closed in the mercury dropped even lower.

The trek back to the car seemed to take forever. Once there, Hamish, Anne, and the children struggled to lift the massive tree onto the roof of their compact station wagon. But it soon became apparent to all that there was no way *that* tree was going to fit on the roof of *that* car. Anne suggested they go home and borrow the neighbour's truck and trailer and come back for the tree. But by this time it was getting dark. Having had enough for one day, Hamish decided the tree would be fine in the ditch overnight.

Driving the neighbour's truck with the trailer in tow, the Murdocks set out for the power lines around noon the next day to collect their tree. As they neared the spot where they'd left it, the thought crossed their minds that the tree might have been spirited off in the night. So when they saw that it was still lying in the ditch, a collective sigh of relief went up. They clambered out of the truck and hurried over to the edge of the ditch, eager to claim their prize. But as they got a little closer, a chorus of "Holy S---!" echoed in the frosty air. Apparently, someone *had* come along and found the tree before the Murdocks returned for it. Searching for a nice average-sized tree, they must have been delighted to discover the perfectly shaped six-metre specimen, load it onto their car, and go. Which was just what they'd done, leaving the Murdocks with nothing but the butt end of their Christmas tree.

Quebec

ig bushy balsam trees are potent symbols of Christmastime. From those who grow them to those who decorate them, people all over Quebec revel in the sight and smell of Christmas trees. For some, a whiff of balsam perfume is all it takes to conjure up vivid memories of Christmases past.

Christmas trees are big business in this province — Quebec is the top producer of Christmas trees in Canada. It is also the home of Canada's first official Christmas tree.

An Avant-garde Christmas Tree
The first Christmas tree in Canada was set up in a modest house in Sorel in 1781 — about 100 years before Quebec families embraced this tradition and more than 60 years before British families began putting up Christmas trees

in their homes.

By a strange twist of fate, a German officer, Baron Friedrich Adolphe von Riedesel, was based at a British garrison in Sorel. Baron von Riedesel was accustomed to the German tradition of setting up a Christmas tree on December 25. Unbeknownst to him and his family, the tree they would set up that year would have historical significance.

The Riedesel family had probably decorated a Christmas tree in their home every holiday season until they travelled to North America. Like other aristocratic German families, the Riedesels would have harvested a tree from their own forest and then decorated it with candles and a variety of natural or handcrafted items, such as paper roses, nuts, apples, gingerbread, and stars formed from straw or gold foil.

Baron von Riedesel first arrived in North America in 1776. He did not have many opportunities to think about Christmas trees and other holiday festivities during his first five years there, however, because of his military service, which included, for a time, a stint as a prisoner of war.

In 1775, American forces were in revolt against their British rulers. Apart from the riotous activity in the United States, these forces also invaded British-ruled Canada. *Les Bastonnais* (as the New Englanders were called) occupied Montreal and laid siege to Quebec City during the 1775–76 invasion of Quebec. King George III of England worried that he did not have sufficient British troops to defeat the rebellious Americans, so he called on his German allies.

In the spring of 1776, German officer Baron von Riedesel, commander of the Brunswick regiment, sailed from Portsmouth with his mercenary army of more than 4000 soldiers. His wife, Baroness Frederika Charlotte von Riedesel, and their children crossed the Atlantic soon thereafter. Unfortunately, by the time the German soldiers arrived, the American threat to Quebec was considerably reduced, so the Germans were garrisoned with some local inhabitants who lived in a strategic area south of the St. Lawrence River, between Chambly and Trois-Rivières. There they waited for the next military opportunity.

In 1777, Riedesel was involved in an offensive action at Saratoga, New York, which ended in a resounding defeat of the British forces (and their German allies). Riedesel's wife and children, along with a few other officers' families, had been travelling with the British army troops. Following the defeat, the British and German soldiers and the officers' families tried to escape. The baroness later recorded the attempt in her journal:

"Profound silence had been recommended to us; large fires were lighted, and many tents were left untouched, to conceal our movement from the enemy. We proceeded on our way the whole night. Frederika (her daughter) was afraid, and began to cry: I was obliged to press a handkerchief to her mouth."

The baroness was so courageous during this terrifying episode that one of the British army officers said it was a pity she was not their commanding general.

Following the British army's surrender, the troops, along with the officers' families, were held as prisoners of war. The baron and his family were treated quite well while they were held prisoner. They were sent to Cambridge, near Boston, where they were accommodated in an abandoned mansion. "[The Americans] greeted us and seemed touched at the sight of a captive mother with three children," wrote the baroness.

But while Riedesel's family fared relatively well, his troops, who were held in barracks on Winterhill, suffered greatly. The barracks were extremely crowded and the soldiers were barely sheltered from the cold and rain.

Finally, in October 1780, the baron was freed during a prisoner exchange. His first assignment after his release was to command British troops who were defending Long Island. However, the baron had so much trouble dealing with the summer heat of Long Island that he requested a transfer back to Quebec.

In 1781, Quebec was still vulnerable to future attacks from the Americans, so Frederick Haldimand, the governor of Quebec and commanding general of the troops in Canada, decided to station Baron von Riedesel in Sorel, a strategically placed town at the juncture of the Richelieu River and the St. Lawrence River. Riedesel had command over the area through which the Americans were most likely to arrive.

In the middle of September 1781, the baron, his wife,

and their four girls — Augusta, Frederika, Caroline, and America — arrived in Quebec City after a gruelling eight-week sea voyage along the eastern seaboard from New York City. The baroness, her children, and their servants stayed with a local family in Quebec City for a month, as there was no accommodation ready for the family in Sorel. They dined every night with Governor Haldimand. Then the family moved to Sorel and lived temporarily with a local inhabitant so that they could be closer to the baron's headquarters.

In mid-November, Governor Haldimand bought the *Seigneurie* of Sorel in the name of the British crown and acquired a house near the Richelieu River that was under construction. The foundation of the house was finished and the main walls had been erected. Haldimand instructed engineers and artisans from the Sorel garrison to ready the house by Christmas.

The Riedesel family was absolutely thrilled when they finally moved into their charming new house a few days before December 25. On Christmas Day, the family invited some British officers from the Sorel garrison to join them in their home.

"To our great surprise we were able to eat our Christmas pie — with which the English always celebrate Christmas — in our new house, although the timber for the building was felled and sawed into boards only after our arrival. Pretty paper was hung on the walls, and we were really very well lodged," the baroness wrote in her journal.

The *Maison des Gouverneurs* (as it is now called) had a very large entrance hall with benches on either side where six guards slept by turns to protect Baron von Riedesel from being kidnapped. It also had a large, stout, wood stove, which heated the house, as well as a large dining room, a spacious sitting room, and a series of bedrooms for the Riedesel family, including a nursery for the younger children. Upstairs, there were two large rooms for the male and female servants as well as two guestrooms.

The house would not have had many Christmas decorations, due to the family's recent arrival. However, on December 25, there was a handsome Christmas tree standing tall and proud in the sitting room. Shortly before Christmas, the homesick baroness had requested that her husband fetch an evergreen tree from the surrounding forest so that the family could enjoy this German tradition on Christmas Day. Evergreen branches, an ancient symbol of faith and hope, must have appealed to this transplanted German family in the rugged Canadian backwoods.

The Riedesels had a lot to celebrate on December 25, 1781: the family was reunited and safely back in Canada, they had just moved into a lovely new home, and, of course, it was Christmas! While not many details are known about the festivities that took place that evening, we do know that they included several different cultural traditions, including the British tradition of plum pudding, the French-Canadian tradition of cranberries cooked with maple sugar, and, of course, the German tradition of an illuminated Christmas tree.

This first tree in the *Maison des Gouverneurs* was decorated very simply. There were small white candles fastened to the branches with special pins or wax, and there may have been a few star-shaped cookies.

It is easy to imagine the Riedesel children's delight as the little white candles were lit one by one and the whole room began to glow with the warm light. Gazing up at the pretty lights and breathing in the rich balsam perfume surely made the family nostalgic for their ancestral German home. The officers who were dinner guests on that Christmas night also shared in the magical scene; they were witnessing their first Christmas tree ever. They may have heard of the Christmas tree tradition from their peers, but they were probably as amazed as the Riedesel children to actually see the decorated tree.

Interestingly, the Riedesel family Christmas tree in Sorel did not start a new trend in Canada. In fact, the second Christmas tree in Canada (put up 65 years later in Halifax) was also set up to satisfy the desire of a homesick German woman. Decades after the Christmas tree tradition was introduced in Britain (1841), bourgeois Quebec families began to decorate small evergreen trees placed on tables. In 1896, a wealthy Montreal family set another precedent by using electric lights to illuminate the Christmas tree instead of the traditional candles.

Then in 1910, the popular department store Paquet mounted a display of Christmas trees adorned with garlands of electric lights. Around this time, many Quebecers began to decorate Christmas trees in their homes with imported glass balls and ornaments. Most Quebecers also incorporated a religious element into the Christmas tree tradition by placing a *crèche* at its base.

Rearing Christmas Trees

Every year just before Christmas, as he was growing up, Lucien Lapointe, along with his brothers and his father, went off in search of the perfect Christmas tree. They would traipse for hours through the woods on the Lapointe family's vast 100-acre property in the Eastern Townships. Each time one of them chose a tree, he would have to argue its relative merit, and if he couldn't convince the others, then they would all plod off again through the dense forest. Finally, after the Lapointe men came to an agreement, Dad would chop down the tree and the children would drag their trophy back through the snow, roughhousing all the way.

Lucien grew up during the Great Depression, so his childhood Christmases were very simple affairs. "No one had any money. People hardly bought anything, they were just getting by," he remembered. "We received stockings with fruits, like bananas, oranges, and a few candies. And we received one or two small presents, like a handmade wooden toy"

However, Lucien did not feel deprived in any way, because his favourite part of the Christmas celebration was the annual hunt for the family tree. He did not know as a boy that he would eventually operate a vast Christmas tree business, but he did know that he had a special rapport with trees. He felt truly at home while walking through the forest, breathing in the rich perfume of the balsam fir.

Once the carefully chosen Christmas tree was brought back to the house, the Lapointe family would set it up and decorate it with a few knitted wool ornaments and a few glass balls "from the store." The traditional wooden crèche, which Lucien's father had constructed, would then be placed underneath the tree.

The tree stood at the centre of numerous family parties during *Les Fêtes.*

Like most traditional families in Quebec in the 1930s, Lucien had a huge extended family, so inviting the relatives over meant an instant party. The more the merrier. After all, there wasn't much to do on the farm during the winter months, so it was an ideal time for social visits. And Lucien loved these gatherings: "I remember trying to avoid bed-time because it was so exciting to see the house overflowing with people dancing. My father played both the violin and the piano."

After a few glasses of whiskey and some conversation about harvests, the dancing would begin. Lucien's father led the dancers through square dances, followed by jigs and reels. While the family elders played cards and Lucien and his siblings slumbered upstairs, young couples danced the night away.

Many years later, when he was a strapping young man of 15, Lucien began to formulate his first vision of operating a Christmas tree farm. His father had just acquired a piece of land near the homestead and he asked his sons to help him plant trees on a section of the land that was bare.

"We had to plant 3000 white spruce seedlings in the forest to produce wood for construction. It was very tough, because there was hardly a proper path to get to the site and we had to carry in all of our stuff on our backs. We had branches jutting out in our faces, and there was so much water on the path that we were practically walking through a stream. It was back-breaking work, but I was absolutely in heaven!"

Lucien decided then and there that he would make his living tending trees. The only problem was money. He had to put his dream on hold to earn some money in order to buy a piece of land. So, in the early 1950s, he studied carpentry and construction in the nearby town of Sherbrooke. That course led to office jobs in Sherbrooke and then Montreal.

"But the trees were always on my mind," he remembers.

Lucien never really felt comfortable in the city, but he plodded on because he knew that eventually he would have enough money to buy his own plot. He was so ill at ease living in Montreal that he did not even drink water from the tap — it didn't taste right to him. Then, in 1969, Lucien attended a meeting of the Vermont Association of Christmas Tree Growers.

"The field was just taking off," he recalled. "I didn't know anything about growing Christmas trees, but I was very excited."

Christmas trees had always been a profitable sideline for Quebec farmers who could cut down wild balsams on their land and then sell them. Then, around 1960, the notion of growing cultivated Christmas trees on plantations became popular. Quebec is currently the top producer of Christmas trees in Canada. Each holiday season, Quebec Christmas tree producers harvest about 1.5 million trees, worth $45 million.

Lucien knew beyond a shadow of a doubt that he would grow his first plantation in the Eastern Townships as the high sloping ground and heavy soil typical of this area are ideal for growing balsam firs. And Lucien also knew that balsam firs were the most popular Christmas trees because they don't lose their needles easily and, more importantly, they boast a heady scent that smells like Christmas.

In 1970, Lucien bought his first piece of land near the Lapointe family homestead in Bury. He took seedlings from the nearby forest and transplanted them onto the field. "The neighbours weren't so happy about me planting trees on that land," Lucien recalled with a laugh. "After all, their ancestors had almost broken their backs clearing the land for agriculture."

Two years later, Lucien bought another piece of land that had belonged to his father and he was well on his way to becoming a Christmas tree grower. Despite a few setbacks due to financial problems and insects that attacked the trees, Lucien Lapointe's plantations have continued to thrive.

Taking care of the Christmas trees is extremely labour intensive. But, for Lucien, it is a labour of love. "All of the trees are beautiful, each tree is different, just like humans," he mused.

Each spring, Lucien transplants seedlings to a field. Then, at two years old, the trees are moved to another field, and at five years old they are moved again. Apart from moving trees around, Lucien and his aides are continually fertilizing the soil, clearing away weeds, pruning the trees to achieve the perfect shape, and dealing with insects and rodents that attack the bark and the foliage. Shortly before Christmas, the trees are graded, chopped down, shaken to remove dead foliage, baled, and shipped out by truck. The trees are perishable, so they cannot stay in transit for a long time.

After about 13 to 15 years of intensive care, Lucien's trees are sold in Christmas markets for about $5 per foot. Managing a Christmas tree plantation is certainly not an easy way to earn a living, but even at the age of 69, Lucien has no intention of stopping work in the fields or the Christmas markets.

"Living with trees is my life," he said.

Ontario

or most of us, one of the most important symbols of Christmas is the tree. The custom of decorating trees goes back to pagan times, when ribbons and coloured objects were hung on them as offerings to the tree spirits. One Scandinavian legend tells how two lovers were killed by brigands in the forest. A fir tree grew out of the bloody soil and flaming lights were seen on it every year. Gradually, families in the area adopted the custom of decorating fir trees in their own homes with candles, a practice which eventually spread to other parts of Scandinavia.

The tradition of the tree is also linked to the Yule log, a ritual celebrated in Britain as far back as medieval times. On Christmas Eve, a large tree was cut down and its branches lopped off. Then it was dragged inside and thrown on the fire, where it was supposed to burn for the 12 days of Christmas. The tradition was still observed when the first permanent settlers reached Ontario. According to Lillian Gray, in 1783 a Reverend Mr. Stuart travelled from Kingston to a log cabin near Maitland to perform a marriage on Christmas Day. "The bare little log house was gay with spruce boughs and sprays of red rowan berries, and the ceremony took place where the dancing light from the Yule log lighted the faces of the bride and groom." The "rowan" berries were actually those of the mountain ash, which other settlers also used as a substitute for bright red holly berries. In 1855, for instance, Grimsby's Anglican church was decorated with evergreens and mountain ash berries.

At this point, Christmas trees were just beginning to become popular in Ontario.

Germany is considered the home of the modern Christmas tree, although stories about the tree stretch back to the time of St. Boniface, the missionary who Christianized parts of Germany around the eighth century. The English saint was determined to eliminate pagan customs from the country. In one town, after he cut down the sacred oak tree, he placated furious citizens by offering them a fir tree as a symbol of the new faith. Martin Luther, himself the founder of a new faith, is also said to have originated the decorated tree. Overcome by the glory of the stars in the winter sky one evening, he rushed home, trying to express his feelings to his family. Unable to do so in words, he chopped a tree from the garden, set it in the nursery, and lighted candles amid the dark boughs.

The German custom of decorated Christmas trees was introduced to the English world in the 1840s, shortly after Queen Victoria married Prince Albert. The new royal consort was German and brought with him the custom of decorating a tree. But parts of Canada were already familiar with the custom by then. In 1781, General Friedrich von Riedesel and his wife introduced the Christmas tree at Sorel, Quebec. Meanwhile, immigrants of German extraction, including Mennonites and others who fled to Upper Canada following the American Revolution, brought their Christmas tree traditions with them. Until the mid-Victorian period, almost the only place in Ontario where a Christmas tree could be found was in a Mennonite or German home. The first trees were usually small enough to fit on a table, but by the late 1800s, sturdy metal stands made it possible to bring enormous trees into the house.

Early decorations were usually handmade, or items found around the house. Straw ornaments or strings of cranberries were popular, as well as candles. Paper and bits of cloth were also used, sometimes shaped into decorative items. By the 1870s, commercial decorations were widely available. Most were imported from Germany and could be purchased at any sizeable store.

One superstition claims that a well-decorated tree ensures good fortune for a household during the coming year. There are also certain superstitions surrounding other Christmas greenery. To avoid family quarrels, holly should not be brought into the house until Christmas Eve. It's unlucky to crush the berries underfoot or to carry a flowering plant indoors. For good luck, the first person to enter a house in the new year should carry a holly sprig, and, once the holidays are over, the plant should be burned.

Kissing under the mistletoe is also said to bring good luck in the coming year. The practice dates back to at least the 17th century, and, although the rules relaxed over the years, there were once certain standard practices. According to tradition, a girl may not refuse to be kissed under the mistletoe, but the man must play fair and pluck a berry as he kisses the lady of his choice. When the berries are gone, the kissing stops.

Of course, a woman who wanted to attract the attention of a particular man could make sure she was "caught" under the mistletoe. Another English custom dictated that any single man who refused to kiss a girl under the mistletoe had to give her a pair of gloves. However, not all immigrants were familiar with the mistletoe custom and first encountered it in Ontario. In her diary, Mary Hallen, who lived in the Penetanguishene area, described an 1852 Christmas gathering where hemlock was hung in a drawing room as a substitute for mistletoe. When two of the young men present seemed reluctant to kiss a certain Miss Hodgett, the lady took matters into her own hands by kissing the gentlemen herself. "How strange," Mary commented in her diary. "It is not English I am sure not Canadian, perhaps it is a wild Irish custom." One of the young men Miss Hodgett kissed was Mary's brother Edgar, who was teased so much by another brother, Preston, at breakfast the following morning that it caused his face "to resemble the rising sun on an Indian summer morning."

Whether or not Ontarians subscribed to the superstitions and practices surrounding Christmas greenery, one thing is for certain: trends in decorating change over time. In the 1920s, theme trees were popular. During the war years, patriotic items, such as small Union Jacks, sometimes adorned Christmas trees. In the 1960s, artificial trees became wildly popular. Some were made of material that resembled toilet brushes dyed green, or, for the more adventurous, pink or white. Aluminium trees were the rage for a time, too. People loved the convenience of an artificial tree — you only had to shop for it once, and there was no need to pick pine needles out of the carpet from December through April. And those who still wanted the lovely fragrance of a real evergreen without all the fuss could buy spray-on scent.

The choice of a Christmas tree and its decorations depended largely on personal taste. Some people simply followed their own fancy, but others looked to experts for advice. In 1966, avant-garde Toronto artist Harold Town discussed his preferences in *Maclean's Magazine*. First of all, he recommended that the Christmas tree be spruce. "Scotch pine is not a Christmas tree, it is an inverted toilet brush." Most of his suggestions for decorating the tree were common sense: start from the top and work down, using the smaller decorations nearer the top and the larger ones at the bottom. He was definitely against handmade ornaments, even those made by children. But he did encourage readers to involve their children in decorating the tree, although he suggested the younger ones handle unbreakable ornaments, which he suggested should be hung deep inside the tree near the bottom.

Choosing the Perfect Tree

Harold Town did not discuss the business of selecting a tree, but it was something most Ontarians knew about from personal experience. As late as the 1960s, in rural areas especially, some people were still cutting their trees in local forests, just as their ancestors had done for generations.

There was relatively little risk involved in harvesting a tree from the wild, although in one case the hunt for a Christmas tree inadvertently led to tragedy. Ernie Elvish was seven-and-a-half and living in Fort William (Thunder Bay). On Monday, December 15, 1924 he went out with a friend, Jackie Saunders, to find Christmas trees for their homes. During their search, the boys argued about the right way home and parted company.

Snow was already falling when the boys separated. A few hours later, Ernie's parents reported him missing. As the temperature plummeted to several degrees below zero, a search party was organized. Jackie, who had made it home safely, led the searchers to the last place he had seen Ernie. Although the snow had covered their footprints, searchers doggedly combed the bush, looking for traces of the missing boy.

The snowfall and the frigid cold soon dashed hopes that the boy would be found alive. Still, the searches continued with city employees, police officers, and private citizens joining in. Walking six feet apart, every man probed the ground in front of him with a staff in an attempt to find some trace of Ernie. Although some believed there was little hope of finding anything before spring, the search continued through Wednesday and Thursday, fanning out five kilometres from where Ernie was last seen.

On Friday morning, the postman delivered a package from a Winnipeg store. Inside were boots and skates that Mrs. Elvish had ordered for her son's Christmas. When she saw them, she broke down. "Bring me back my son," she told searchers. "Get his body even though he is dead. I cannot stand the thought of him lying in the snow." That afternoon, three Finnish volunteers with the search party spied a dark area in the snow. On closer inspection, they found Ernie's body, partly covered by a snowdrift. He had apparently walked more than two kilometres by himself in the storm before collapsing.

Despite Jackie's safe return, Ernie's death was a tragic ending to what should have been a happy holiday outing. Fortunately, for most people, choosing a tree was a pleasant experience, one that was often filled with nostalgia. Writing in the *Sault Ste. Marie Star* in 1929, Isabel Peycott ruminated on how much town residents owed country folks for their Christmas cheer. She described a scene at the local market on a Saturday in mid-December when Joseph Roberts of Korah brought in a sled filled with balsam and spruce. "Even people who had no idea of buying one just then, gathered around the sleigh and there was an understanding smile around that meant such a lot, as if they were thinking, 'Remember how we used to go out and get one like this and haul it in, and put it in place'." Various comments passed as the people made their selections. Some of the "old boys" talked about how they liked cedar at Christmas, while "an old girl" preferred spruce and another woman insisted balsam was essential "to make the right Christmas fragrance."

In more recent years, Christmas tree farms have become increasingly popular. Today, almost all trees sold in the province come from farms. Only about 10 percent of a tree farmer's crop is harvested in any one year. The rest remains in the field, waiting for another holiday season. Many of these farms are family-run operations where customers can pick out their own tree before it is cut. Like other kinds of farming, it is a business operation, but that doesn't mean the owners lack Christmas spirit. In 2003, the Victorian Country Christmas Tree Farm in Scugog donated $5 from every tree to Habitat for Humanity of North Durham.

Christmas trees have been turned into fundraisers

in other ways, too. Since 2000, Sharbot Lake has held an annual festival of trees sponsored by the Villages Beautiful Committee, which looks after all the communities in Central Frontenac county. Participants, both individuals and organizations, buy trees in three different sizes — four feet, six feet, and eight feet — then decorate them at their own expense, usually following a theme of some kind, such as teddy bears or candies. Once the trees are decorated, the public is invited to view them at a local community hall. They are also able to buy tickets for a chance to win their favourite tree. After three days, the winning names are drawn. The event raises money for community causes and also brings in donations for the area food bank.

Food and Feasting

While Christmas trees provide a feast for the eyes, the holiday simply is not complete without a real feast as well. A few centuries back, the English celebrated with a boar's head. To Christians, the animal symbolized Satan and its slaughter recalled Christ's triumph over evil. Apparently, the English custom was a Christianized version of a Germanic folk tale, for it was said that the god Freyr rode his boar Gullinbusti, and during Freyr's festival of Yuletide, a boar was slain in his honour. About the only trace of the legend to reach Canada was a song celebrating the event, "The Boar's Head Carol," which is seldom heard today.

They may have preferred to leave the tradition of the

boar's head behind them, but Ontario's early settlers still went all out to pack the table with holiday goodies. Many women spent weeks preparing for the holiday, hoarding various dried fruits, sugar, and other items to make into plum pudding, fruitcake, and mincemeat tarts. One early Niagara Peninsula settler, finding he had no raisins or spices, added several cakes of maple sugar to his pudding. It turned out just fine.

Plum pudding was often made on the last Sunday before Advent in order to give it time to ripen, and was one of the most popular Christmas dishes through much of the 19th century. Even the prisoners at Kingston Penitentiary received a share — in 1886, a half-ton of pudding was prepared for their Christmas dinner.

In 1837, Catharine Parr Traill's Christmas dinner consisted of "A glorious goose, fattened on the rice-bed in our lake." Years later she noted that, in this period, "turkeys were only to be met with on old cleared farms in those days, and beef was rarely seen in the back-woods." Yet, when the extended family of Georgina and Frederick Hyde of Port Maitland sat down to their Christmas dinner in 1841, their sumptuous menu included a number of wild turkeys, which are considerably smaller than the modern domestic variety. The Hydes also enjoyed home-cured ham, applesauce made from their own orchard, and plum pudding that had been liberally doused with brandy and set afire

Christmas Cheer

Aside from food, an integral part of the holiday is Christmas cheer. Beverages particularly associated with Christmas are mulled wine and mulled cider. Adding sugar and spices to wine and cider then heating them creates warm drinks that are especially welcome in chilly December. Mulled cider is a distant cousin of wassail, from an Anglo-Saxon phrase *waes hael*, which means "be whole" or "hale." In England, it was the custom to raise a toast to apple orchards in the middle of winter in order to ensure a bountiful crop in the coming months. In some areas, a formal procession went from orchard to orchard. In each place, a special tree was selected and some of the drink was sprinkled on its roots while revellers chanted lines commanding the trees to grow.

By the 20th century, wassailing was just a dim and distant memory, probably best known in Christmas carols. Ontarians still had a strong thirst for alcohol at Christmastime, although it was a bit of a trick to satisfy that thirst during the prohibition era. Some turned to non-alcoholic drinks, such as O'Keefe's Dry Ginger Ale, while others found a creative way to stock up on stronger beverages. Because liquor could not be legally sold, except for medicinal purposes, prohibition Christmases usually brought an upsurge in minor ailments. In 1924, the Ontario department of licences estimated that there would be 40,000 more orders placed in the province's dispensaries than there had been in November. Figures from previous years bore out their predictions: in November 1923,

57,715 doctors' prescriptions for liquor had been filled, but in December of the same year, the prescriptions jumped to 87,877. In most cases, each prescription was for a quart of liquor.

"The pressure on the doctors becomes so great about Christmas for prescriptions that they must give in to a certain extent," licence commission spokesman James Hales told a reporter from the *Evening Telegram*. According to a city druggist, the increase had more to do with housewives wanting alcohol for their Christmas plum pudding than drinkers trying to obtain their favourite beverages. But there were plenty who disputed that theory. According to one report, the line-up at a Wellington Street dispensary looked more like the queue in front of the post office. The crowd at the dispensary not only looked pretty healthy, but happy to boot. The reporter who covered the story overheard one businessman explaining he had picked up a cold driving from Hamilton. Apparently his wife had caught the same bug, too.

London also experienced a sudden increase in "sick" people just prior to Christmas; the government dispensary on Talbot Street was doing a booming business! Officials probably knew exactly what was going on, but, as one of them told a *London Free Press* reporter, "It is not up to us to question the sale of liquor made through a bona fide doctor's prescription. Of course, there is a lot of liquor being sold, but as far as we are concerned it is all for medical purposes." Meanwhile, in Windsor, there was a huge upsurge in rum running. From early morning until late at night, trucks and cars brought caseloads of liquor to waiting boats. The boats raced across the river, bringing an estimated extra 40,000 quarts of bootleg booze to thirsty Americans.

Ontarians could also opt for bootleg booze, especially if they did not want to stand in long line-ups at government dispensaries. But there were definite risks. On December 16, a Studebaker owned by a Toronto woman was seized by police. Inside, they found 279 bottles of liquor that were being transported from Montreal. The driver, Joe Simmons, pleaded guilty before a Whitby magistrate on December 23. Convicted, he took three months in jail rather than pay a $600 fine.

Two days after the liquor was confiscated, a reporter for the *Evening Times* conveyed the news of a Toronto magistrate's court with tongue firmly planted in cheek. One of the cases involved John Warden's Royal Edward Hotel on Queen Street West. Beer that exceeded the legal alcohol limits had been found on the premises and Warden was given the choice of a $500 fine or three months in jail. As a result of the sentence, Warden was forced to close the Royal Edward, prompting the Crown Attorney to predict "that all hotels would now become apartment houses." It is doubtful that any of the people present in the courtroom at the time really believed the statement. The writing was already on the wall — prohibition was not working, and, as it turned out, came to an end a short time later. Once again, Ontarians could buy their Christmas cheer with little fuss, although there were still occasional problems.

In 1945, there was a fire in the Lombard Street building in which one of Toronto's liquor stores was located. Apparently caused by an electrical problem, it broke out in a second story business and was quickly stopped after firefighters turned their hoses on it. Meanwhile, business went on as usual in the liquor store. Clerks kept selling and customers kept buying, even though, as one witness reported, water from the fire hoses poured down through the ceiling onto the people in the liquor store. It seems no inconvenience is too great when Ontarians are determined to swallow some seasonal spirit.

The Prairies

hether it is lifted from a cardboard box or taken home from a shopping mall parking lot, today's prairie residents tend to take their Christmas tree for granted. Christmas without a tree is almost unthinkable, but scarcely three generations ago, the reverse was true. As recently as the early 1940s, a farm family that had a Christmas tree and placed presents beneath it was actually celebrating more than Christmas. That fortunate family was celebrating its ability to afford those traditional symbols of the season.

The First Christmas Tree of the Prairies
Somehow, with grit, determination, and stoicism, the Red River colony, the Canadian West's first agricultural settlement, had survived it all: scurvy, animosity between Irish

and Scottish factions, near starvation, and warfare between the Hudson's Bay Company and the North-West Company. In 1862, 50 years after the first colonists had set up camp on the banks of the Red River (near present-day Winnipeg) much had changed. And that year, at Christmas, there was another change in store.

Alexander Grant Dallas, the new governor of Rupert's Land, had arrived in the colony to oversee the immense 1.5 million square mile Hudson's Bay Company land grant that extended to the Rockies. Dallas did not come to Red River alone. He brought his wife, Jane. Faced with the task of making her drab surroundings more festive for Christmas entertaining, Jane was saddened to realize that the colony had never had a Christmas tree. As the daughter of Sir James Douglas (the governor of the colony of Vancouver Island), Jane's childhood Christmases in and around Fort Victoria undoubtedly included Christmas trees. She set to work with a will.

Finding a tree was not a problem for Red River settlers, but decorating it in suitable fashion was another matter. At that time, ingenuity and handicraft skill substituted for packaged ornaments. Jane and her friends carved hearts and stars from cakes of yellow soap, and made garlands from beads and berries. But Jane also wanted something shiny to put on her tree, so she scavenged foil lining from empty boxes at the Fort Garry store. Still not satisfied, she commissioned the fort's tinsmith to make small candleholders and then cut regular candles down to fit them.

Then she turned her attention to gifts. After all, what would Christmas be without toys for the children? For miles downriver, shops were scoured for playthings. Jane and her assistants scrounged a few dolls and Noah's arks and added them to the homemade gifts arrayed in and around the first Christmas tree of the Prairies.

Christmas Trees as Big Business

One of the first entrepreneurs to turn Christmas trees into cash — certainly the first in Calgary — was a Sarcee man named Brave Foxtail. In the early 1900s, plenty of small spruce trees grew on the Sarcee reserve lands near Calgary. Foxtail knew that city people wanted these trees at Christmastime. He and other band members also wanted something at this time of year: funds for the December 26 communal celebrations on the reserve.

Foxtail, soon christened "The Christmas Tree King," came up with a way to please everyone. The Sarcee men set to work. They felled the trees, took them to the city, and sold them to the city folk. As Foxtail predicted, this raised enough funds for their own Christmas celebrations.

Brave Foxtail lived to the ripe old age of 91 — long enough to see Calgary's Sarcee Christmas tree trade grow far bigger than his original vision. Every December, horse-drawn sleighs full of evergreens slipped slowly down the snow-covered streets and avenues of the city's residential neighbourhoods. As they went from house to house, band members didn't have to press people to buy the fragrant trees.

After answering the door and peeking past a smiling band member, sons, daughters, or parents would duck back inside and announce excitedly that the Christmas trees had arrived. There was a scurry to the front windows. Dad or Mom would reach for some cash, put on a coat, slip into boots, and tromp down the wooden front steps. There, in the cold early evening or Saturday afternoon, a careful curbside inspection took place. Meanwhile, a patient horse snorted clouds of white vapour into the air while waiting for each family to lighten the sleigh's load.

Brave Foxtail's descendants carried on the profitable business until the mid-1930s, when other entrepreneurs realized there was a profit to be made in Christmas trees. Farmers began selling trees wholesale to other growers and suppliers. In this era of the automobile, it was far more cost effective for growers and suppliers to set up shop in a vacant lot, or make a deal with a service station, than to painstakingly take their wares from door to door.

"Business no good ... too many trees in Calgary; so many they not half sold," Chief Joe Big Plume complained to the *Calgary Herald* in 1936. Unable to compete, the Sarcee Christmas tree merchants gradually gave up their seasonal trade, and Calgary's unique door-to-door Christmas tree business became a memory.

The "Reasonable Facsimile" Trees

During the first 30 years of the 1900s, few prairie families had Christmas trees in their living rooms at Christmastime; at least, not Christmas trees we would recognize today. The first reason was that, on the bald prairie, there were no evergreen forests where settlers could take their hatchets and help themselves. The second reason was the ever-present lack of money.

Nobody was more surprised at this woeful state of affairs than the thousands of immigrants who stepped off the boats and trains to make their new homes on the Canadian Prairies.

"Oh, it was the land of milk and honey," says Dorothy Hodgson with a laugh, while recounting her own 30-odd years of meagre Christmases. Immigrant farmers soon discovered that a parcel of 160 acres wasn't enough to keep a family going. "Although they didn't know it at the time," Dorothy adds. "These young boys, coming from England didn't know anything about farming. My own brothers didn't know anything about farming. They said they farmed, but they didn't really … My husband was another one. He was not interested in farming. He had more of an engineering mind. He could have done very, very well in engineering."

Not one of Dorothy's neighbours was the ideal farmer envisioned by Clifford Sifton when he launched his marketing campaign to fill the West. Instead, these were Birmingham machinists, Glasgow shipwrights, and derby-hatted London office workers. The failure rate, something that is not talked about much today, was enormous. Thousands of acres of the free land were simply abandoned. "Have given up the unequal task. Help Yourself." was one note left nailed to an empty two-room house. Hundreds of rotting, tumbled-down shacks and farmhouses dotted the Prairies, mute testimony to naivety, inability, and the unforgiving land itself.

In these hard times, having any extra money to spend on a Christmas tree was unthinkable. Even today, Dorothy, who is over 100 years old, scoffs at the idea. However, that didn't mean her family went without something festive to put in the corner of the large area that served as kitchen, dining room, and living room: "We cut little poplar saplings and we made paper chains — coloured paper; pages of the Eaton's catalogue — and we had little candles — I don't know why we didn't burn the house down. That was our decoration."

While Dorothy and her family were making paper chains, other farming families in the neighbouring province of Alberta were doing what they could to bring some Christmas cheer into their homes. In the small settlement of Brooks, south of Calgary, two young men, J.A. Hawkinson and Carl Anderson, went Christmas shopping after delivering their loads of wheat.

Hawkinson had a wife and kids at home, and he knew that a Christmas tree would mean a lot. Back in Minnesota, where the family had emigrated from, there were evergreens everywhere. But not here! The two stores in Brooks had none, and he was getting frustrated. Desperate for a tree, or at least to voice his complaint, Hawkinson went to the only symbol of authority in the tiny hamlet of 200: the CPR station. But there was no help to be had there, either.

It was too far to travel back to their farm that night, so the men stayed in Brooks. The next morning, they got up early, harnessed the horses and set out for home. It was bitterly cold, so the men chose to walk beside their wagon, simply to keep warm. For the family man, it was a depressing journey. He knew his family would be disappointed at his failure to find a Christmas tree. Finally tiring, Hawkinson jumped up on the wagon, and just as quickly jumped to the ground again in shock and surprise.

"Why'dja do it?" he yelled happily to his friend. Anderson, bewildered, demanded to know what Hawkinson was talking about. Getting no answer other than a beaming smile, Anderson jumped up onto the wagon and looked inside. There, at the bottom, was a beautiful spruce tree. It probably took a while for him to convince his happy friend that he hadn't put the tree in the wagon.

As soon as the men got home, Hawkinson proudly showed his family the beautiful tree. Much to his surprise, they were not thrilled. While he and his friend had been away, the kids had carried home a tumbleweed, placed it in the corner of their two-room cabin, and decorated it with Christmas ornaments they had brought all the way from Minnesota. To them, the tumbleweed was a real Christmas tree!

Despite his family's surprising reaction, Hawkinson still treasured his tree and wondered who had put it the wagon. Years later, he discovered the "secret Santa" was CPR district engineer Augustus Griffin. After listening to the young father's lament, he had gone out and cut down one of the hundreds of trees he had planted for the CPR and had placed it in the wagon.

A Simply Beautiful Christmas

By the mid-1950s, trekking into the woods to chop down your own Christmas tree was, for most people, merely a fond memory. However, things were different in Grey Campbell's household.

Campbell, a retired Alberta RCMP officer, had made the decision to take up ranching. He moved to the C7 Ranch in the foothills of Alberta's Rocky Mountains. For 12 years, the Campbell family — Grey, his wife Eleanor, and their four children — lived in relative isolation, 90 kilometres from any large store and 30 kilometres from the nearest village. Far from feeling disadvantaged, the family loved the isolation. That was the sheer beauty of it! Life was simple, clean, and uncomplicated.

"We made a ceremony out of everything," Grey recalled when writing about his ranching experiences years later. And that included getting the Christmas tree. Living so far away from civilization, the Campbell family couldn't buy one from a city parking lot. And they wouldn't have done so, even if they could.

"Getting our tree was a very special occasion," Grey wrote. "And that meant team and sleigh." After harnessing the horses, the family set out in the crisp, cool breeze. Their horses, Prince and Brownie, plodded through the snow to the top of the ridge and climbed up the valley through the Campbells' herd of Herefords. The sight of the rancher and his family meant only one thing to the cattle: extra feed! Within a few seconds, cows were plodding along, too, following the sleigh at a respectable distance at the rear. Laughing and clowning, son Dane, who was snug in his own sleigh tied to the larger one, waved the cattle away. Once the horses had climbed up the gentle slopes of the valley, Campbell tethered them out of the wind, and the family set off into the trees.

The kids inspected each tree closely. After careful deliberation, family members took a vote and chose their tree. The boys ran through the snow to the sleigh for the axe and saw. The fir came down within a few minutes, and Grey dragged it to the waiting sleighs.

At the memory of their first year on the ranch and that first Christmas tree, Grey Campbell echoed the age-old familiar prairie refrain: "There was little enough money and nothing for frills," he wrote. They decorated the tree with whatever they could find: "... some strands of tarnished tinsel Eleanor found among our effects, which had been stored throughout the war. She added color and a measure of enchantment by hanging toys and rattles."

Inspired by the novelty of the Christmas tree, Dane threw on his coat and gloves and raced outside. Soon, he was busy collecting small boughs that had been trimmed off the tree. Crouching down in the snow in front of the house, he painstakingly tied bits of fat and peanuts onto the miniature limbs. The clever result: a Christmas tree birdfeeder.

"I suppose," Grey mused years later, "a city dweller used to elaborate displays in stores, and the lights and shiny balls and tinsel one may purchase would find ours a shabby effort. But the children were satisfied, and that was all that mattered."

Of course, the tree the Campbells put up in their modest ranch house didn't have to be elegant to bring them pleasure. It gave them an opportunity to have fun as a family. The Christmas tree meant fond memories in the making; memories of family love.

British Columbia

mong the most-loved activities of the
Christmas season are trimming the tree
and feasting on holiday treats. For more
than a century, both the Christmas tree and Christmas dinner have served as warm, welcoming symbols of holiday
merriment and togetherness.

An Enduring, Adaptable Tradition
Since the 1840s, the Christmas tree has been an endur-
ing focal point of Christmas celebrations. In fact, in many
instances, this green and living Yuletide tradition has often
given its very name to a particular event or celebration, as it
did in the Vernon area in 1896. As Alice Parke recorded in her
diary, "the Christmas tree" was well worth making the trip
into town by cutter (a large open sleigh) from the BX Ranch

where her husband, Hal, was the manager: "We went in to the Presbyterian Xmas Tree last night. A whole load from here went — all except Furniss and Orr. Orr came over & kept house for us. Hal asked him to have the kettle boiling, so when we got home from the tree I made a cup of coffee and we had coffee, cake and apples ..."

As times and circumstances changed, the ever-adaptable Christmas tree has been there, to conveniently serve and promote special, timely needs. In Nelson, and perhaps in dozens of other British Columbia communities, the Christmas tree became a symbol of support for thousands of men in uniform and their families back home, during times of war.

On December 15, 1916, the *Nelson Daily News* reported: "All a-glitter to its topmost peak which reached away up into the skylight. In Eagle Hall, a huge Christmas tree was provided by the women of Nelson for the kiddies whose names are on the District Patriotic Fund Lists. The Festive tree delighted 125 youngsters' hearts yesterday afternoon and Old St. Nicholas himself attended, and distributed parcels and good things."

Today, the "tree" often comes out of a box and is quickly assembled. In early days, the tree, likely as not, came out of a forest, no assembly necessary. Decades later, the former acts of searching for, selecting, and cutting down the tree became fond and cherished memories. For Clare McAllister, the Christmas trees of her turn-of-the-century childhood in

Nelson left an indelible mark upon her memory.

"The particular thing about Christmas in those days was the smell of Christmas," Clare remarked. Nelson, like so many British Columbia communities, was small. The town was surrounded by forest. Clare remembered nostalgically that, "all the trees were fresh cut, so that when the tree came ... out of the frosty, snowy winter air, into a warm house, it smelled of Christmas."

First Chopping, Then Shopping

Obtaining a live Christmas tree was a true Christmas adventure. It was a special occasion, not, as it often is today, simply another complication to be jammed in on the hurried commute from work or while dashing into a big-box retailer for an extra set of lights.

Major J.S. Matthews, the founder of Vancouver City Archives, placed enough importance on the cultural rituals surrounding the Christmas tree that he left details of Christmas tree excursions behind for future generations. Labelling his reminiscences "A cursory memorandum before I forget," he wrote:

"There was no Christmas tree problem before the Great War; it was more a matter of 'where should we go to get one?' Those who had horse and buggy found it easy; others took the streetcar. Frequently, school boys called, usually at the front door, either with a small fir tree they had cut somewhere, or 'getting orders' as they called it. And their price ranged from twenty-five cents up to as much as one dollar; often their childish limit was the 'immense' sum of ten cents for something very scraggly they had dragged a long way.

"The more fortunate, who lived in Hastings, Grandview, Mt. Pleasant, South Vancouver, the new Shaughnessy or Kitsilano, simply went out in the clearing and cut one; it was a little trouble; the weather may be inclement, but there was some fun about it; to go with the children — next Saturday afternoon, or Sunday morning when Father was not at work — and get Mother a Christmas tree; large or small, as she wished.

"But one day, I recall the first occasion, when, at Kitsilano Beach, we took a small axe and started off, with the children, to cut a Christmas tree in the Indian Reserve. We came back with empty hands; we could not find one; they had all gone. That was about 1913."

By then, tracts of wooded land were marked out for roads and residential lots. What was once rural was now urban. Nevertheless, where there is a need, there will be those ready to fill it.

"After the war [World War I], and about Christmas 1918 or a year or so later, there were men who went out and gathered Christmas trees; just one or two, and, if memory serves correctly, the first I saw was a man who had a few stacked together on what was afterwards called, 'Victory Square,' but before the Cenotaph was erected." The man was clever: the street traffic in that part of downtown would have been heavy, even then. "He had a few [trees] for sale, and later, perhaps the same year, was to experience competition." Obviously, others recognized a good thing when they saw it.

At the start of the Depression, competition for a good location — and the extra income that you simply had to have to buy a few Christmas presents and a turkey — became fierce. "The street-corner Christmas tree trade developed until, about 1935, or so, men contested for street-corners; some started earlier than others; some said they had held a certain corner for years, and when another man 'jumped' his corner, there was a squabble; even a fight, and the police were called to allay the disturbance."

So much for the "season of goodwill." Then things changed, yet again. In late November 1939, Major Matthews was walking up the hill toward Vancouver city hall when he noticed a group of about 30 men waiting patiently in the rain beneath the steps of the building's north entrance. He walked up to one of the men and asked him what was going on.

"His reply astonished me," the major remembered. The man said they were lined up to get permits to sell Christmas trees.

Sophisticated Dining

Traditional Christmas dinners are always a sight to behold. Laid out on fine tablecloths are dishes filled with Brussels sprouts, carrots, turnips, broccoli, mashed potatoes, cranberry sauce, and stuffing. And then, of course, there is the turkey, which is carved at the table, or served, steaming, on large platters. This is the meal that countless families in British Columbia have enjoyed for years and years on Christmas Day.

But picture this for Christmas dinner: oysters on the half shell and chicken bisque, followed by baked stuffed salmon, delicious lobster, and banana fritters with vanilla sauce. Next, "stuffed young" turkey, loin of pork, tamed goose, duck, sirloin of beef, as well as lemon snow pudding and custard sauce.

In what fine establishment could a hungry patron find such a sophisticated feast? Not the Vancouver Hotel, or any of the up-scale restaurants on Granville Street; not inside Victoria's Empress Hotel, or even across the street at the Union Club. Instead, this was the dinner offered to patrons of the Kalamalka Hotel on Barnard Avenue, in Vernon, in 1925.

"A Real Christmas Dinner without the trouble of cooking at home," the headline of the hotel's newspaper advertisement enthused. In 1925, the hard-working folks at the north end of the lake might have been a little "rough around the edges" compared to the big city folks on the coast, but they knew how to do it up in style — if they could afford to. The cost of the Christmas dinner at the Kalamalka was one dollar per plate, but that didn't seem to deter the good people of Vernon. Small wonder the ad advised making "your reservations early. Phone 24."

Throughout British Columbia, there were other special

dinners associated with the Yuletide season. In Nelson, there were "game suppers" held before Christmas. "These were for the gentlemen only," long-time Nelson resident Clare McAllister later recalled, "and you would have everything from bear, mountain goat, venison, grouse, trout, salmon, char, sturgeon ... a great mass of protein."

But that wasn't all.

"A distinction of festive meals in those times was the incredible number of desserts," Clare continued. "You had white Christmas cake, dark Christmas cake, mince pie, plum pudding, and sherbet cups of jelly with whipped cream on top, and heaven help you if you did not consume at least a mouthful of all these kinds of sweets that came at the end of the meal."

Culinary Creativity

Christmases in the early 1900s were a time for men to relax and for women to work. Usually, women would spend countless hours preparing meals and desserts for their large families. "My grandmother used to make all the Christmas puddings and all the cakes," Duke Ackerman remembered fondly. "Everything was homemade. You didn't go in a shop in them days, you made it yourself. The house was full at Christmas. In my mother's family, there were 11, and they had sons and daughters and everything; it was a big affair, coming around the house every Christmas."

Doris Smith, who grew up in Revelstoke in the early

1900s, remembers how hard her mother worked during the Christmas season and how her father couldn't even perform the task of carving the turkey. "Christmas was more for the men," she stated rather bluntly, recalling the Christmases when the men of the neighbourhood took things a little too far. "I don't know how, one must have started it ... [the men would] go to somebody's house and this man would join them and they'd go to the next house. By the time it was two or three in the afternoon, there would be about a dozen men and they'd come and call at the house and there was always hot drinks or Tom and Jerry's ...

"Mother had to stay home and cook the turkey, which was then, of course, *not* enjoyed by the head of the household." Doris laughed at the memory. "He felt no pain, then, you see. He didn't care for his dinner. I remember that so well because we had many a Christmas dinner spoiled."

A Turkey By Any Other Name...

In British Columbia's pioneer days, turkey and goose were not always the main entrees at Christmas dinner. While chicken and duck were often worthy substitutes, some early settlers were forced to come up with more original alternatives.

Among the settlers in the Chilcotin were "Bunch" Trudeau and her father. One year, 18 bachelors came from near and far to enjoy Christmas dinner at the Trudeaus' log cabin. Bunch's father had taught his daughter cooking. That Christmas, she prepared an elaborate, but mysterious feast.

"They all came for supper and we had roast of bear — of course, we never told them it was bear — and we had a roast of goat and a roast of deer." Bunch recalled the dinner included stuffed potatoes, vegetables, and "pies of all descriptions." The bear meat went unnamed, but not unnoticed. Guests ate most of the goat, a little of the venison, but by meal's end, the bear meat had completely disappeared.

Two or three weeks after the holiday, on the regularly scheduled mail day, their Christmas guests returned to the cabin to pick up parcels and letters. Bunch's father decided to have a little fun.

"Daddy brought the conversation around, as he could, to eating bear meat. Oh, there were some that wouldn't eat bear, no sir, you couldn't get them to eat bear, and at last, Daddy quietly told them, 'Oh, I think you've eaten bear.' 'No, I've never eaten bear,' you know, and, 'Oh, I think you have, in fact,' Daddy says, 'I know you have. At Christmas dinner.'

"Do you know that three of them went outside and were sick and they just still couldn't take it, and yet it was really awfully good bear, and it was just done to a turn, just nice and crisp. It was just like pork, really. Maybe they figured it was pork, but I don't know where in the world they ever thought we got pigs."

Chapter 4
Here Comes Santa Claus

Atlantic Canada

or over a century, children everywhere have gone to bed on Christmas Eve dreaming of Santa sitting at the helm of a great sleigh loaded with presents, sailing across the heavens and shouting, "On Comet! On Cupid! On Donner! And Blitzen!" Santa Claus is such a familiar icon in popular culture that we often take it for granted that he's been around forever. But in fact, the Santa Claus we know and love today wasn't even conceived of until the early 19th century. Prior to that time, there were various incarnations of the Christmas gift-giver, such as Saint Nicholas and Sinter Klaas. But it wasn't until 1822, when Clement Clark Moore wrote his famous poem, "A Visit From St. Nicholas," or, as it is better known today, "The Night Before Christmas," that the figure of Santa came into being. The poem was written as a Christmas present for

Moore's six young children. And although he refers to the bearer of gifts as St. Nicholas instead of Santa Claus, it was Moore's poem that first defined the character:

> He was dressed all in fur, from his head to his foot,
> And his clothes were all tarnished with ashes and soot;
> A bundle of toys he had flung on his back,
> And he looked like a peddler just opening his pack.
> His eyes how they twinkled! His dimples, how merry!
> His cheeks were like roses, his nose like a cherry!
> His droll little mouth was drawn up like a bow,
> And the beard on his chin was as white as the snow;
>
> ... He had a broad face and a round little belly,
> That shook when he laughed like a bowl full of jelly..."

Much later, an American illustrator by the name of Thomas Nast created the first visual image of Santa Claus. One of Nast's illustrations, which appeared in a book of Christmas poems in 1863, depicts the portly old fellow on the roof of a house about to make his descent down the chimney. On Santa's back is the toy-stuffed sack, and just over his shoulder is a church steeple topped with a cross. It didn't take long for merchants throughout North America to catch on to the marketing appeal of this loveable gift giver. Images of Santa soon began popping up in advertisements for all kinds of goods during the festive season.

Eventually, Santa made his way to the Maritime Provinces where, in addition to climbing down the region's chimneys on Christmas Eve, he also made appearances at stores and Christmas parties. In the late 1800s, a live appearance by Santa Claus had an effect similar to that of a major rock star appearing unannounced on our streets today — roads were blocked off, fans screamed and cried, women fainted. Back then, live appearances by Santa normally occurred only in major centres such as Fredericton, Saint John, and Halifax. Children living in outlying areas had little hope of ever seeing the mythical figure in person. Instead, they wrote letters addressed to Santa Claus at the North Pole telling him how good they had been all year and what they wanted for Christmas. Most letters to Santa were sent via the conventional postal route. However, many children in Atlantic Canada preferred to send their wishes up in smoke. Once their letters were written and ready to go, they were tossed into the woodstove in the belief that the thoughts expressed therein would fly up the chimney and be carried on the wind to the North Pole.

Santa Arrives in Outport Newfoundland
Back in the early days, merchants weren't the only ones responsible for introducing Santa Claus to the children of Atlantic Canada. Missionaries working in remote areas of Newfoundland and Labrador also shared that pleasure. In the late 1800s, when a young English doctor by the name of

Wilfred Grenfell arrived in northern Newfoundland to establish the mission hospital at Cape St. Anthony, he was shocked by the impoverished conditions he encountered. In the small, scattered settlements, people lived in rough shacks without even the most rudimentary conveniences. There were no schools or medical facilities for hundreds of kilometres, and stores were simply non-existent. All goods were bartered for. In fact, there were so few goods in the area that, according to Grenfell, many of the children of St. Anthony had never even possessed a store-bought toy.

When the Christmas season approached that year, Grenfell's thoughts turned to home and the "conventional pleasures of the season." In that remote northern outpost, where just putting food on the table was a daily struggle for most, there would be no plum pudding or holly and mistletoe, no lavish Christmas dinners or exchanging of presents. And, perhaps worst of all, there would be no visit from Santa. Although the children of Cape St. Anthony may have *heard* of Santa Claus, they certainly had no expectations of him visiting their community. As the doctor brooded on the situation, it occurred to him that it was within his means to bring a little joy into the lives of these children. Grenfell decided he would introduce Santa Claus to the children of Cape St. Anthony.

The mission soon became a hive of activity. A room at the hospital was secured for the event, a tree was picked out, and preparations were made. When the mission workers announced that Santa Claus would visit Cape St. Anthony that year, there was such a hubbub in the community that Grenfell feared there wouldn't be enough gifts to go around or enough space to accommodate the crowd that was eagerly anticipating the event.

The day before Santa was to arrive, Grenfell and his assistant were called away to tend a patient on the Straits of Belle Isle. They were travelling by dogsled, the only mode of transportation in the region at that time. And since their route that day was awash in areas covered with dodgy ice, the trip took much longer than it should have. The doctor began to worry that he would not make it back to St. Anthony in time for Santa's arrival the following day. But the next morning dawned bright and clear, and the men set out early, feeling optimistic that they might make it back in time after all.

That notion went by the wayside, however, when they met up with a man from another community seeking the doctor. He explained to Grenfell that a boy in his community had accidentally shot himself in the leg and was in critical condition. Without a moment's hesitation, the doctor changed course and rushed to the wounded boy's side. One look told Grenfell the wound was bad. He feared the child would develop blood poisoning and die if he wasn't taken to the hospital immediately. So the boy was bundled up and carried out to the doctor's sled. Once again they set out for St. Anthony.

Meanwhile, in St. Anthony, the anticipation of the crowd waiting at the hospital for the arrival of "Sandy Claws" had reached a fevered pitch. Men, women, and children crowded round the doors watching anxiously for a sign of the mythical figure and his sled. When word spread that a sled was approaching, everyone rushed out front expecting to see the jolly, bearded figure of Santa. Their disappointment was palpable when they realized it was only the doctor and his patient. But Grenfell told them not to worry; he'd seen the big man headed their way. Indeed, within minutes, another dog sled carrying the unmistakably rotund figure of Santa glided up to the front door. For the underprivileged children of that isolated community, it was a truly magical moment, one they undoubtedly cherished for years.

Wilfred Grenfell's experience of introducing Santa Claus to the children of a remote Atlantic outport was not entirely unique. Around the same time that the doctor was conspiring to have the legendary figure visit Cape St. Anthony, another missionary, Samuel King Hullon, described a similar visit to the church at Hopedale, Labrador: "At just the right moment the door opened, and in came the well-known figure of picture and story — red and furry gown, long white beard and a sack of presents." The youngsters of Hopedale were completely dumbfounded by the appearance of Santa in their midst. "The children gaze in some little awe at the portly bearded figure," Hullon recorded. "Some of them forget to say their 'nanomek' (thank you) as they clutch the parcel which he hands to them, just as children in England sometimes forget under similar circumstances!"

For Hullon, the experience of bringing such joy to these children was tremendously satisfying. "Surely one of the most lovely things in the world is to make little children happy," he wrote.

Special Santas

Santa Claus, the kind-hearted, fatherly figure who spreads joy wherever he goes, is the very embodiment of the Christmas spirit. Over the years, thousands of men and, on occasion, women have donned the red suit and portrayed Santa, passing out presents at parties and listening to the wishes of children who line up in malls and department stores for the chance to sit on his knee and confide in this magical being. But there's much more to the part than simply wearing the outfit. For many, like Eddie Aulenback and Victor Bernard, Santa Claus isn't just a role they enact once a year and then forget about until the next December; it's a way of life.

On January 31, 2004, Eddie Aulenback woke up in the middle of the night surrounded by flames. His century old home in Martin's Point, Nova Scotia, was ablaze. Somehow, the 55-year-old managed to make it down the stairs and out the front door with only minor burns. But once outside, he realized his most precious possession was still in the house. Without a thought for his own safety, he dashed back into the burning building. Smoke stung his eyes and flames singed his hair as he struggled through the blaze to the room where his Santa suit was stored. He had just about reached the suit when smoke and flames drove him back outside empty handed. Although losing his home and all his possessions was devastating, it was the loss of that Santa suit that Eddie regretted most.

Eddie Aulenback comes from a long line of "Santas." At least six people in the Aulenback family have assumed the role over the years, including Eddie's own father, who used to dress up for his children, as well as others. Eddie was just 26 when he first donned the Santa suit himself. He was in the mall one day shortly before Christmas when he had a revelation about Santa Claus. As he passed by the long line of children waiting for a chance to spend a few seconds on Santa's knee, he realized it would be really special if Santa went out to the children and took them by surprise, rather than making them come to him. So, dressed in the bright red suit and carrying a sack filled with teddy bears, Eddie began visiting the homes of handicapped and underprivileged children all over the South Shore of Nova Scotia. For this soft-spoken Santa, the joyous reaction of the children at his unexpected arrival has been a truly heart-warming experience.

Like Eddie Aulenback, Victor Bernard also donned the red suit for the first time in his mid-20s, and has been doing so every year since. It was shortly before Christmas 1947 that 24-year-old Victor got his first taste of portraying Santa Claus. That night, he was among the audience at a Christmas concert at Alberry Plains School in PEI when one of the teachers approached him. She explained that the person who was supposed to play Santa that evening hadn't shown up, and that there were going to be a lot of very disappointed boys and girls in the audience if someone didn't fill in for him. Then she asked if he would mind playing the part.

Victor was reluctant. He knew nothing about playing Santa, he told her. He suggested she try someone else. But the woman persisted, saying he was the only one there that night who was about the right size for the outfit. Victor looked around at all the expectant faces in the crowd and thought of what a letdown it would be if Santa didn't show up. After all, he was the star of the show. Finally, he relented. The teacher rushed him backstage, thrust the red costume and a rubber mask into his hands, and told him to get dressed. The next thing Victor knew, he had a bulging sack slung over his shoulder and was being instructed to sing "Jingle Bells" as he was propelled out onto the stage.

Despite his reluctance to play the role that first night, Victor ended up repeating his performance five times that week. That was 56 years ago, and the jolly 80-year-old is still at it. Victor, who was raised in an orphanage until the age of four and then shunted from one temporary home to the next, gets tremendous pleasure out of brightening the lives of others. And to his mind, there's no better way of doing that than playing Santa Claus.

Quebec

anta Claus has been a magical bearer of gifts during the holiday season since his arrival in Quebec around the mid-19th century. During the first few decades following his arrival, Quebec children expected Santa Claus to arrive on New Year's Eve and not Christmas Eve, because December 24 was primarily a religious event. Now, Quebec children, along with other Canadian children, expect Santa's arrival on Christmas Eve. Santa Claus makes an appearance in numerous Quebec Christmas stories, as a purveyor of love and magic.

Santa Brought a Doctor's Kit
It was snowing on New Year's Eve. Giant snowflakes resembling perfectly formed crystals floated down gently, piling up on top of each other until it looked like billowy clouds had

fallen to the earth. Mont-Ste-Hilaire (just east of Montreal) and all of the surrounding countryside was soon blanketed with the pure-white mounds of snow.

Dr. Ernest Choquette was used to working at all hours — that was simply the life of a country doctor — but he was still surprised that on that New Year's Eve, at the tail end of the 19th century, someone was knocking on his door. The evening was so magical that Dr. Choquette could hardly believe someone in his community was suffering.

An elderly woman was at the door, covered from head to foot with the soft new snow. She accepted Dr. Choquette's hospitality immediately and entered the sitting room, where she almost collapsed on a parlour chair. After she caught her breath, she was able to explain why she had come out and walked across several fields during a snowstorm.

Dr. Choquette had treated the old woman's husband, as well as her daughter, numerous times, and the old woman had never been able to pay for the doctor's services. She was obviously embarrassed to ask Dr. Choquette for another favour. The doctor patiently encouraged her to talk and to explain the nature of the problem. He knew why she hesitated to tell her story. She was a very honest and very poor woman. Moved by the old woman's love and dedication to her family and her willingness to risk rebuff for them, Dr. Choquette was genuinely saddened to see this loving grandmother in such a desperate state on New Year's Eve — a night normally reserved for festivity and exchanging gifts.

Finally, he asked her if her grandson was sick, and the floodgates opened. Yes, she replied right away, he had become sick all of sudden. She explained how her grandson had gone to school as usual, but when he'd arrived home in the afternoon, he had developed a very high fever. The boy had been transformed — he lay in bed screaming out in agony and he appeared to be having terrifying dreams

As her grandson suffered, the old woman had come up with a possible explanation for his raving. On Christmas Day, Santa Claus had brought beautiful trees — the boughs laden with brightly coloured presents — to the homes of her grandson's English classmates. The children had brought their new toys to school the next day. Her grandson had been absolutely devastated because *Père Noël* had never brought him a tree or any presents. The poor child was going mad trying to understand why Santa Claus had forsaken him, and he had worked himself into a frenzy.

The old woman had tried to cheer up her grandson by going out to the woods and chopping down a little evergreen tree. However, the only things with which she'd had to decorate the tree were apples and acorns. Her sick grandson had not been at all interested in this little tree that she'd set up for him and had continued to moan about how *Père Noël* did not love him.

After she explained the situation to Dr. Choquette, the old woman suggested that maybe the doctor could provide her with some of the medicine that her neighbour's boy,

Louison, had been prescribed recently. The doctor, however, knew that there was really only one appropriate response — to make a house call to see her sick grandson.

The old woman's radiant smile was the only reply that Dr. Choquette needed. She was overjoyed to hear that the doctor was willing to examine her grandson and find out what ailment was tormenting her darling boy.

While they waited for the doctor's horse and carriage to be readied for the journey, Dr. Choquette secretly went over to his children's tree, which was decorated for New Year's Day. He removed some of the toys and candies that were hanging from the branches. The doctor then sorted through the toys his children had received the year before and he chose a few items that were still in good condition, including a puppet, a music box, and a mechanical horse. As he looked at his children's toys thrown pell-mell into the toy chest, he couldn't stop thinking about the fact that the old woman's sick grandson had never received a present from *Père Noël.*

They set off in the carriage, bundled up under buffalo pelts. The snowstorm had abated somewhat, however the horse balked at the huge snowbanks and the slippery conditions underfoot. The old woman's cottage was only a few miles away, but due to the difficult weather conditions, the journey took almost twice as long as usual.

Finally, they arrived at the humble cottage, which was built up against a rock-face. Just before they entered the house, Dr. Choquette pulled some cotton batting out of his little black bag and twisted it into his mustache and beard. Then the doctor pulled up the collar of his fur coat, which was speckled with fresh snow, and took hold of the bag of presents.

As the old woman led the doctor to the sick boy's room, she turned and gave him a beatific smile. Not only had the doctor brought medicine to relieve her grandson's suffering, he had brought some magic.

When Dr. Choquette entered the little room, the sick boy sat up startled. He could not quite believe his eyes. Was it really *Père Noël*? Was he dreaming? Was his family no longer poor? His face flushed with fever, the young boy turned to his grandmother with a look of disbelief. He wanted her to say what was going on, but was afraid that he might break the spell and that *Père Noël* and all of the toys would disappear. He kept looking to his grandmother for some kind of explanation, so finally, Dr. Choquette began to speak with the sick boy in a most gentle tone. He asked the boy about where it hurt the most and whether he had been able to sleep, and suddenly the boy looked convinced.

The doctor knew the boy's belief that the legendary *Père Noël* was really standing beside him in his bedroom was due as much to his feverish state as to the doctor's convincing impersonation.

"*Père Noël*" began to examine the boy's chest and take his temperature. The boy had the glassy eyes of one hallucinating with fever. Shortly before Santa arrived, he had been tossing and turning in physical pain and emotional anguish. But now, not only was he being tended to by *"Père Noël,"* but he had been given magnificent toys as well. *"Père Noël"* must surely love him after all. As the doctor worked his healing magic, the boy relaxed and began to breathe easier.

Keeping the Magic Alive

Mme. Danielle Simard taught kindergarten in Sainte-Anne-de-Beaupré, near Quebec City, for 35 years until her retirement in 2003. She had spent dozens of Christmas seasons reading Christmas stories to her pupils, making Christmas decorations with them, and bringing them Christmas cookies. Simard had also gone above and beyond the call of duty — she'd managed to convince Santa Claus to pay a visit to her class at the École Primaire de la Place de l'Éveil for 22 years in a row. And every year, Santa had arrived in a novel way.

Once, Santa Claus had arrived all bundled up in horse-drawn carriage, like a picture out of the 19th century. On another occasion, he had zoomed in on a thoroughly modern Ski-doo. Santa had even driven a dogsled one time, calling out to the dogs like a natural.

"It depended on my whim that year, and it depended on the weather," said Simard. For instance, one year Santa Claus walked through a blinding snowstorm because that was the only means of transportation possible. It was one of the simplest plans, but it made for a very dramatic entrance.

"One time I wanted him to arrive by sleigh, but then it

was raining just before the event so we had to use a car ... I really had to adapt fast," she recalled.

In December 2002, Simard enlisted the support of the local firemen and policemen for her Grand Finale. Shortly before the beginning of the Christmas holiday, the 20-odd children in Simard's class were invited to spend the night at school. The children arrived promptly at 7 p.m., wearing pyjamas and clutching their teddies or dolls. They were so excited about the upcoming evening, they appeared barely concerned about sleeping away from home.

After enjoying some Christmas entertainment in the *Grande Salle*, the children came across a note from Santa Claus: "I do not have the keys to your school, so you will have to come out and look for me." But it wasn't time look for Santa just yet. So the children took a little rest in their sleeping bags.

At 11:15, Simard woke the children with the jingle of little bells, and they all put on their snowsuits, mittens, and winter boots to go out and find Santa Claus. They were traipsing around the school when suddenly a police car stopped by. When the police officers heard about the children's mission, they asked if they could help out.

After pursuing several false leads, the children discovered that Santa was asleep on the roof of the school! "The children were amazed. They were looking everywhere on the ground, in the snow; then as soon as the children looked up to the roof, they were yelling and screaming with excitement that they had found him! What should we do? How will we get him down? The kids were very excited that they had found him and they were not worried about his situation," said Simard.

The children never even wondered aloud how Santa had ended up on the roof of the school. But Simard had a story just in case that question came up — she was ready to tell them that Santa's naughty reindeer had left him there as a prank.

The next step was to save Santa. The children had lots of ideas on how they might get him down from the roof. They thought of using a stepladder, but that wasn't long enough. Finally, one little girl piped up with the suggestion that they should call the fire department. Of course! Soon, a couple of fire engines arrived on the scene, and no less than six firemen helped Santa and his big bag down from the roof.

After all that hard work, Simard, the children, the firemen, the policemen, and Santa Claus were happy to go back into the school to share a little *réveillon*. Now, Simard knew that five-year-olds would not necessarily want *tourtière, cretons*, and other authentic *réveillon* dishes in the middle of the night. So her kindergarten class *réveillon* consisted of juice boxes, party sandwiches, and carrot sticks.

After their snack, Santa pulled presents out of his giant sack. "He gave them colouring books, crayons, little games; nothing was very expensive, but it was special because it came from Santa," said Simard.

The enterprising teacher persuaded the children to get back into their sleeping bags for a few more hours until sunrise. The next morning at eight o'clock, when the parents came to retrieve their children, Simard's class was filled with a joyous cacophony as each child, in turn, tried to tell their version of the previous night's events.

Remarkably, in 22 years, everything has always gone according to plan. "Children never even got homesick in the middle of the night because we started to prepare everything from the first of December," Simard explained. For instance, Santa Claus would telephone several times during the weeks leading up to his arrival. Simard would put on the speakerphone so the children could all listen to his calls. The children had oodles of questions for him — "When will you arrive?" "How will you find our school?" and "Will you bring presents?"

In the last few years, Santa Claus also sent Rudolph's harness to the children in mid-December. He told them that if they shook it around Christmastime, it would help him to find their school!

"Santa" was often one of Simard's friends, but there were a few different ones, including a professional Santa, with an appropriately round physique, who played the role in a lot of different settings, from senior citizens' homes to daycares.

"The last one was the best one," remembered Simard. "He was young, but well-built and he really put on the Santa performance extremely well and convinced the children completely ... he was almost an acrobat and the children loved that."

The annual Santa Claus visit has had a significant impact on Simard's pupils' siblings, too! Once, the mother of one of Simard's pupils called her and said that when her daughter, Véronique, had come home from kindergarten, she'd told her brother (who was in sixth grade) about how Santa Claus had telephoned that day. Apparently, Véronique had been so enthralled with the whole experience that she'd managed to convince her brother that Santa Claus really does exist.

Véronique's mother told Simard: "I could see he was really wondering about this and, while Véronique was telling the story, he asked me if it was true. After dinner, when Véronique had left the table, my son said 'Mommy, I think I believe in Santa Claus again'."

"The magic of Christmas is really there! I still wonder myself if Santa Claus exists," laughed Simard.

Ontario

A saintly bishop was the inspiration for our modern Santa Claus. St. Nicholas, the story goes, lived in Myra, in southwestern Asia Minor, in the fourth century. A kind-hearted and generous man, he once gave three bags of gold to three noblewomen, providing them with the dowries they needed to marry. A number of miracles were also attributed to him, including one in which he restored three boys to life after an innkeeper had killed them and tried to turn them into bacon. As a result of that miracle, he was made the patron saint of boys and later, of all children.

The name Santa Claus is derived from the Dutch version of his name, Sanct Herr Nicholas, or Sintirklaas. In the early 19th century, he was often portrayed as a tall man in fur-trimmed clothing, usually looking more regal than jolly.

226

Traditionally, he was depicted dressed in red bishop's robes, travelling across the sky as fast as the wind on a white horse. (In some accounts, Sleipnir, the horse, had eight legs and originally belonged to the Germanic god Odin.)

Transplanted to New York State, Dutch traditions became firmly entrenched in North American culture through the work of two writers. One was Washington Irving, who wrote frequently about Santa Claus. The other was Clement Clark Moore, a scholarly man whose poem, *A Visit from Saint Nicholas*, revolutionized the image of Santa. In his poem, most commonly known as *'Twas the Night Before Christmas*, Moore transforms St. Nicholas into a jolly old elf. He becomes smaller and plumper and, instead of travelling by horse, he gets around in a sleigh pulled by eight tiny reindeer — Dasher, Dancer, Prancer, Vixen, Comet, Cupid, Donder, and Blitzen.

Irving and Moore were writing at a time when educational levels were rising, when newspaper readership was growing, and when the newly developed middle-class had more money to spend and more items on which to spend it. All these factors helped entrench the new image of Santa Claus in the public's imagination. Many parents encouraged their children's belief in Santa Claus, partly as a means of extending childhood, but also as a way to maintain discipline in the weeks leading up to Christmas. Meanwhile, there were always a few spoilsports around, including older children who thought it was their duty to tell their younger comrades that Santa was nothing but a pleasant fable.

Virginia O'Hanlon, an eight-year-old American girl, was one of these younger children. In 1897, when she asked her doctor father if there really was a Santa Claus, he suggested that she write to the *New York Sun* for an answer because if she read it in the newspaper, it had to be true. The response she received from editor Francis Pharcellus Church became a classic. "Yes, Virginia, there is a Santa Claus," Church wrote. "He exists as certainly as love and generosity and devotion exist, and you know that they abound and give to your life its highest beauty and joy."

The editorial ran on September 21, 1897, and has probably been carried in dozens of newspapers in Canada and the United States almost every year since. At a later time and place, Virginia's dad might well have recommended a different expert and she might have received a completely different answer. In the 1940s, an Ontario psychiatrist created a furore, not just by denying the existence of Santa Claus, but by insisting that parents were harming their children by encouraging them to believe in him.

George Brock Chisholm (1896–1971) was a doctor and veteran of two world wars. The Oakville native was Canada's federal deputy minister of health when he stirred up the controversy about Santa Claus, stating that, "A child who believes in Santa Claus, who really and literally believes, because his daddy told him so, that Santa comes down all the chimneys in the world on the same night has had his thinking ability permanently impaired if not destroyed."

Canadians were furious at what they saw as an attack on a cherished myth and demanded that Chisholm resign from his cabinet post. Chisholm did not, and the calls for his resignation ended when he was appointed the first director of the World Health Organization (WHO). Far from being a crank, Chisholm was a respected physician who worked on the committee that formed the WHO. At the time, the organization was considered revolutionary because its constitution stressed that health meant more than the absence of disease. It also meant complete physical, mental, and social well-being. Chisholm played such a major role in the establishment of the new organization that he was elected to the position of director by a vote of 46-2.

As a psychiatrist, Chisholm was naturally concerned about mental well-being, including the mental health of children. That mental health, he was convinced, relied partly on children being treated with complete honesty by their parents. Catching their parents in a lie — even a seemingly harmless one about Santa Claus — would, in Chisholm's opinion, be a shattering experience for youngsters. Although some people followed Chisholm's thinking, others were extremely confrontational. In 1954, he described one dinner where another guest attacked him on the topic of Santa Claus. According to Chisholm, the man claimed he had believed in Santa until he was seven and it hadn't done him any harm. Later in the evening, though, he mentioned that he suffered from gastric ulcers and bad nerves. This, as far as the eminent doctor was concerned, simply proved his point. In Chisholm's opinion, children were quite capable of coping with reality. The real harm came when dealing with those who misrepresented reality, thus "crippling their ability to think clearly and honestly."

In spite of Ontarians' growing reliance on child psychology and child-rearing manuals, almost no one was willing to abandon Santa in favour of modern ideas about mental health. Besides, some would argue, at the time Dr. Chisholm was making his recommendations, there was ample proof that children had a solid grasp on reality. In a 1947 article for *Maclean's Magazine*, writer Robert Thomas Allen described a department store Santa at work. Patrick Joseph Murphy had worked for the Robert Simpson Company department store in Toronto since 1931 and, at the time of the interview, had plenty of experience with children and their antics. Although many of them were mesmerized by Murphy's Santa, truly believing he was the genuine article, others weren't so sure. Boys in particular asked all kinds of questions about *other* Santas. Murphy explained that as Santa, he had the power to pop up anywhere he chose at very short notice. However, at least one pair of young skeptics decided to verify that explanation themselves. While one watched, the other ran across the street to Eaton's, then ran back to report that he had seen Santa there. The boy who had been keeping his eye on Murphy then confirmed that the Simpson's Santa had not moved from his seat. When they confronted Murphy, he told them that the other Santa was his brother.

Here Comes Santa Claus

Patrick Murphy was one of a long line of department store Santa Clauses who dazzled and amused children. In Ontario, the tradition of visiting Santa at a store goes back to the late 1800s. In some cases, he was an invisible presence — one Toronto bookstore billed itself as Santa's depository for gifts. But stores that featured a real live Santa had a definite edge, especially if his arrival was marked by a special event.

The most special event of all was Eaton's annual Santa Claus parade, which started in 1905. Prior to that time, Santa was enthroned in the Toronto department store's Toyland in the weeks leading up to Christmas, but in the late fall of 1905, a series of Eaton's newspaper advertisements hinted that something extra special was about to happen. Santa was on his way to Toronto from the Far North.

A *Toronto Star* newspaper ad which ran on November 29 announced that Santa's train would arrive at Union Station at 9:59 sharp on Saturday morning. Every child who met St. Nick at the Front Street entrance or greeted him along the route to the store was promised a small memento. Meantime, the ad listed items that youngsters could put on their wish lists — toy pianos, magic lanterns, dolls, wooden horses, and carts, all priced at 25 cents each.

Santa arrived as promised on Saturday, December 2. He was a little later than anticipated, but was still "welcomed royally" by crowds of boys and girls. The float on which he rode was simple — a wagon drawn by a team of horses carrying a red and black checkered packing case that served as Santa's seat. The wagon carried Santa to the store on Yonge Street, where Santa could be visited in Toyland every day from 9 to 10:30 a.m. and from 2:30 to 4 p.m.

Eventually, Eaton's sponsored parades in Montreal, Winnipeg, and Edmonton, but the Toronto event was the first and frequently the most lavish. In the early years, organizers played with Santa's mode of transportation. In 1906, he arrived in a coach drawn by four horses. In 1913, eight live reindeer, brought in from Labrador especially for the occasion, pulled Santa's sled down Yonge Street. Fifteen years later, the parade consisted of eight floats.

By 1955, the year it marked its 50th anniversary, the parade was a mile long, comprised of some 44 floats and 88 nursery rhyme and storybook characters. A full-time staff of carpenters, artists, and paper sculptors were employed year round to plan and implement the event. All kinds of details had to be considered, including municipal regulations. One of the best-loved floats in the Toronto parade at this point featured Mother Goose. However, although the float met Toronto regulations, it was too big to ship by rail to Montreal.

Timing was crucial once the parade got underway. It had to move past any given point within 20 minutes in order to minimize traffic disruptions. Although store employees had once marched in the parade as costumed characters, at this point Toronto high school students were involved. There were also a number of marching bands. By the mid-1950s, walkie-talkies were making it somewhat easier for organizers to communicate, but they still relied on their own eyes and ears to spot any problems. As an additional safety measure, a doctor and nurse, as well as a stand-in, always travelled close to Santa's float.

Starting in 1928, Eaton's employee Jack Brockie headed up the parade arrangements, overseeing all the details that turned the annual event into a cherished Christmas tradition. Brockie had definite ideas about what was appropriate and what was not, leaning heavily towards traditional depictions of holiday themes. Under this management, Santa always arrived in a sleigh pulled by reindeer. New attractions were added only after considerable thought. In the 1950s, one of the most popular was Punkinhead, a tow-headed little bear that had been created by a company copywriter in 1949 to promote a Yuletide giveaway. By the mid-1950s, Punkinhead was showing up on all kinds of children's merchandise, including T-shirts and mugs.

Preserving a half-century-old tradition in the booming post-war period was a bit of a challenge. As television swept into Ontario homes, there were fears that people would stay in their living rooms rather than risk frigid weather to watch the parade. Some did, although in the early years black-and-white television images were a poor substitute for the vivid colours of the parade. Another concern for parade organizers was the increasing interest in space exploration. In 1955, Jack Brockie told an interviewer, "when space ships and super-men come in, I go out." Four years later, in another article about the parade, Margaret Munnoch stressed that the organizers deliberately steered away from science fiction themes and "have kept rockets, planets, and missiles completely divorced from Santa's Parade." By this time, Sputnik had been launched, and the U.S. was about to become deeply involved in the space race; but to organizers it seemed there was no connection between space and Santa — a Christmas icon from the days before planes, automobiles, and even trains. Yet the integration of holiday tradition and hi-tech travel and communication had already begun.

It started with a typographical error in 1955 when a newspaper in Colorado Springs, Colorado, printed the telephone number of the local Santa Hotline. At least it was supposed to be Santa's number. Instead, callers found themselves connected to the hotline at the Continental Air Defence Command, the predecessor of NORAD (North American Aerospace Defence Command). When the senior officer on duty took the very first call, he heard a small voice at the other end of the line asking to speak to Santa. Rather than disappoint the owner of the voice, he explained that he was one of Santa's helpers and that he was tracking him on the radar screen as he started his journey from the North Pole. Other calls followed, and the local news media picked up the story. The next year, more children called to find out where Santa Claus was on the radar screen. Caught up in the spirit of the season, military personnel established a tradition of issuing reports on Santa's whereabouts. Eventually, NORAD also established a web site so youngsters could track Santa for themselves.

In 2000, the NORAD site received more than 200 million hits. According to the site, "Santa Cams" located around the world keep an eye on Santa and his reindeer, taking pictures of them as they enter a country and downloading them to a web site so boys and girls can see their progress for themselves. There is also special infrared tracking that can locate Santa and his sleigh by pinpointing the heat from Rudolph's nose.

Along with providing information to anxious children, NORAD's tracking system provides advance information for fighter pilots who form the official escort for Santa and the reindeer. In 2002, those pilots were alerted by the Canadian Air Defence Sector Operations Centre in the underground complex at 22 Wing North Bay, Ontario. Two of the pilots took off from Bagotville, Quebec, to meet Santa as he crossed over Labrador, while a third waited at Cold Lake, Alberta, to escort him out of Canadian airspace. As a courtesy to his escort, Santa always slows down the sleigh so the CF-18 Hornet fighters can keep up with him.

Most of the time, NORAD's Santa watch proceeds without a hitch. But technical problems struck in 2003. A Sudbury boy, eight-year-old Matthew Breczki, was terribly disappointed when, after several attempts, he was unable to track Santa on the web site. His father took action and called NORAD headquarters in Colorado Springs. Major Douglas Martin, deputy director of public affairs, responded by e-mail, saying the technicians were working on it. Apparently three of the Santa Cams were down, but there were hopes that they could be restored to service quickly so that tracking could continue. Eventually, the Santa Cams were back online.

Of course, fighter pilots aren't Santa's only helpers. Generations of children have heard tales of others, including elves who help make toys for good little girls and boys. To assist department store and mall Santas, very large "elves" help out by calming crying children and taking photographs. Then there are those anonymous helpers who function as Santa's secretaries, answering the thousands of letters from hopeful children. Some have regular jobs on the staff of local newspapers. Others are Canada Post employees. Each year, about 13,000 postal elves answer letters addressed to Santa at the North Pole. In 1999, one of the elves apparently was a little late getting into the Christmas spirit. When Jonathon Comeau, a seven-year-old Oshawa boy wrote to Santa asking for a number of presents, he received the standard reply, plus something more. A particularly wicked elf added a postscript to the letter, "You are one greedy little boy." Jonathon and his mother asked for and received an apology from Canada Post. As for the elf, he probably got a lump of coal in his stocking at Christmas.

The Prairies

anta, as every kid knows, can't be everywhere at once. So, he has helpers. These Santa stand-ins come from all walks of life and travel all over the place. You just never know where you'll find a great Santa. He — or she — could be anywhere: at a school concert, in a Doukhobor village, or hiding in somebody's imagination.

An Interview with Santa

In 1982, Myrna Morris was working as a reporter for a newspaper in Fort Qu'Appelle, Saskatchewan. A few weeks before Christmas, she was given an assignment to write a feature story based on an interview with Santa Claus.

Myrna remembered how strongly she had believed in Santa when she was a little girl. But she was no longer a child.

She was an adult reporter covering important local stories. When she told her friends about this assignment, she suffered some good-natured ribbing. After that, she judiciously decided she wouldn't tell anyone else. As she began thinking about how she would handle the story, she heard a booming voice, "Hello, Little One!" Her "interview" with the Jolly Old Elf was about to begin.

"I knew Santa Claus would have a booming voice!" she wrote in the story that appeared in the *Fort Qu'Appelle Times* three days before Christmas Day that year. "He looked me square in the eyes and said, 'The reason I chose you to visit me, Little One, is because I have a message for you to take back to everyone' So that was it," Myrna concluded, "I had been chosen.

"'Here is my message,' he continued, tugging thoughtfully on his snow-white beard and settling his glasses comfortably on his nose. 'It has come to my attention that some folks are losing their enthusiasm for the Christmas season,' he stated. 'They worry that it is being too commercialized, and that it may someday lose all of its meaning and importance. But you know, Little One, that will never happen, as long as you all remember to do one thing; and that is to see Christmas through the eyes of the children,' said Santa.

"'As long as there are little ones who put on school Christmas concerts, who write me letters each year, who set out their stockings on Christmas Eve, who leave me snacks and listen carefully for my reindeer on the roof until they fall asleep, Christmas will never lose its magic. That is why I was created,' said Santa, 'to make sure that the spirit of Christmas can be kept alive through children's belief in me, in good times and bad.

"'So tell everyone,' Santa instructed me, 'not to feel discouraged. I know it must be difficult at times, with Santas on every street corner, and the monetary value that has been attached to having a good Christmas. I know there are poor people and lonely people who despair at Christmas, and evil people, who use Christmas for themselves. But above all else, there are still the children. They don't see the greed, the evil or the commercialization of the season. They only feel the spirit of love and giving that is the spirit of Santa Claus. It is there,' he assured me, 'I see it every year, in their trusting faces, and read it in their letters to me.

"'So you see, Little One,' concluded Santa, 'as long as we have children and a Santa Claus we will still have the spirit of Christmas. And I intend to be around for a long, long time,' he chuckled."

Outstanding Stand-ins

John Wilson, a transplanted British newspaperman, was looking forward to Christmas 1908 — his second festive season on a farm near Prince Albert, Saskatchewan. It wasn't because the food would be better, and it wasn't because he was expecting expensive gifts. It was because some single women had moved to town! This fact brightened the lives of

Prince Albert's bachelors considerably.

That Christmas Eve, John and his friends joined the high-spirited girls in a special sleigh ride. One of the young women was very dressed up and adjusted her festive garments as they reached their destination — a nearby Doukhobor village. Once there, the girls eagerly set about their Christmas Eve task of visiting each of the homes and leaving toys for the children. The one girl's finery impressed the village children. She was dressed as Santa Claus, beard and all, and the others were her elves!

In another area of Saskatchewan, a quarter of a century later, Jim Storey saw a special Santa — his first — at a school concert. The concert was pretty much the only place rural kids saw Santa's helpers in those days. It was not until after World War II that Santa-suited men appeared in department stores or stood on street corners in aid of charity. Street corners were few and far between in rural Saskatchewan, and the closest most people got to a department store was browsing through the Eaton's catalogue.

Jim remembers that the gas and coal oil lamps people had brought into the school had given the room a warm, somewhat mysterious glow. He was looking at the shadows the lamps were throwing here and there, when in came Santa Claus with a booming "Ho Ho Ho!"

"He scared me right out of my mind!" Jim laughs, the memory still fresh 70 years later. It's a good bet that young Jim wouldn't have been worried had he realized it was his own father under the beard and red hat.

Every once in a long time, though, a very special pseudo-Santa emerges. One of the best remembered in rural Alberta was a travelling salesman who worked for Love Feeds Limited. His name was Jack Fulton. He was built a lot like Santa, and his voice, reportedly, boomed just the way Santa's should. He was very friendly, laughed a lot, and loved the kids. Legend has it that, in the month of December, Jack had more than seed catalogues and samples in the trunk of his car. He had an entire Santa Claus suit tucked away in there, too. Now, here was a man who was prepared.

One December while in Drumheller, Jack was invited to dinner by a farm family on the very evening of the school Christmas concert. It was all the three daughters in the household could do to eat their supper. They were performing that night, so excitement was running high. The family invited him to the concert, but Jack declined, saying he couldn't be in the audience because he had another appointment to keep.

He didn't actually fib. Jack really wasn't going to be in the audience — he was going to be on the stage. His "appointment" was to play Santa Claus at the concert. He made his way to the school, quickly changed into his costume, and made his grand entrance. Did he worry that the girls would recognize him? If so, he needn't have. They were as delighted as their other classmates when the Jolly Old Elf marched onto the stage. They had no idea that this was the same man who had sat across the dinner table from them three hours earlier.

In another part of the province, some years before Jack was doing his rounds as Santa, Jeane Jervais, a teacher at Sedalia, was having trouble finding anyone to play the part at her Christmas concert. She told her fiancé, John McLeod, about her problem. John said he could convince a friend of his to play the part. Jeane must have been dubious: John worked in Calgary, more than 300 kilometres away. What friend would travel that distance in the middle of winter to play Santa?

The big night came, and — much to Jeane's relief — so did Santa. Not just any old Santa, either; this Santa was terrific! He charmed the children; therefore, he also charmed their parents. Jeane was pleased, but her delight turned to shock as she discovered that under that red hat and behind that white beard was her fiancé, John!

Happily, most Christmas concerts were held at night, which meant that organizers could use the cover of darkness outside to enhance the reality of Santa's arrival. One Cotswold, Alberta, school-board-trustee-turned-Santa would race around the schoolhouse shouting, "Whoa there, Prancer, Whoa, there Vixen!" at the top of his lungs, while an accomplice made scraping sounds outside, high on the school wall. There could be no doubt about it, you could actually hear those reindeer pulling Santa's sleigh right onto the roof! All eyes flew up to the trapdoor in the ceiling. Sure enough, the trap door opened and, with considerable huffing and puffing — the trap-door entrance was a tight squeeze — down came Santa!

A Santa Sighting

One Christmas Eve in the late 1950s, Edmonton radio morning-show host John Barton was driving home with his wife Lesley, and their children, Juley (seven) and Reid (five), after visiting an aunt and uncle. John remembers that trip clearly:

"It was after dark, and we had to hurry home because Santa was on his way. The kids were in the back seat, punching each other." John laughs and corrects himself. "No, they were excited all right, but behaving themselves. After all this was the night of nights! They just wanted us to hurry home, hurry home! We were maybe ten blocks from the Edmonton Municipal Airport, and it was pitch black outside. Lesley looked up and spotted something in the sky. What she had seen, of course, was simply the blinking red light of an airplane coming in for a landing. 'Oh look!' she said."

John had seen the light at the same time. Before Lesley had a chance to give the game away, he turned to the kids and said, "Do you see what I see?" The children stopped their excited babble and silently leaned forward, their eyes following their father's outstretched arm.

John then said, "If you're very careful, if you look hard, directly ahead and up into the sky … what do you see? Do you see something that looks like a nose?" Both kids looked hard and said, "Oh, my gosh!"

"They couldn't believe it," says John, smiling at the memory. "Their jaws just dropped and they just stared!"

The right time, the right place, and the power of suggestion was all it took. To Juley and Reid Barton, there was no doubt. It just had to be Rudolph leading Santa's team of reindeer! Now the kids were really in a panic to get home. John had a ready answer that calmed them down: "I said, 'You don't have to worry too much, because Santa's working that end of town right now.'"

Leslie rolled her eyes at her husband's slick act. "I just thought it was a hoot," John recalls with a laugh.

British Columbia

very year, children across Canada go to bed on Christmas Eve eagerly anticipating a visit from Santa Claus. With their eyes squeezed shut and their spirits hopeful, they wait for the jolly man in the red suit to slide down the chimney and leave gifts for them under the tree. Most spend the weeks leading up to Christmas preparing for this most important of visits. They comb through catalogues and race through toy stores, eyes peeled for the perfect gift to ask for from Santa. Acting on their best behaviour, they visit his look-alikes at nearby shopping malls and department stores. Those who do not have access to one of Santa's helpers might chose instead to write a letter to the man himself, detailing the gift or gifts they would like to receive. This eager anticipation of Santa's visit, this build-up of excitement, has been present in British

Columbia for well over a century.

Nothing — and everything — from Santa

Bad behaviour meant that Bert Williams and his brothers and sisters wouldn't find anything on Christmas morning, or so their parents told them. When the big day came, there was evidence that Santa had, indeed, paid a visit: all that was left of the cake the kids had left out for him was a few scattered crumbs on an empty plate. One look in the stockings, however, turned Christmas morning anticipation to abject disappointment. The stockings weren't filled with toys, they were filled with wood-shavings!

"Well, I declare," Bert Williams said as he recounted this tragic Christmas tale, "he [Santa] was getting a calling down, I'll tell you, about how mean he was, and all this sort of thing. We wouldn't be good. We wouldn't be good anymore! We wasn't gonna be!"

It didn't matter what day it was, when you were a member of a Langley farm family, there were chores to be done. Hop to it, his parents said. Bert stomped out to the stable to feed the horses.

"There's a hay loft overhead ... hanging from the ceiling, there was the biggest Christmas tree you ever saw, and it was absolutely loaded. Well, of course, down I went to the house and my eyes were sticking out like saucers and I couldn't talk plain or tell them what it was. I remember that year I got a mouth-organ and an axe. My brother got an axe and a little gun. And other things, candies and things, all tied up. Wonderful presents."

In later years, that fondly remembered Christmas seemed even more miraculous when Bert understood the special efforts his parents had made. Gift-giving wasn't as simple as going to a department store or ordering items from a catalogue. Mr. Williams packed those presents home on his back, and it wasn't a short walk, either. It was a long, arduous journey by foot and ferry to New Westminster. Making the journey down to the Royal City was the easy part. Coming back was much more difficult. Once off the ferry, it was an eight-kilometre hike through the bush with those awkward, heavy parcels.

As children do, there were sly comparisons made later on that day and in the days that followed. "Some of the richer kids had better [gifts] and nicer shoes or something like that," Bert said, "but we were always satisfied, and it was a wonderful time."

The Letter to Santa

The Tatangelos, and other Italians living in Trail, called it *span-iolla.* Most other people called it "the flu." In any case, it was the 20th century scourge that authorities are only now recognizing as one of the worst epidemics of any century, anywhere. Giuseppe Tatangelo was a husband, father, and one of Trail's tireless community volunteers. When the epidemic claimed him just a week before Christmas, it was the hardest death of three that had crushed the family since they had immigrated to the Kootenays nine years before. First, four-year-old Enrico had drowned in a rain barrel. Then, five years later, little two-year-old Peter had succumbed to a rare illness.

Now, while other households in the mining community prepared for the festive season, Pasqua, the Tatangelo children's mother, was inconsolable in her loss. To take the children's minds off the tragedy, one of their uncles suggested they should all write a letter to Santa Claus.

Eight-year-old Enrico (named to commemorate his deceased brother) finished his letter and carefully placed it in the oven. Why not? That way, it would be magically whisked up the chimney to Santa. Six-year-old Mary thought she knew better. She was adamant she was going to mail her letter to the North Pole, and so off to the post office she went. The postmaster noticed the address on the letter. Of course, in the small, tightly knit community, the latest Tatangelo tragedy was on everyone's lips. The postmaster took the liberty of opening up Mary's letter.

A few days before Christmas, Mary found a little note in the Tatangelo mailbox addressed to her. The note asked her to please come to the post office on Christmas morning. The date did not surprise her: in those days the post office was open between ten and noon Christmas morning.

Obediently, on December 25 Mary walked down to the post office with her older brother Enrico. Mary showed the postmaster her note. Inside the post office were dozens of toys and gifts, money tied around a doll, mitts, socks, and a hat to keep Mary warm in the winter. Thank heavens she had brought her bigger brother along to help her carry everything home!

At 92, Mary still makes her home in Trail and can recall that special Christmas with crystal clarity.

"I was six when my father died," she said, "and I remember that Christmas like it was yesterday."

The Magic Of It All

Could anything be more memorable than Christmas stocking treats and presents under the tree? One of three little girls living near Peachland at the turn of the century, Adelaide Treasure discovered there was more to Christmas than gifts. There could be magic as well.

"One Christmas I went with another girl, to stay with a little girl by the name of Mary Miller," Adelaide began. "They lived way, way up in the mountains. They had a big ranch up there. They wanted to have some other little girls there for Mary's sake, because she was an only child, you see. The other girl's name was Jean Pollard. We went in a sleigh, all covered up with fur rugs in the back to keep us warm. It was a long trek up that mountain, I'm telling you, in deep snow. It's a wonder the horses ever got up there."

The Millers had a large Christmas tree all decorated by the time the little girls climbed down from the sleigh. This was the night Santa was to come. That was exciting enough, but when Mrs. Miller announced that when Santa arrived, she would come in and wake the girls so they could visit with him, all hope of sleep was banished.

Not long after the three girls were tucked into the one big bed, the silence outside was broken by the sound of bells. Mrs. Miller hurried into the bedroom. Look out the window, she urged. The girls scraped little holes in the frost-covered windows.

"I can remember peering through these little holes that we'd made, wiping them off, to see him," Adelaide recalled. "We went out and here was Santa Claus standing by the fireplace, with a great big sack of all kinds of stuff. We wanted him to stay and have breakfast with us, and he said, 'oh, [I] couldn't possibly do that', because he had to go to Peachland before a certain time, you see.

"Mrs. Miller said that if we went back and looked through the window we would see him leave. Well, they must have taken deer horns and put them on the horses, and when he was leaving the bells were ringing and he was waving to us.

"It was really a fantastic thing. They went to an awful lot of trouble. It was a fantastic Christmas. I can't remember any child ever having a Christmas like it."

Does the magic of a child's Christmas exist today? Perhaps it still does, if you are a child, if you believe. Kids don't talk about it, and won't, until 40 or 50 years later. Then, they smile and say, "I remember this one Christmas ..."

And they relive the magic all over again.

Chapter 5
Gifts and Giving

Atlantic Canada

he tradition of exchanging gifts at Christmas is as old as the holiday itself. Changing social values over the centuries, however, have greatly influenced the gift giving tradition. Prior to the mid-1800s, goods were not terribly plentiful or accessible in Atlantic Canada. In addition, Christmas was still viewed as a sacred holiday, so gift giving was restricted to the exchange of a few trinkets and essential items. But it was also around that time that local merchants began placing lists of "Seasonal Goods" in newspapers in the weeks leading up to Christmas. Unlike the advertisements yet to come, these lists were not usually illustrated. They simply consisted of items the merchants had in stock, such as different types of fabrics, ribbons, and hats. In addition, they invariably included items such as "rum, spirits, brandy and gin," as well as nuts, fruits,

and spices for Christmas baking. It wasn't until late in the 19th century that the commercialization of the holiday began in earnest.

In the Victorian era, the exchange of "Christmas boxes" was common among the upper classes. Still, these gifts were quite modest in comparison to the extravagance of today's Christmas gift giving. In 1853, Sarah Clinch of Boston was spending Christmas with her cousins in Halifax. Her diary entry for December 24 described the presents exchanged among the family that year: "The Christmas boxes were given out today, as tomorrow is Sunday. Mine, besides the shoulder ribbons and belt, and the six pounds from Uncle Morton, were a papeteur from Heber and a neck ribbon from Aunt Mary ... and also a pretty little almanac ..."

The gifts Sarah gave were equally modest: "I gave Uncle William a book of blotting paper, Aunt Mary a bottle of lavender, Charlotte a bottle of mignonette, Louisa a papeteur ... Miriam some velvet bracelets, Heber Laurt's 'Essays of Elia', Bella and Tory collars and the three boys neck ties." The gifts she received from home, however, were slightly more lavish: "... a large music book, a pair of shoes & stockings, velvet raw silk for my New Year's dress."

Gifts from the Heart

The Great Depression hit Atlantic Canada particularly hard. For most families on the East Coast, purchasing Christmas presents was simply impossible during the 1930s. Many children received little more than a handful nuts and raisins for Christmas. If they were lucky, they'd get an orange in their stockings, or perhaps a few store-bought necessities, such as hankies, hair ribbons, or a comb. Gifts given in addition to the stocking stuffers usually consisted of handmade items, such as woollen socks, mittens, and hats, or handcrafted toys. Despite the humble nature of these gifts, they were often treasured long after store-bought presents had been forgotten.

Among the most prized homemade gifts that Florence Cormier and her sister Bernette received during the Depression was a pair of handcrafted matching doll cradles. Even though there were six children in the Cormier family, there was always something special for each of them beneath the tree on Christmas morning. Their parents, Fidele and Elise Cormier, were both creative and resourceful. Elise was an excellent seamstress and Fidele enjoyed working with his hands. Together they created many treasured presents for the children.

Marvels of recycling, the little doll cradles were created out of wooden fruit baskets. The Cormiers owned a corner store in Moncton, New Brunswick, so there was always a surplus of these baskets on hand. One year, Fidele decided to put two of them to good use. He started by removing the arched handles from the top of each basket. The handles were then cut in two and attached to the bottom of the baskets, making perfect rockers. More handles were used to form canopy frames at the head of both cradles.

Once the basic construction was completed, Elise took over. She covered the canopies and outsides of the baskets with a bit of shirred fabric. A miniature quilt and pillow completed each cradle. Florence and Bernette were delighted when they discovered the cradles under the tree on Christmas morning. Their dolls were already tucked beneath the tiny quilts, sleeping contentedly.

The Most Precious Gift

In the weeks leading up to Christmas, six-year-old Jessie Cameron sensed that something was wrong in the Cameron household. As usual, her mother Katie was busy cooking and cleaning. With seven children — one a newborn — there was never any shortage of chores to be done around the house. But Jessie noticed that the delicious aroma of Christmas baking didn't fill the kitchen like it usually did at that time of year. Whenever the children brought up the topic of Santa Claus and the gifts they were certain he was going to bring, a mournful look would cross her mother's tired features. Christmas isn't just about getting presents, she would remind them.

It was 1950, and employment on Cape Breton Island was scarce. Jessie's father, Dan Cameron, had to travel all the way to the town of Mulgrave on the mainland to find work as a security guard. The Camerons lived in Glenco Station, nearly 50 kilometres from Mulgrave.

At that time, the railway was an integral part of the Cameron family's daily life. Since he didn't own a car, Dan relied on the train to get to and from work. And because the station was just a stone's throw from their house, the family had become friends with many railway employees over the years. Two people in particular that Dan had befriended were Murdock Skinner and his son Basil. Father and son were both train engineers, and often on the long trip to and from the mainland, Dan would ride up in the engine with them.

For the children, the trains that passed by the Cameron house two or three times a day were an exciting diversion from the daily routine. At the sound of the whistle blowing down the line, they would race out to watch the long procession of cars roll by. They liked the passenger train best, as that was the one that always brought their father home. In addition, the passengers often threw candies or coins out the windows to them. For John Allan, who would later become a well-known Canadian musician, the passengers were a receptive audience. A born performer, he would often step dance and pretend to play the fiddle for them as they passed by.

Like many rural Maritime families back then, the Camerons were struggling financially. With seven children to feed and clothe on one meagre salary, there wasn't much left over at the end of each month. After the birth of their seventh child in 1950, Dan and Katie found themselves in dire financial straits. As Christmas approached, the couple came to the realization that store-bought gifts would be out of the question that year. And with more to do to keep the household going than she could manage, Katie had no time to create homemade presents. The thought of the children's disappointment on Christmas morning when they discovered that Santa Claus hadn't come to their house was more than Katie could bear. She decided they had to be told before they got their hopes up. One morning at breakfast, as the children were once again speculating on what Santa would bring them, she announced as tactfully as possible that Santa probably wouldn't be coming that year. A howl of protest went up from the children. Like the rest of her siblings, Jessie was bewildered by this news. She knew they'd been good all year, so why wasn't Santa going to make his annual stop at their house?

For the next few days, the children struggled with the notion that Santa wasn't going to visit their house that Christmas. In an effort to cheer them up, Katie reminded them that there would still be midnight mass on Christmas Eve, something they all looked forward to each year. And perhaps a special treat for Christmas dinner. But this did little to raise their spirits.

Then, just two days before Christmas, something completely unexpected happened. The afternoon train had just pulled into the station, and the children were out on the bank beside the tracks collecting the candies the passengers had tossed out the windows. Suddenly, Jessie noticed the stationmaster's son running towards them. The boy was so excited that by the time he reached them, he could barely speak. Between gasps for breath he managed to blurt out, "There's a big box just came in on the train for you people!"

Forgetting all about the candies, they dashed towards the station. John Allan, being the fastest, was the first one there. Before the others had reached the station, he and the stationmaster's son had already picked up the box and were struggling to carry it back up the hill to the Cameron house. The children couldn't ever remember receiving a parcel like this before. The excitement of it all was overwhelming.

Mere seconds after they'd wrestled the box through the door and set it down, they ripped it open. Nestled inside were seven presents, each one wrapped in glossy Christmas paper with a nametag attached. For a few moments, the children just stared at the gifts in disbelief. It wasn't long, however, before squeals of delight filled the room as the gifts were passed out and dolls, toy trains, and watercolour sets were pulled from their wrappings. When Jessie unwrapped the package with her name on it, she almost cried. Inside was a porcelain doll dressed in a long gown. She'd never seen such a beautiful doll before and could hardly believe it was hers. The children were beside themselves with joy at this unexpected windfall. It seemed Santa had received their wishes after all.

A few days after Christmas, however, Jessie happened to overhear her father telling her mother that he'd found out where the presents had come from. "It was Basil Skinner who sent them," he said. The statement puzzled Jessie. Just who was this Basil Skinner, and what was his role in the gift giving? After all, the nametags had clearly said "From Santa."

At that time, Basil and his wife Evelyn hadn't started their own family yet. And as an engineer, he made enough for the two of them to get by. He knew his friend was struggling, but had no idea how bad things were until Dan let it slip that there wouldn't be much of a Christmas at the Cameron house that year. The thought of his friend's children receiving nothing for Christmas was intolerable to Basil. He'd learned from his own father that it was better to give than to receive. Murdock Skinner was well known in the community for his generosity. If Murdock knew someone was going through a rough time, he was always the first to offer whatever help he could.

Basil, it seemed, had inherited his father's generous nature. He decided that if *he* had anything to do with it, Santa would be paying a visit to the Cameron house that year. He recruited a friend to find out the names, ages, and interests of each of the Cameron children. After making up a list, he gave it to Evelyn and asked her to go out shopping for appropriate gifts for each of them. Delivering the gifts was easy. All he had to do was drop off the package, addressed to the Cameron family, at the station.

It wasn't until she was a little older that Jessie realized just how big-hearted Basil's gesture had been. She vowed that one day she would seek him out and thank him in person.

But as fate would have it, she ended up moving to Ontario and having a family of her own before she had the chance to thank him for his kindness.

Nearly 50 years later, Jessie was at a Christmas party in Windsor, Ontario, with some old friends from Cape Breton when the subject of that long-ago Christmas came up. After telling the story about the box of presents arriving on the train, she suddenly felt remorseful that she never *had* thanked Basil. She hoped it wasn't too late. That night, after the party, she went home and poured her feelings out in a letter to the man who had brought such joy to her family that Christmas of 1950. Of all the gifts she had ever received in her life, she wrote, his was the "most precious."

Christmas Spirit All Year Round

Just three days before Christmas of 2003, Erica Tung was diagnosed with an extremely rare disease known as Langerhans Cell Histiocytosis. The disease, which consumes tissues and bones, can only be controlled with chemotherapy. Since it had been ravaging two-year-old Erica's system unchecked for some time, the doctors informed her parents that chemotherapy would be necessary immediately. However, the only hospital in the region equipped to treat her was the IWK Children's Hospital in Halifax, Nova Scotia, and the Tungs lived in Prince Edward Island. Since Erica's mom, Sandy, had just given birth to her second child, there was no way she could leave home for an extended period. She and her husband, Lewis, decided he would take Erica to Halifax, where they would spend the next six months while she received treatment.

It was a traumatic Christmas for the young couple that year. Worry over Erica's condition was compounded by financial stress. The Tungs owned and operated a restaurant in the small community of Souris. Lewis did the cooking and Sandy waited on tables. Like most small business owners, they had no safety net to fall back on in times of crisis. With Lewis away in Halifax and a new infant to care for, it was impossible for Sandy to keep the restaurant open that winter. And with the restaurant closed, she had no idea how she was going to manage to pay the bills for the next few months.

When it came time to pay the rent, Sandy approached the landlord and explained the situation, hoping he would allow her some extra time to scrape together the money. To her surprise, he seemed completely unconcerned about the rent money. "Don't worry about it," he said. "Just make sure your little girl gets well." And later, when the pipes in restaurant froze up and she had to call in a plumber, the man astonished her by refusing to take a cent for the job.

In a tiny community like Souris, little goes unnoticed by the residents for long. When the Bonsai Restaurant failed to re-open after the Christmas holidays, customers and neighbours began to worry. Although they had only lived in the community for six years, the Tungs were liked and respected by everyone who knew them. Word about Erica's illness soon spread, and before long the community united in an effort to raise funds to help out the young family. The local schoolchildren started a penny drive; the Legion held a fundraiser; the women's auxiliary of a church in Charlottetown made Erica a quilt. Even rival restaurateurs in the area began collecting for the Tungs. Sandy was overwhelmed by the outpouring of generosity.

When Erica was finally released from the hospital six months later, she and Lewis returned home to a warm reception from the community. Although the two-year-old had lost her hearing in one ear and the disease had damaged her jawbone, neck, ribs, hip, and one leg, the chemotherapy had at least temporarily halted its progression. And the doctors hoped that, in time, the damage would be reversed with steroids.

Life slowly returned to normal for the Tungs. They reopened the restaurant, and Erica spent most of her days there with them. The sweet-tempered girl, who followed her mother around with a pad and pencil in hand pretending to take orders, charmed everyone who came through the door.

When the Christmas season rolled around again, and the *Christmas Wish Book* arrived on the Tungs' doorstep, Erica eagerly flipped through the glossy pages in search of the gift she hoped Santa would bring. She paid scant attention to the dolls, ignored the games and clothes, but stopped dead when she came to a picture of a boy and girl cooking up a storm in a play-kitchen. Here was the Christmas present of her dreams. The life-like kitchen came complete with fridge, stove, sink, and cupboards filled with dishes, utensils, and pots and pans. To Erica, it was a perfect replica of her father's kitchen in the restaurant. But when she showed the picture to her mother and said that that was what she wanted for Christmas, Sandy's heart sank. The Tungs were still struggling to catch up with the bills from the past winter, and Sandy knew there was no way they could afford such an extravagant gift that year. But how could she explain that to the three-year-old? She tried to direct Erica's attention to more affordable gifts, but the child's desire for the kitchen was unshakable. Erica lugged the catalogue around with her everywhere. When customers asked her what she wanted from Santa for Christmas, she would whip it open and point to the play-kitchen. As Christmas drew closer, Sandy worried about how Erica would react when she opened her presents on Christmas morning and found no play-kitchen among them.

Then, a few days before Christmas, a friend of the Tungs showed up at the restaurant and asked Sandy to bring Erica outside. Curious, Sandy got Erica dressed in her jacket and mittens and the two stepped out into the frosty air. In the parking lot, a circle of friends and customers stood smiling broadly. And there, in the centre of the circle, was Erica's play-kitchen. For a few seconds, the child just stared at the gift, dumbfounded. When she realized it was for her, she toddled right over and began opening the cupboards and pulling out the pots and pans. The look of joy on her daughter's face at that moment brought tears to Sandy's eyes. All that they'd been through that past year came rushing back to her, and suddenly she was overwhelmed with gratitude. She was grateful for having her daughter and husband home for Christmas. She was grateful that Erica's disease was in remission for the time being. And last, but not least, she was grateful that they lived in a community that had been there to help out in their time of need. Christmas spirit wasn't something the community of Souris adopted once a year and then forgot about for the remaining 11 months, she realized. It was something that flourished there all year long.

Quebec

hristmas gifts come in all shapes and sizes. They can also arrive in a variety of ways; some are delightful surprises and others are special because they have been anxiously anticipated. The simplest things can be gifts; they need only be treasured by their recipients. Some presents endure well beyond the end of the holiday season — especially those that come in the form of kind gestures and thoughtfulness.

Made With Love

> *Il est né, le divin Enfant!*
> *Jouez haut-bois, résonnez musettes;*
> *Il est né, le divin Enfant!*
> *Chantons tous son avènement.*

The choir sang with great affection as one more wooden sculpture was carefully placed into the Christmas *crèche*. The parishioners of St-Jean-Port-Joli (a town on the south shore of the St. Lawrence River midway between Quebec City and Rivière-du-Loup) were rapt with joy upon hearing the traditional Christmas melodies once again. They were also thrilled to view their new wooden *crèche* of human figures and animals that had all been crafted by local sculptors.

In mid-December 1987, the sculptors gave this *crèche* to the Église Saint-Jean-Baptiste as a testament of their faith and of their pride in the town's handsome 18th century church, with its fieldstone, red roof, and twin steeples. Yet the *crèche* project did not begin in solemnity — it was actually the result of a battle of wits between *curé* Sarto Lord and renowned local sculptor Benoi Deschênes.

The two men were great friends and they spent lots of time together, as Deschênes was involved in organizing a number of church activities.

"One day in December 1986, I was working on a large life-size *Christ Glorieux* (a type of sculpture portraying the Resurrected Christ) for a parish in Rivière-du-Loup. That parish wanted to have a symbolic cross above Christ's back," recalled Deschênes.

The *curé* walked into Deschênes's studio, looked up and down at the work in progress, and then teased the sculptor by telling him that he shouldn't put a cross there because, after all, Christ had risen!

Deschênes had a saucy comeback ready: "I don't tell you how to give sermons so you shouldn't tell me how to create my sculptures."

The next day, Deschênes was at the parish church for a meeting regarding midnight mass preparations, and the *curé* casually inquired if he was still doing *Christ Glorieux* sculptures with crosses in the background. Deschênes happened to notice that the church's plaster Christmas *crèche* was being unpacked at that moment. The crèche had fallen on hard times — it was dusty and dilapidated, and some of the plaster figures were chipped. So Deschênes blurted out to the *curé*, "What are you doing with a plaster *crèche* in the capital of wood sculpture?"

"If you don't like our *crèche* then make us another one!" was the *curé*'s simple reply.

Deschênes realized that it would be unrealistic for him to create an entirely new *crèche* for the church, so he contacted a group of his fellow sculptors. "I told them the whole story and then I said that there is no budget or anything; and they were all interested!" he recalled.

The St-Jean sculptors contacted by Benoi Deschênes had many different reasons to commit themselves to the *crèche* project. Some were moved by their Catholic faith to recreate a scene of Christ's birth on that most holy night. Others liked the fact that the *crèche* was a gift for their parish church.

Naturally, the sculptors were also motivated by the joy

of friendship and collaboration. "We had worked together before for symposiums and exhibitions ... but nothing on this scale," mentioned Deschênes.

There is a rich tradition of wood sculpting in this region of Quebec. Back in the 1670s, Bishop Laval was instrumental in encouraging the teaching of arts and crafts in St. Joachim. At that time, there was a high demand for wood sculptors to decorate local churches, public buildings, and the homes of the ruling class. With the advent of mass-production, the woodcarving profession suffered a decline, although many Quebec farmers and sailors continued to carve for their own pleasure.

Médard Bourgault, a famous wood sculptor, was born in St-Jean-Port-Joli in 1897. As a boy, Médard was mesmerized by the beautifully carved, gilded wood interior of the St-Jean parish church. He spent years travelling around the world as a sailor, but in 1925, Médard realized that carving was his true vocation and so he came back to work in his father's carpentry shop. A few years later, Médard and his brother Jean-Julien opened a woodcarving studio in St-Jean. They were later joined by their brother André.

The Bourgaults were the fathers of a wood carving revival in St-Jean. Today, this small town on the south shore of the St. Lawrence River boasts 23 wood carving studios which produce many different types of sculptures, including wooden model sailboats, *habitant* farmers on snowshoes, and life-size historical figures.

Gifts and Giving

When it became apparent that there was a popular interest in the creation of St-Jean's new *crèche*, the *curé* decided to open up the planning process so that any local sculptor who wanted to participate could execute one of the human figures or animals from the nativity story.

Deschênes decided to create the Joseph figure, Jacques Bourgault chose Mary, Nicole Deschênes-Duval wanted to create the infant Jesus, and Denys Heppell was interested in sculpting the gentle cow in the manger. By the end of a series of meetings, 17 wood carvers had taken on the creation of 23 sculptures.

Selecting the character was the easy part. Reality set in during the fall of 1987, when the sculptors had to complete their piece (or pieces) in time for the Christmas celebration. The main directives were that the figures had to be sculpted of linden wood, that they were to be left unfinished (not painted or varnished), and that each sculpture had to be about two feet high. Linden wood has been a choice material for European and Canadian sculptors for generations. "We wanted to use a traditional medium so that it would fit in the church," explained Deschênes.

The sculptors picked up their chisels and their wood carving knives and set to work. It was not always easy to find enough hours in the day to complete the carvings. Some sculptors also had to work on other projects simultaneously.

Nicole Deschênes-Duval had offered to sculpt the baby Jesus because she specializes in sculptures of children and adolescents. "After all the meetings and the sketches were presented it took me two to three weeks of intensive work to create the baby Jesus in his bed of straw, with a simple cover. I sculpted a baby with his eyes open and his arms and feet in the air, like a happy baby kicking his feet," she explained.

Finally, it was time to present the sculptures to the church. On December 12, 1987, the sculptors arrived with their precious woodcarvings for a special early midnight mass. (The television station Radio-Canada wanted to film the presentation so that it could be aired at Christmastime.)

"Each sculptor arrived at the church with their sculpture. During the mass, the churchwardens did a little presentation of the sculptor and their creation and then each sculptor placed their own work in the *crèche*," Nicole Deschênes-Duval recalled.

The sculptures were brought to the *crèche* following the order of the nativity story. First, the gentle cow with big eyes was placed in the manger. Next came the proud parents, Mary and Joseph, and then Nicole brought the infant Jesus to rest in his little bed of straw.

"The music and the Christmas carols during the presentation corresponded to the sculptures. So when I presented the sculpture of baby Jesus, *Il est né le divin enfant* was performed," recalled Deschênes-Duval.

After the babe, the shepherds were presented, and all of the other sculptures followed in the appropriate order.

Several other sculptures have been added since 1987,

including a pregnant virgin who appears during advent, another shepherd, a shepherd dog, and a star. Apart from their own satisfaction at a job well done, Deschênes and the other sculptors all benefited from the *crèche* project in the form of new wood carving projects. Deschênes was even commissioned to create a complete *crèche* for the nearby town of La Pocatière.

When asked whether any of the original sculptors plan to contribute anything else to the St-Jean *crèche*, Deschênes chuckled and replied, "The next generation will do their part."

Christmas Cards Came Raining Down

The fishermen, trappers, missionaries, and other inhabitants of the Côte-Nord were accustomed to isolation in 1927. After all, east of Portneuf-sur-Mer there were no roads connecting the dozens of little villages dotted along the north shore of the St. Lawrence River. During the summer months, when the St. Lawrence was open water, mail was delivered by boat. However, during the winter months mail was delivered by a runner on snowshoes or by dogsled. Letters often took weeks or months to arrive.

So on Christmas Day, 1927, when mailbags full of Christmas cards, presents, and New Year's wishes came tumbling out of an airplane and parachuted down to the villages along the Côte-Nord, it was like some kind of miracle. Although the Christmas mail drops were announced in the

Quebec City newspapers, most villagers living on the Côte-Nord were so isolated that they had not heard about the new airmail service.

L'Action Catholique, a Quebec City newspaper, reported the event the next day: "The first airmail delivery of letters and parcels to destinations on the North Shore occurred yesterday, Christmas Day. The letters and parcels were dropped in mailbags, which were attached to parachutes. The first plane G-CAIP of the Canadian Transcontinental Airways left Lac Sainte-Agnès, near LaMalbaie at 10:15 yesterday morning and it successfully delivered the mail to over six destinations between LaMalbaie and Sept-Îles. At 2:15 p.m., the delivery was complete and Captain (Charles) Sutton who piloted the G-CAIP with Dr. Cuisinier as a passenger had successfully completed the first flight of this kind on the North Shore."

Canadian Transcontinental Airways (CTA) was founded in Quebec in 1927. CTA's chief pilot, Charles Sutton, had recently emigrated from England. The technical director and soul of the new airline was the French aviator, Dr. Louis Cuisinier. Soon after it was formed, CTA was awarded several airmail delivery contracts from the postmaster general of Canada, including the first contract to deliver airmail on the North Shore. Her Majesty's mail would be delivered twice a week during the winter season.

Sutton began the historic Christmas Day trip at Lac Sainte-Agnès, where he loaded almost 800 pounds of mail into a Fairchild plane. The small plane was simply stuffed right up to its weight capacity. All of the letters and packages had already been neatly sorted into mailbags that could easily be attached to parachutes for delivery. Then, the mailbags were placed in the airplane cabin in reverse order to the anticipated sequence of the drop: Sept-Îles, Shelter Bay, Pentecost, Trinity Bay, Godbout, Baie Comeau, Outardes, and finally, Bersimis.

It was obvious that parachute drops were the best way to deliver the mail to avoid wasting time landing and taking off from each village, and also because there were no proper landing fields near the North Shore settlements. The main disadvantage of the mail-drop system was that outgoing mail could not be picked up at each village, so the North Shore villagers had to take their outgoing mail to a central collection spot, such as Sept-Îles.

Sutton, accompanied by Dr. Cuisinier, was flying a brand new machine for this flight — a single-engine monoplane that he had picked up in New York City a few days before. It was a beautiful machine in its day, but it was not equipped with the sophisticated cockpit instruments that are standard on modern airplanes, or with radar to help with navigation. Sutton had to rely on his own vision to guide the plane safely. And if, God forbid, he ever lost his way, there was no radio available in the cockpit to call for help.

A pilot with 13 years experience, Sutton had flown in difficult situations before — he'd flown over German lines in WWI and had some experience transporting mail in the

Middle East between Cairo and Baghdad. But the North Shore of the St. Lawrence is a serious challenge for any pilot; the rugged coast has always had a reputation for nasty storms and fog as thick as pea soup. In 1534, French explorer Jacques Cartier found this region so inhospitable that he called it the "Land of Cain."

Sutton was pretty busy during his flight — cruising along the North Shore, locating the villages that were due to receive mail-drops, steering clear of fog patches and gusts of wind, and doing his best to stay warm in –20 degree Celsius weather. And of course, he also had to help deliver the mail.

Once he located a village, he alerted the inhabitants by "buzzing them" (flying very low over their houses). Then he probably made a low-level practice pass near where the mail was supposed to land. On the second pass he would have reduced his altitude to about 50 feet and tossed the rolled-up mailbag with an attached parachute out one of the plane's windows.

Naturally, Sutton never saw the villagers' reactions as they opened their mail, but he knew he was transporting a precious cargo of sentimental illustrated Christmas cards, family letters with all of the latest news, and gaily decorated Christmas packages.

As the Fairchild neared the town of Sept-Îles, a nasty squall blew up and dampened the jubilant moods of Sutton and Cuisinier, who were nearing the end of a successful flight. As wind howled and buffeted the little plane, Sutton and Cuisinier got into a heated argument. Sutton wanted to turn back because he feared for their safety. But Cuisinier — who was acutely aware of the financial implications of this inaugural route — wanted Sutton to land the plane. The first bundle of outgoing mail was waiting at Sept-Îles and Cuisinier was determined that the inaugural voyage of this mail delivery route would be a great success. CTA had invested a lot of money in the new planes and they could not afford to lose the postal contract.

As the argument between the two men intensified, the storm outside began to build. Sutton and Cuisinier yelled at each other above the roar of the wind. Neither man was prepared to back down and they continued to argue their positions. Yet the storm was more furious than either man, and it threatened to destroy both of their lives. As the plane careened down towards the icy St. Lawrence River, Sutton and Cuisinier began to tussle. The two men were so embroiled in their fistfight that they seemed to ignore the fact that they were headed towards certain death.

Finally, Cuisinier threatened Sutton (according to some sources, the threat was at gunpoint) and Sutton managed to land the plane in the bay at Sept-Îles on a bed of broken ice. Eyewitnesses at Sept-Îles reported that the plane floated along the St. Lawrence for a bit until some fishermen noticed it and towed it to shore. After the plane arrived at Sept-Îles, it picked up the outgoing mail for the return flight.

The next day, after the storm had abated, Sutton and

Cuisinier returned to the base at St. Agnès, and then Sutton stormed off. History does not reveal exactly what Sutton did after that fateful Christmas Day run. However, it seems he was angry enough that he left the province.

Barely one month after the Christmas Day incident, Sutton is reported to have completed an inaugural air-mail delivery flight in western Ontario. After a very brief career, Sutton died in a tragic accident while racing a Fokker Universal on floats at the 1930 Canadian National Exhibition in Toronto.

A couple of replacement pilots delivered the mail along the North Shore in January; and then in February 1928, Canadian aviation pioneer Roméo Vachon took over the route. Vachon said that he wanted to do in the winter what the Clarke Steamship line did in the summer when there was open water. For more than 11 years, Vachon faithfully transported Her Majesty's mail to the North Shore every winter season between December 15 and April 15. And the villagers on the North Shore soon came to expect regular mail delivery.

Christmas Shoeboxes

Graham Reynolds and André Bellerive have been playing Santa every Christmas season since 1998. But the Christmas greetings and the presents hiding in their big red sack are not for children — they are for international sailors.

Reynolds and Bellerive are volunteers at the Maison

du Marin at the Port du Quebec (port of Quebec City). This centre, founded in 1850 as the Seamen's Mission, provides a host of different services for the seamen, including access to recreational activities, reading material, free clothing, and visits with a chaplain. For the last 21 years, the Maison du Marin has also provided Christmas "shoebox" presents to the crews of international ships.

At the beginning of December, Reynolds and Bellerive start to deliver the gift-wrapped shoeboxes to the crews of ships that will either be in the Port du Quebec or out at sea on Christmas Day. After December 25, the two Santas give out boxes to ships with crews of Greek or Russian orthodox origin so that these sailors receive gifts for the Orthodox Christmas on January 6. In 2003, Reynolds and Bellerive brought 896 boxes onboard 39 different ships. "For many seamen, the present that they receive from us is their one and only present," said Reynolds.

In the fall, people all over Quebec prepare their shoeboxes for the Maison du Marin. School groups, women's church groups, nuns, and a multitude of individuals fill their boxes with about $20 worth of little gifts, such as pens, playing cards, shampoo, razors, shaving lotion, stationary, mittens, and *tuques* (woollen hats). Many donors also include a little note with Christmas greetings.

"The boats are pretty cold in the winter, so the sailors are very happy to find a scarf or a *tuque*," said Bellerive.

"And they love to receive little hand-held pocket

calculators," added Reynolds. Electronic gadgets are fun novelties for sailors from developing countries.

Reading material is not usually included in the boxes, as the sailors speak a great variety of languages and there is no way of knowing where a certain shoebox is going to end up. Also, sailors can visit the Maison du Marin, to read *National Geographic* and other magazines, books, and bibles in more than 10 languages.

Before joining the Maison du Marin, Graham Reynolds worked as an electrician onboard ship. When he was approaching retirement, a friend of his, who was also the Protestant chaplain at the Maison du Marin, suggested that Reynolds help out with the shoebox delivery. André Bellerive was the director of student services at l'Université Laval prior to his retirement. Bellerive's best friend, the harbour master of the Port du Quebec, suggested that he volunteer at the Maison du Marin. Now, Reynolds and Bellerive are at the centre every morning and sometimes in the evenings or on weekends, depending on ship arrival times.

Although Reynolds and Bellerive do not dress up in Santa Claus costumes, the sailors await their arrival with the same anticipation as small children awaiting the mythical Santa on Christmas Eve. In 2003 when the two volunteers were approaching a ship, some sailors called out, "Santa Claus has come!"

Reynolds and Bellerive bring presents onboard ships that have come from around the globe — Russia, Liberia,

Greece, Ukraine, and the Philippines. Of course, not all sailors celebrate the Christian holiday of Christmas, but that is not a problem. "We put some Christmas shoeboxes onboard Chinese ships, and they were just as happy to get a present as anyone else," recalled Reynolds.

"Their reaction depends on how their work is going, and sometimes on their nationality, too. The Filipinos — who are numerous in the shipping business — always have a smile and they are ready to joke. The Ukrainian crews are very thankful for the presents, but they can be quite taciturn," explained Bellerive.

Reynolds and Bellerive are delighted to be able to provide the crews with a little fun at Christmas, but they do miss the old days when they could really get to know the individual sailors who worked on charter ships that had regular routes. "They are mostly tramp ships now," explained Reynolds. "They (the sailors) never know where they are going next."

A container ship might travel to Brazil, then to Spain, then to Turkey, then to England, then to the U.S., and then to Canada. Reynolds and Bellerive almost never see the same sailors on a regular basis.

"There used to be a ship, the *Daishowa Voyager*, that came in here every three weeks for 13 years with a Filipino crew. The local pulp and paper mill had a big export for paper and chartered this ship. But now to cut down on cost, the mill just brings in ships when they need them."

The *Stolt Aspiration* is one of Reynolds's favorite ships.

This Liberian ship comes to Quebec about three or four times a year to pick up tallow and transport it to ports around the world. The boat smells horrendous due to its cargo of animal fat, but the ship's crew is an extremely friendly group of men.

Of course, regardless of whether the crews have ever met the Maison du Marin volunteers before, they are always extremely appreciative. After Reynolds and Bellerive have brought the presents onboard, they are usually invited to join the seamen for some coffee, tea, or vodka, depending on the ship.

The Maison du Marin receives hundreds of letters and faxes of thanks, and sometimes the sailors are so grateful for the shoeboxes, they give the volunteers a present in return.

One time, after the volunteers brought presents onboard a Chinese ship, the chief engineer came back two days later with a model of a junk that he had made himself. It was made of bamboo and mahogany, without any nails whatsoever.

"Some people put their names and addresses in the shoeboxes and they receive a letter of thanks. One woman who prepared a shoebox even received a marriage proposal from an appreciative sailor," said Bellerive.

The Christmas shoebox project gets underway every September, when Maison du Marin volunteers send out information letters to interested individuals and organizations across Quebec. Each year, the Maison du Marin typically receives about 850 to 1000 filled boxes. Most people mail or hand-deliver their boxes to the Maison du Marin, but Reynolds also hits the road to go and pick up some boxes. Last year, he picked up about 150 boxes from the Eastern Townships and the Gaspé.

The Maison du Marin volunteers never know exactly how many boxes they will receive each year, and they cannot predict how many they will be giving out, either. Incredibly, they are almost never short of gifts.

"We give them out until they are all gone," explained Reynolds. "We used to give out the last ones around Christmas; now, we often have some left over, even after Epiphany. We don't keep any for the following year, we simply give away any extra boxes to sailors who are especially poor."

Ontario

iving and receiving gifts has been a signifi-
cant part of Christmas from time imme-
morial, inspired by aspects of well-known
Christmas stories. The holiday tradition of helping the poor
can be traced back to Bethlehem. Joseph was a humble carpenter, not wealthy by any standard, and when he and his
pregnant wife, Mary, travelled to the City of David at census
time, they were unable to get a room at the inn. As a result,
Jesus was born in a stable, and ever since, Christians have
made an extra effort to dispense charity in memory of the
poor couple and the miraculous child they produced.

In 1860, the St. George Society of Toronto turned a
store on King Street into a temporary distribution centre for
"Christmas cheer for the poor." Starting at two in the afternoon and continuing until after dark, the English immigrants

who belonged to the society gave out 5000 pounds of beef, 10 sheep, 150 bushels of potatoes, 3000 pounds of turnips, 200 cabbages, and 600 loaves of bread, plus vast quantities of flour, tea, coffee and sugar. The *Globe* reported that those who received the donations "belong to all the various nationalities, and the appearance they presented gave striking evidence of the amount of misery which at present prevails in this city."

As immigrants, some of the members of St. George's Society may have known loneliness or want during their first years in Ontario. It seems anyone who has ever experienced a bleak or lonely Christmas, or even imagined one, is willing to help out those in need during the holidays.

One individual who puts charity first at Christmas is Joanne Pettes. She knows firsthand what it is like to do without during the holiday season. In 1993, Joanne and her husband, Bruce, were facing a bleak Christmas. They had been living in Oshawa, but when they heard about a job opportunity for Bruce, they moved with their two young sons to Minden. Then the job fell through. With both of them unemployed, they could barely make ends meet. In desperation, Joanne went to the local food bank. A short while later, the food bank delivered boxes of food, clothing, and toys. Joanne made a promise right then that she would do the same for someone else one day.

Ten years later, back in Oshawa, she tried to keep that promise. The boys were older, and both she and Bruce were working. Although not wealthy, they were comfortable. So Joanne rounded up a turkey, trimmings, and other items, and set aside some money to buy hats and mitts for needy children. Then she tried to find a suitable family. She started by calling the local newspaper and was told they could not give out names. Instead, they gave her the number of a local charity. For the next several hours, Joanne called one organization after another. In every case, she was told to bring items to the agency office or put them in a drop box. Finally, in frustration, she called the newspaper again.

This time, she was told they could provide the names and contact information for local people in need. The newspaper also sent out a reporter, who wrote about Joanne's experience in Minden and her desire to help someone in Oshawa.

When the article was published, it included Joanne's e-mail address. The result was a flood of requests for assistance — and something extra. A number of people also contacted her to see how they could get involved in making Christmas better for needy families. Joanne passed along the information she had, and several people selected families to help. One man eventually conducted his own toy and clothing drive, providing items to several families.

Choosing just one family to help was difficult, Joanne recalled. She finally settled on a young single mother whose situation had been described by a friend. The woman was attending college, determined to make a better future for herself and her daughter. When she was not studying, she devoted all her time and energy to her child. Joanne, who runs a daycare, told her clients about the young woman and several of them pitched in to help. One donated a bag full of beautiful clothing for the little girl.

The young mother and her daughter were invited to the daycare Christmas party, where Santa gave the little girl a gift. Then Joanne loaded up her car with presents and other goodies and drove them back to their apartment. At a glance, she knew how much they needed a little help at Christmas — the young woman could not even afford to replace lightbulbs in her apartment.

It was, Joanne said, "the most amazing Christmas ever." Along with the other people who helped spread Christmas cheer, she is planning to do it again.

The Kindness of Strangers

Sometimes, strangers provide the best Christmas presents. Shortly before December 25, 2003, a Christmas light ignited the Smith family Christmas tree. As fire swept through the Pembroke area house, the family scrambled to safety. Three-year-old Gerry-Lee Smith watched the flames engulf the home from his parents' car. Despite their best efforts, firefighters from the Tri-Township Fire Department were unable to save the building. The Smiths lost everything, and to young Gerry-Lee, it seemed he might lose Christmas as well. "How's Santa going to know where to find me?" he asked his parents.

Santa, of course, knows everything, and in this case he had a little help from the fire department. The firefighters fundraising association donated more than $150 for presents for the family. A short time later, Santa appeared at the door of Gerry-Lee's grandmother's house. Although the jolly old elf bore a striking resemblance to fire captain Tim Sutcliffe, Gerry-Lee did not notice. All that mattered was that Santa had found him and had brought gifts as well.

Two years earlier, a Windsor family had a similar experience. On December 15, thieves broke into the home of Trisha Thompson and Frank Simpson, stealing 16 gifts purchased for three-year-old Zackery and four-year-old Mackenzie, as well as food and a television satellite receiver. Payday was several days away and there was no money to buy more gifts. But when the community learned of the family's loss, they made up for the thieves' lack of Christmas spirit. They donated hundreds of dollars, food, and dozens of toys. Overwhelmed by the generosity, the couple replaced the items that had been stolen, then donated the rest, including nine boxes of toys, to other needy families.

For those in need, food and clothing are always much appreciated at Christmastime, but youngsters also need something to play with. A Dryden senior citizen makes sure they get it by spending months restoring toys for Christmas hampers. Gladys Johnson loves dolls and spends most of the year cleaning up old dolls and plush toys. She carefully hand washes the dolls, shampoos their hair, and often makes new clothes for them. The toys come from other people in the community, some of whom have brought garbage bags full of them to her for restoration. Some years, she donates as many as 200 toys to the Christmas Cheer drive.

Many people love to give handmade items at Christmas, but lack the time or skill to make them. Fortunately there are other options, including special craft fairs. Fort Frances has a smaller effort called "Spirit of Christmas" It's a silent auction featuring between 250 and 300 handcrafted items, which typically raises about $15,000 for the local Canadian Cancer Society and the Fort Frances Community Chest.

In the hustle and bustle of preparing for December 25, generosity may be temporarily forgotten, but it usually takes just a little nudge to remind people of those less fortunate. A week before Christmas 2001, the Salvation Army in Wallaceburg had only 80 toys to distribute to needy children. But there were 300 children on the list. Many people were facing a difficult Christmas because of layoffs at area companies. Still, it took just one request and the organization had more than enough toys to fill their Christmas hampers.

The Mind of a Child
Sometimes adults are very well meaning but simply cannot fathom the mind of a child. One Christmas present that did not work out quite the way it was planned was a hamster purchased by a Dryden newspaper editor. Typically, fathers play Santa to their kids on Christmas Eve, drinking the milk and

cookies left out for them and perhaps leaving large footprints in strategic locations. As a single mother, Laurie Papineau had to take on this role herself. One Christmas, she didn't get around to that pleasant duty until 2 a.m. Christmas morning. That's when she discovered that Delaney, her seven-year-old daughter, had left a note for Santa. Since her pet hamster had died just two days earlier, Laurie expected Delaney to ask for a replacement and had secretly purchased a new one. But the request specifically asked Santa *not* to bring a hamster, out of respect for the dear departed rodent. Instead, could Santa put a candy cane on the dead hamster's grave?

Laurie hesitated. The hamster was buried in a clearing in the woods three-quarters of a kilometre away. The spot was selected because it was the only piece of ground that wasn't frozen. The family had located a small burrow, put in the hamster, and topped it up with four bags of cat litter.

It was dark and cold outside. Laurie hesitated, but her older children, then in their late teens, reminded her she would have gone outside for them when they were Delaney's age. Laurie gritted her teeth, grabbed a flashlight and candy cane, and headed into the darkness. It was freezing cold. Trees and bushes blocked the way, scratching Laurie as she pushed on. Then the flashlight went out. But she still managed to find her way to the tiny grave, deposit the candy cane, and stumble back through the bush before collapsing into bed in the wee small hours of the morning.

The next morning, the first thing Delaney did after

getting up was put on her jacket and run out to check the hamster's grave. There was the candy cane, along with an unexpected addition. Santa had left a note, thanking Delaney for giving her departed hamster such a loving home and asking her to adopt a new one. The replacement hamster was accepted happily, and Delaney's faith in Santa remained unshaken.

The Prairies

n most homes today, gifts are piled high under the Christmas tree and long, fat Christmas stockings hang heavily above the fireplace. But scarcely two generations ago, the Christmas morning scene was quite different. Gifts were few. And compared to today's expensive items, they seem meagre, indeed. The reason is simple. Any time before the 1950s, most Prairie people suffered deprivation 12 months of the year — Christmas included. Perhaps that's why the few small gifts opened on Christmas morning were valued far more than most of the gifts we give or receive today.

Gifts From The Heart

During the 1930s, many gifts were handmade. As Christmas approached, the clever craftsmanship of thousands of creative mothers and fathers became a meaningful and especially heartfelt way to compensate for a lack of cash. This was certainly the way it was at the Storeys' place just south of Saskatoon.

"We had nothing. Most people had nothing," says Jim Storey. "But you know, we were actually better off than the town people. We had gardens and animals," he adds, voicing the typical hard-times sentiment.

What Jim and his sisters also had were creative, caring parents. When the Storeys couldn't afford to buy gifts, they made them. One Christmas, Jim's dad made him a wooden horse, brightly painted, with real horsehair for the mane and tail.

"That was the highlight of my life," says Jim. "He made it out in the horse barn. That's where he hid it, you see, so I never knew."

Another gift made an impression: a "store-bought" toy. "Later on, I got a dump-truck that had actual lights on it; lights that really worked!" To young Jim, this gift was magic. As the years passed, the gift became even more amazing to Jim because he realized his parents couldn't have afforded it. "My dad must have really scrambled to buy it. I'm sure my mother and dad went without so we had those kinds of things. But they never talked about it."

The Lost Gift

In the Logan household in Calgary, late on Christmas Eve

The Prairies

1933, Lila Logan surveyed her living room to make sure everything was ready for the next morning. While checking the gifts under the tree, the mother of seven experienced a sudden pang of remorse. Somehow, it seemed that little Ila wouldn't have quite as much to open the following morning as the other kids. The stores had long since closed. But she had to do something. She went to her husband and they came up with a solution.

Reluctantly, Jim Logan pulled out a two-dollar bill from his wallet. He didn't begrudge his little girl the extra gift, but two dollars was a lot of money in those days. A nickel bought a chocolate bar, a dime got you into a movie, and 50 cents filled the car's gas tank. Too proud to go on relief, Jim had accepted a minimum-wage job for the City of Calgary. Ironically, he was a clerk in the department responsible for handing out welfare cheques. With seven children to feed, he could have earned more money as a relief recipient than his job paid.

That precious two-dollar bill was slipped into a crisp white envelope. The envelope was hidden away in the branches of the Christmas tree — one more present for Ila.

Christmas morning! After all the laughter, the cries of delight, the happy confusion of torn wrapping paper and swiftly emptied boxes, came the burning question: Ila, what will you buy with your two dollars? Only a blank stare in return. What two dollars?

Lila's face went white. It was difficult enough to part

with an additional two dollars, but now, to lose it? Surely not. The hunt was on.

And hunt they did, going belly-to-the-floor to peer under the couch and chairs. They searched all over the house and then went into the backyard, where the discarded wrapping paper and boxes had been deposited. The wrappings were brought back in and strewn over the floor again. Hands flew this way and that in this desperate Christmas Day quest, anxious eyes scanning the refuse for the elusive white envelope.

That envelope was never found. The saga of the missing gift became an oft-repeated story at get-togethers with friends and neighbours well into the New Year.

Santa Outdone

The following year, as Christmas approached, the Logans were determined that Ila would have a doll from Santa. Mr. Claus must have agreed. Under the Christmas tree on that next exciting Christmas morning was a big, bright, beautiful doll. But due to an unusual event in Ontario, there was more — much more!

In May of that year, in a rural Ontario hamlet, an astonishing biological miracle had occurred. Inside a log farmhouse, Elzire Dionne had given birth to five tiny babies; living, breathing quintuplets! The phenomenon known as "the Dionne Quints" sparked the wonder of people all over the globe. Some of those people were in business, and business was booming. The quints were featured on fans, plates, spoons, pens, books, and t-shirts, as well as in news-reels and documentary films. Most of all, there were dolls, tens of thousands of them. Singly and in sets of five, the quint dolls were worth millions to their makers.

Just as the real babies fascinated adults, the doll babies captured the imaginations of little girls everywhere. The first sets of quint dolls made their very timely and profitable appearance in the gift-giving weeks just before Christmas. They became the hottest toy on the market, outselling even the Shirley Temple doll. Among the captivated in Calgary were young Ila Logan and her sisters. The girls would press their noses against the windows of McGill's Drugs. There, on the other side of the pane, in all their cuddlesome baby-doll glory, were the quints, snuggled into their own little wooden bed. Price: $4.95. However, if you were a loyal McGill customer, the dolls could be yours, absolutely free.

As a shopping incentive, McGill's offered customers points for cash register tapes. The shopper with the highest number of points would win those dolls.

"Poor little Ila," friends and neighbours must have thought, as they remembered the lost two-dollar bill of the previous Christmas. "Poor little Ila," they thought again, as they scribbled her name on their drug-store receipts.

Weeks later, waiting for Ila under the Logans' tree on Christmas morning, was not one, not two, not even five dolls, but six! That lost envelope, McGill's Drugs, and the miracle in North Bay had unwittingly conspired to outdo even Santa Claus. Ila was beaming. This particular gift from her family and friends was too big to lose!

Prairie Prosperity Returns

By the late 1940s and into the mid-1950s, it appeared that the good times had returned at last. Canadian wheat was king again, as it had been in the 1920s, when the Canadian Prairies were known as "The Breadbasket of the Empire." By 1960, more than 80,000 combines reaped an average of 25 bushels an acre of the golden harvest the world clambered for. In the country, outhouses were disappearing as flush toilets were installed in even the most modest of farmhouses. Construction cranes swept the city skies over Regina, Calgary, and Winnipeg, as new, tall buildings reached upwards. There was even talk of an international airport in Edmonton.

Of course, there was no better time to celebrate the long-awaited good times than at Christmas. The gift-giving holiday was a made-to-order opportunity to celebrate new-found prosperity.

Santas Anonymous

However, "good-times Christmases" brought with them the sobering reminder that not everyone was able to celebrate in the modern, affluent way. In large cities, neighbour didn't always help neighbour as they once did in villages and small towns. (All too often, neighbour didn't even know neighbour.)

Service clubs and what most people still called "the press" lent a hand.

The press now included radio and TV stations. In those pioneering days of rock-and-roll, radio in Edmonton meant CHED. Listening to CHED any weekday morning, anytime between 1955 and 1964, meant listening to John Barton.

"We really dominated the town," recalls John. "We did a lot of stuff nobody had ever thought about before."

One of the innovations the Edmonton station implemented in the late 1950s was a special Christmas charity program called Santas Anonymous, a concept that, in the decades since, has been implemented successfully in other cities and towns across Canada. John and other DJs took their cues from program manager Jerry Forbes.

"I don't know how the idea came up, but to the best of my knowledge, Jerry came up with the name," John explains. "Jerry and I sat down and we put the idea together. He said, 'wouldn't it be nice if people could donate gifts and remain anonymous?'"

Santas Anonymous remains today and is a unique way of helping those less fortunate. The main concept of the scheme, which made it so compelling, was that donations weren't cans of food left in boxes in grocery stores. They were gifts for children, given directly, one-to one, to the needy families.

"It became personal; it was a very personal way of giving." John remembers, explaining that donors could determine the gender and age of their recipients. "On the item, it would say, 'girl, seven to nine', or 'boy, twelve to four-teen', this sort of thing. Then, there was a blank card attached for the parent to sign as well, you know, 'from Mom' or 'from Santa'. And when we found out that a particular family had two boys and girl, we would package this up and it would be delivered to them."

Social agencies and church groups were delighted to provide names and addresses of needy recipients. John's role in all this, as the host of the morning show, was to sell the idea to the city, "bringing people on-board" during his shift and "in the commercials" he recorded later in the day. Not long after John went to work behind the microphone to promote the concept, the city's biggest radio listening audi-ence began to respond. Then, others went to work behind the scenes.

"We had a huge space upstairs on the third floor of the radio station, and I remember staff and volunteers up there wrapping the gifts. It was very, very labour intensive." However, it was, in the true sense, a labour of love, and the labour was shared. When it was time to distribute the gifts, different groups in town volunteered to help.

The mountain of gifts was high enough that deliveries became a challenge and John became one of the many vol-unteer distributors. As Christmas approached, there was one more shopping bag left in the car, and one more name left on his list. One evening, John decided to make the last delivery, and he took along his six-year old son, Reid.

"I think I just brought him along for the ride, and I also thought, 'it's kind of a neat thing, you know.' I wasn't trying to teach him a lesson, but I just thought it would make Christmas mean a little bit more. The whole Santa Claus thing was just huge in his mind, and it was just a little difficult to explain to a six-year old, 'Well, why are you Santa?' So, I probably said, 'well, Santa can't get to absolutely everybody and the odd person could possibly be missed.'"

When they got to the address, John asked his son to go to the house with him. Carrying the shopping bag full of parcels, John and Reid trudged through the snow and up the steps. "A woman came to the door and she had the little children around her. I explained to her that I was from Santas Anonymous. She immediately sent the little children off into another room to play because she knew the gifts were for them. We handed the gifts to the lady. There were tears in her eyes, and my son, I remember him looking around, and wondering why the little kids were gone, he really didn't know how to handle all this. It baffled him; you take so much for granted at that age. The woman cried; she hugged Reid and she hugged me, and thanked us very much, and said it was going to be a wonderful Christmas."

John and Reid got back into the car and started for home. Reid sat quietly, looking out the passenger-side window.

"Did you enjoy this evening?" John asked, finally.

"Yup."

A pause.

"So," John started. "You happy with everything?"

"Yeah."

"So, what's on your mind, right now?" John asked. Reid turned to his dad.

"The woman and her little girls," he said quietly. "How much she liked what we just did. I didn't know that everybody doesn't have a Christmas like we do."

"As a little child, he thought everybody was the same," says John. "That [visit] really hit him."

British Columbia

Exchanging gifts is a major part of the Christmas season. From searching for that perfect item, to wrapping it up in festive paper and placing it under the tree, the steps of gift-giving have become holiday customs unto themselves. Of course, some of the most treasured holiday gifts are the ones that cannot be wrapped. Instead, they come in the form of kind words, bighearted gestures, or generous donations.

Gold And Christmas Giving

In 1858, a twist of fate changed the colony of Vancouver Island forever and ended its dependence on the fur trade: gold was discovered on the Fraser River. For the '49ers and those who had followed them to the California gold fields, the news of the find had 20,000 dreamers and schemers fighting their way aboard every kind of ship and boat that could carry them north to the tiny British colony. They weren't all bent on digging and sluicing. Men had to be equipped, had to be clothed, had to eat, and, when the winter chased them down through the Fraser Valley back to Victoria, they had to have places to live. So, while the adventurous tramped upriver, the enterprising — the merchants, tradesmen, and builders — set about building a city on the slopes beyond the fort's bastions.

Everybody was, quite literally, from "somewhere else," and at no other time of the year were bitter regrets mingled so poignantly with fond memories as they were at Christmastime. Publisher Amor de Cosmos, self-proclaimed Lover of the Universe, exploited these feelings effectively in his Christmas editorial in his newspaper, the *British Colonist.* "From the cradle to the grave," he wrote, "Christmas always presents pictures of family re-unions, social endearments and universal festivity. It is the season when the benevolent always remember the needy; the old wardrobe becomes warm and new; the scanty table partakes of plenty; the sick and distressed are comforted ..."

The "benevolent" of de Cosmos's editorial were none other than the new citizens of the burgeoning city, and their spirit of giving would glow most brightly in December of 1861. Miners had now followed gold's lure hundreds of kilometres up the exhausting Harrison-Lillooett trail into the wilds of the Cariboo. That meant the trip back to Vancouver Island to escape winter's freezing clutches was now longer and more arduous than ever. Upon their arrival in Victoria, many who had journeyed from Antler Creek, Williams Creek, and the tent settlement that would be Barkerville, were already ill. Others would soon become so. A Christmas fundraiser was organized to help those lying in hospital beds. Under the authorship of "Santa Claus," the city's newspaper published a Christmas Day poem to help encourage the generosity of its readers.

> Here is to your Christmas joys,
> Ye gallant ones and true,
> Ye merry boys, ye jolly boys,
> The boys of Cariboo.
> And here's to wives' elation,
> So they be leal and true,
> And here's to those awaiting
> The boys of Cariboo.
>
> Were I a woman young and smart,
> And lovely as I'm true,
> I know I'd keep a faithful heart
> For one from Cariboo.
> Here's to the nuggets you have got,
> And those that yet remain,
> They ne'er shall bless the lout or sot,
> But be the brave man's gain.

Gifts and Giving

The manly sons of manly toil,
The stalwart and the true,
Whether they plough the main or soil,
The boys of Cariboo.
And as to those who have no gains,
I would my song were gold,
And I would buy up all their gain
As quickly as 'twas told.

But, ah! For those, the sick and weak,
That in a darkened room
Have no kind wife to fondly speak,
And kiss away their gloom,
I would I were a prophet now,
To whisper in each ear,
Calming each fever heated brow —
"Look up, the boys are near.

"There is not one e'er sunk a shaft,
But kindly thinks of you,
Remembering how in hope's fair craft,
Ye cruised for Cariboo.
With helping hand and cheering voice
They've come to succor you."
The kindly boys, the friendly boys,
The boys from Cariboo.

Giving in Needful Times

With hard work and frugality, countless returning World War I veterans and their families bettered themselves throughout the 1920s.

"It has been a good year," the *Victoria Times* reported cautiously on the last day of the last year in the tumultuous decade. "In spite of a greatly reduced wheat crop in the west and the spectacular fall of stocks in the last week of October, Canada faces the coming year with optimism and confidence ..."

Yet, just one year later, Lieutenant Governor R. Randolph Bruce's Christmas message was a far-from-jolly reminder that things were not what they once were: "In our province blest with a generous people, we can rest assured that every care will be taken of both our unemployed and our needy ... Let us this Christmas test the truth of the saying that true happiness is only found in giving happiness to others. Let us count our blessings, rather than dwell on our adversities."

However, as the 1930s progressed and the Great Depression deepened, many families had fewer and fewer blessings to count.

Married at the tender age of 16 to a dashing, older, Vancouver fireman, but divorced just a few years later, Adelaide Treasure was, in the late 1920s, a member of a very small minority of women who would be called, two generations later, "single moms." As a mother of three — Dick, Phil, and little Norma — there was no "career path" open for Adelaide. If she wanted work, she would have to create it herself. "Norma wasn't going to school, you see, and I didn't know how I was going to look after them and work, too. I had never worked," she explained.

The house the four moved to was a large, twelve-room, two-storey home on Bidwell Street in Vancouver's West End. There was plenty of room — but not much else. Adelaide had just enough money to pay the rent. She decided to take in borders, and "do whatever I could do," to enable her to stay home and look after the children.

If you listen to the audio tapes in the BC Provincial Archives, you can hear the tone of pride in Adelaide Treasure's voice, as, half a century earlier, she related her own successful efforts at self-sufficiency. It took courage, ingenuity, and perhaps a little desperation.

"Do you know that we never went on relief; never once did I ever ask for relief. We just took people as they came. If they came and they wanted board and room, we gave it to them. If they just wanted a room, we just rented it to them. If somebody wanted the downstairs, we'd let them have it and we'd move upstairs. Oh, accommodating? I'll say — as long as they had a buck!"

Christmas shopping was just one more challenge that Adelaide began to meet as soon as summer was over. "Well, I used to always have a system about clothing the children. I used to get everything when they started school in September. I'd get everything they needed in winter clothing at the Hudson's Bay; I took out an account there. Then I'd try by Christmas to have that account cleared off. Then I'd get them some new things — I always got them some things that they needed, as well as some other things and toys — and then I'd clear that off. They never went without.

Adelaide went on to recall that the family always had a "little Christmas tree." And one Christmas, a particularly special present was placed beneath it. Her oldest boy, Dick, bought a little black-and-white terrier puppy as a family gift. "How he kept it a secret, I can't remember, but I think he must have left it with the neighbours or something. But anyway, when the kids went to look under the tree for their things, this little pup just popped up out of the box. And the children! I can remember they looked so ... they didn't know what to think about it!"

That Christmas — and most of the others for Adelaide's kids — was experienced without a father at home. "Well, I think the children missed their father," Adelaide admitted, "but we never made it a sad thing in our house. We just went along the best way we could, but we never were sad; we never had a sad household because of it. For one thing, I had to work too hard. I was working dreadfully hard."

Thousands of other parents demonstrated the dogged determination of Adelaide, and others who substituted ingenuity and skill for the money they didn't have during the Depression.

Then, as now, service clubs and the media worked

diligently to help the needy at Christmastime — and to persuade others to do the same. In Victoria, the Gyro Club distributed hampers to the destitute. Archie Wills, campaign chairman, enlisted cycle-racing champion Torchy Peden to promote the Christmas cause on the city's radio station. Not all listeners were sympathetic. "We got so annoyed ... a fellow wrote a letter complaining about having no turkeys for these poor people," Archie Wills recalled. "Well, we used to get the best joints of meat and figured it far better than having turkeys." Joining the others, Archie helped make deliveries. It was a humbling and occasionally frustrating experience. Hefting 50-pound hampers up flights of stairs wasn't easy work.

Things were tough for many in the city and for many more in the country. Still, people discovered that although they didn't have much, they did have each other.

"You know the Depression, in some ways, it brought people together," Notch Hill resident Henry Copeland explained. "Nobody had any money. You couldn't go anywhere. So, the local things got going again, people got visiting amongst themselves a lot more. They'd put on a dance; everybody'd go."

Turkey and all the trimmings? Perhaps ... but probably not.

"Well, they had chickens," said Henry. "Sometimes they'd get a deer, although they weren't supposed to shoot them out of season, but, during the Depression," he laughed, "the game warden was smart: he stayed in town! No, there were not turkeys around there, not then. Oh, if you lived in town and had a job, you could get a turkey." Henry Copeland shook his head. "Unless you lived through the depression, you've no idea what it was like."

For years, Henry had worked, schemed, scrimped, and saved, and he finally managed to open a store at Notch Hill. "We went on good until the Depression came," he remembered. We used to stock up on lumberjack's clothes, heavy pants and jackets, crosscut saws, peeves, axes, everything." Whether by accident or design, Copeland's General Store was strategically located. "About three or four hundred lumberjacks used to come into Notch Hill and go across the lake and log for the Adams River Lumber Company."

But the loggers stopped coming when the mill shut down. Then the banks closed their doors. The door of Copeland's General Store was still open, but fewer people were walking in. Unsold stock weighed heavily on the shelves — and on Henry's mind. When most of your neighbours were hard-up, retailing was hardly a road to riches. The Copelands owed one particular Christmas dinner to a man with debt. He paid Henry off with leghorns, and the family sat down to roast rooster. But the gifts that Christmas, and most others, were minimal.

"Buy presents?" Henry scoffed. "You made something up yourself, if you could. You couldn't afford to buy presents. Oh, I'll tell you, it was tough."

The Magical Ten Dollars

Henry Copeland's family had a battery-operated radio. It was, in the days before television or even telephones in most homes, a wonderful link to the outside world. That is, as long as there were batteries to light up the tubes and reach out to bring the world in through the speaker. This was a generation before the small, lightweight radios of the 1950s and 1960s. The first battery-operated radios were big — and expensive. One year, the Copeland radio fell silent. And somehow, that cold, silent radio became the embodiment of all the family's frustrations and perceived failures.

However, Henry had promised his children that the family would have music for Christmas. One day he went into town to visit a friend who operated a service station. The station had batteries for sale. Henry arranged to buy the $10 batteries on credit until New Year's Eve.

"As long as you pay me by New Year's, you can have a couple," the operator said nervously, "but be sure to pay me by New Year's or I'm in Dutch!"

"I'll pay you somehow, I don't know how, but I'll pay you," Henry remembered telling him. Now, added to all his other worries, he had another weight to bear: the $10 he owned his friend at the service station. Soon, there was something more: his wife's outrage.

Mrs. Copeland had been hoping that a little extra business at the store around Christmastime would provide her with money for Christmas presents for the children. There was no room on her gift list for radio batteries, and now there was $10 less for the items that were already on the list. This meant she would not be able to buy most of them. At a time when men were being paid eight dollars for a month of relief work, a $10 bill represented a considerable sum.

With Christmas around the corner, Henry was sweeping up the store at the end of another day when something caught his eye, something that, as he recalled, "looked like a dollar bill." Thinking it was impossible that someone would lose a dollar during these desperate times, he swept the dust from the other direction, and there, among the pile of dirt on the floor, was the bill. Henry picked it up and was instantly thunderstruck. What he was holding in his hand was a $10 bill.

"Well, I knew nobody local had a $10 bill to lose, so it must have come in 'off the road.' Somebody had dropped it in the store."

Here was the money to pay for the batteries, Henry thought. Then he had another thought. His wife had already "cooled down" from her anger over his decision to buy the batteries, but this lucky find was just the thing to smooth over the whole affair once and for all. He locked up the store and hurried home.

Mrs. Copeland was wide-eyed with amazement. Henry hid the money away and needlessly urged her to tell no one. "You daren't say anything," he told her, "because everybody would have lost the $10 bill!"

The next few days were long ones, indeed. Henry was on tenterhooks, waiting for some desperate friend or neighbour to dash into the store and start looking around the floor, to plead for help in finding the lost treasure. But nobody reported any missing money. Henry's assumption appeared correct. In his mind, that settled it. It was finder's keepers. The money was his, "... and we had music for Christmas."

Just before New Year's, Henry made a surprise visit to his friend at the service station and made good on his promise to pay him for the batteries that gave his family that special gift of Christmas music.

Chapter 6
Holiday Adventures

Atlantic Canada

hristmas adventures invariably occur in the wilderness, it seems. In Atlantic Canada, the wilderness has many different faces. It can be pristine and pastoral, bleak and barren, or rough and rugged. It may be brutal, harsh, and unforgiving or, just as frequently, gentle and benevolent. For those who spend Christmas in the wilderness, the holiday is often a reflection of the surroundings.

Rosebank Cottage Christmas

In 1816, Lord Dalhousie, the governor of Nova Scotia, decided it was time the large tract of wilderness in the centre of the province was settled. Since the end of the Napoleonic Wars, the British had found themselves with a surplus of soldiers and insufficient labour to keep them occupied. Dalhousie felt the perfect solution would be to offer the disbanded soldiers land grants in the midst of the wilderness, in the hope that they would carve out a settlement. Many renounced this idea, maintaining that military men were highly unsuitable for this type of undertaking. Charles Lawrence, a former governor, was one of the biggest opponents of Dalhousie's settlement scheme. The former governor even went so far as to call the disbanded soldiers "the King's Bad Bargains." But this didn't deter Dalhousie. Determined to carry out his plan for a settlement, he appointed Captain William Ross to lead a group of 172 disbanded soldiers into the wilderness.

In August of 1816, Captain Ross, along with his wife, Mary, and four small children, and the other soldiers and their families, sailed from Halifax to Chester. From Chester, they set out on the 30-kilometre journey inland on foot. Because no one in the party owned a horse, and wagons couldn't be pulled over the densely forested terrain, the men, women, and children made the trek with all of their worldly possessions on their backs. Years later, young Edward Ross would make this journey in half a day in fine weather. But that first trip took much longer. The terrain was rough; stumbling over boulders, wading through rivers and streams, and skirting around dozens of lakes along the trail slowed the group down tremendously.

The settlers arrived at Sherbrooke (later renamed New Ross after its founder) on August 7, 1816. With winter fast approaching, it was essential that the backbreaking labour of clearing the land by hand and erecting temporary shelters be started immediately. As luck would have it, that first winter turned out to be one of the most severe on record. It was fraught with hardship and suffering for the settlers. Their hastily erected cabins were dark and drafty, providing little protection from the bitter winds and cold temperatures. And, since there were still no roads into or out of the settlement, and no horses, all of their supplies had to be carried in on the backs of the men. Given the circumstances, Christmas that year likely consisted of just another day of struggling to survive.

By the following spring many of the settlers had abandoned their claims and moved on. But Captain Ross and several others remained on the land, despite the hardships. Unfortunately, just six years after leading his men into the wilderness, Captain Ross fell ill and died. Mary Ross was left with five children to care for on her own, the youngest less than a year old.

Years later, in 1835, the settlement at Sherbrooke was still a rough outpost with a rugged, frontier-town atmosphere. By that time, Captain Ross's sons were in their late teens and early 20s. Edward, the second eldest, was 22. A keen observer, he kept a diary describing the details of daily life in the settlement.

According to Edward's diary, Christmas of 1835 was a sorry affair at "Rosebank Cottage," the Ross family home. There were few — if any — presents exchanged, and apparently no special preparations made. On Christmas

Eve, the Ross brothers started drinking rum early in the afternoon. Later that day, several neighbours and friends dropped in. "In the evening Francis and George Price, Dick and Francis Rufsel, John and Francis Baggs, George Corey, George Driscoll, Jacob Burgoyne, and Andrew Kiens were here drinking," Edward wrote. The party, it seems, quickly deteriorated into a drunken brawl: "Francis and George Price afforded the company considerable amusement for a while with their drunken pranks, at last they went home and nothing would do but Burgoyne and George Corey must begin to wrestle, from wrestling they came to fighting."

Before long, the house was in an "uproar" as several of the guests jumped into the tussle. While Edward and his brother George tried to "part the combatants," the women fainted, cried, and made futile attempts to stop the fisticuffs. Finally, Edward and George managed to break up the fight. Still, the tone of the evening didn't improve much: "At last ... peace was restored, Andrew went home in a fret and I went home with Mary. In the meantime Frank Baggs and F. Rufsel were stretched on the floor along side of the other two. After a while they all recovered but George Driscoll, and all went home, we then ate our supper and went to bed and left George Driscoll lying on the kitchen floor — thus closing Christmas Eve 1835."

According to Edward, Christmas Day at Rosebank Cottage was even more miserable than Christmas Eve that year:

Atlantic Canada

Friday, December 25, 1835

Christmas day. Raining almost all day. William and Rachael dined at Mr. Walker's. We had not a morsel of bread nor a cake nor a pudding this Christmas for the first time in our lives. In fact it appeared to be a dull Christmas altogether.

Christmas on the High Seas

On Christmas Day, 1868, Angeline Publicover found herself in the most terrifying situation imaginable. The 18-year-old was aboard a foundering schooner in the midst of a raging gale in the mid-Atlantic. The little schooner, *Industry*, had been at the mercy of the storm for a full 14 days by that time, and the meagre supply of food and water was all but exhausted.

Having been ravaged by the storm for so long, the vessel was beginning to break up. She was taking on water so badly that all aboard believed they wouldn't survive the night. A single potato was the last edible thing found onboard. Angeline and her six male companions divided the potato equally between them for what they believed would be their last Christmas dinner. However, their tongues were so swollen from thirst that they could barely swallow the morsel of raw potato. Following the pitiful meal, they said a prayer together, shook hands, and huddled in the frigid darkness of the cabin waiting for the end.

It seemed as though a lifetime had passed since Angeline

Publicover, Lawrence Murphy, Captain Lewis Sponagle, and the three crewmembers had set out on the morning of Friday, December 11 on what should have been a short jaunt from LaHave to Halifax, Nova Scotia. In favourable weather, the 88-kilometre journey would have taken less than a day. Angeline had been filled with excitement as they'd pulled away from the wharf that morning. She had never been away from home on her own before, and this was a very special trip. She had recently become engaged and was on her way to Halifax that weekend to shop for her wedding gown. Captain Sponagle had gladly agreed to give her a lift to Halifax aboard the *Industry*; he was making a run down to the farmer's market with a load of dried fish and firewood that Friday, and planned to return early Sunday morning.

December 11 was one of those typically capricious Nova Scotian days. The weather was fine and winds favourable as the *Industry* set out, but before long the wind dropped. The passengers and crew found themselves becalmed off the coast of Sambro Island. Then, a few hours later, a vicious storm blew in. By that time, evening was coming on. The driving snow made it almost impossible to navigate in the growing darkness. Not wanting to take a chance on being dashed on the rocks while trying to enter Halifax harbour blind, Sponagle decided to turn and head for home. Just as they were veering around, a gust of wind swooped down and snapped the schooner's foremast in two. One calamity followed hard on the heels of the last for the hapless vessel. As they pitched and lurched on the wild sea, the cargo and supplies onboard broke free of their lashings and began tumbling around. The group's only canister of kerosene was knocked over and spilled out onto the deck, leaving no fuel for the lanterns. Worse still was the loss of most of their supply of fresh drinking water. Once the crew managed to secure the water barrels, only two gallons of the precious liquid remained.

They were nearing the mouth of Lunenburg harbour on the morning of December 12 when the wind suddenly veered to the northwest, driving the little craft out into the open waters of the Atlantic. For the next three days, the *Industry* tossed about helplessly on the towering waves. Since the trip was only supposed to take a few days at most, Captain Sponagle hadn't laid up much in the way of supplies. So, after the first few days at sea, those scant supplies were all but depleted. The captain began rationing the remaining water and the bit of hard tack left in the stores. For the next two weeks, the passengers and crew survived on a few bites of hard tack washed down with a mouthful of water each day. It wasn't long before their strength began to fail.

On December 15, their hopes were raised when they spotted an American schooner. The two ships managed to get close enough to communicate, but the seas were so rough that a rescue attempt was impossible. The most the American captain could do for them was to give Sponagle his position and directions for a course to Bermuda before the two ships were wrenched apart. Doing the best he could with no fore-sail, no charts, and no stars to steer by, the captain set off in the direction of Bermuda. For a couple of days the weather turned favourable, and the group began to believe they might survive the ordeal after all. But before long, another gale blew up, dashing their hopes. This one was even worse than the last. Severely battered by wind and waves, the little vessel began to founder. The crew worked frantically to keep her afloat, manning the pumps night and day. By December 25, the situation looked utterly hopeless. Starving and exhausted, they gave up the fight.

But the *Industry* didn't go down that night as expected. Somehow, the little schooner stayed afloat for another four days. And on December 29, a cargo vessel out of Nova Scotia crossed her path. The aptly named *Providence* was en route to London carrying a load of kerosene. She was 1120 kilometres east of Nova Scotia when her crew spotted the beleaguered *Industry*. The minute he laid eyes on it, Captain Hiram Coalfleet knew the small schooner was in trouble. Her foremast was gone and her few remaining sails were in tatters. Although it appeared the ship was abandoned, he decided to check it out anyway. When they were close enough, he hailed the vessel and after a few minutes the captain and crew of the schooner appeared on deck. The heavy sea made launching a small boat impossible, so in a daring move, Coalfleet manoeuvred his vessel alongside the *Industry*.

As the wind lashed the sails and the ships pitched and

rolled alongside one another, the main yard of the *Providence* became entangled in the schooner's rigging. At that moment, Coalfleet knew they might all go down in the rescue attempt. But there was no turning back. Captain Coalfleet's brother and first mate, Abel, volunteered to shimmy up the main-mast with a line and cross over on the yard to the *Industry*. The captain watched anxiously as his brother inched his way across the narrow yard. Once aboard the small vessel, Abel quickly attached the line to Angeline first. She was hauled up and over the hull onto the larger vessel. Soaking wet and weak with hunger and fear, the girl collapsed the minute she landed on the deck of the *Providence.*

One by one, the remaining survivors were hoisted over onto the rescue vessel. Once they were all safely aboard, Abel climbed up and freed the *Providence* from the little schoo-ner, managing to swing over to his own vessel just before the two ships parted. Although the *Providence* sustained a great deal of damage in the rescue effort, it could have been much worse. To the survivors, it must have seemed truly providen-tial that the cargo vessel came along when it did. Shortly after they were plucked from her deck, the *Industry* went down.

Three weeks later, on January 20, 1869, the *Providence* sailed into the port of London. After a brief stay, the survivors of the *Industry* managed to catch a lift home aboard another vessel. And a full three months after setting out for their weekend trip to Halifax, Angeline Publicover and her fellow survivors finally arrived back home in Nova Scotia.

Cargo Ship Christmases

For three-year-old Forrest Ladd, Christmas of 1893 was sensational. Despite the fact that they were onboard the cargo ship *Belmont* en route to Java, Captain Frederick Ladd and his wife Grace had managed to arrange for some special Christmas treats for Forrest. This was the boy's second Christmas at sea, and when Santa Claus showed up in person aboard the *Belmont*, Forrest was overjoyed. In a letter to her father back in Yarmouth, Nova Scotia, Grace described the events of this rather unconventional Christmas: "Last evening Fred dressed Ralph up as Santa Claus — filled him out, and with a [manila] wig and long beard, he made a splendid one. Forrest was so excited. We had prepared for his coming by making doughnuts, etc. and had some ginger beer ready for him. Forrest asked Santa 'where he had left his rein-bow?' This morning he was awake at half past five, his delight at seeing his stocking full and a large basket trimmed in popcorn (which Willie and he had popped and strung) also full, you can imagine."

Christmas of 1893 was Grace's fifth onboard a cargo ship. She had married her childhood sweetheart, Captain Frederick Ladd, in 1886. Faced with the prospect of remaining home in Yarmouth waiting for her husband to return once or twice a year between voyages, as most other captain's wives did, Grace chose to travel with him instead.

By 1893, Grace had celebrated Christmas in such exotic locales as Wellington, New Zealand, and Calcutta, India. Most

Christmases, however, were spent at sea. Her letters home to her father offer glimpses into these unusual Christmases, as well as those back home in Yarmouth. On December 23, 1886, she wrote from Shanghai: "I suppose you are all very busy preparing for Christmas. I shall think of you all tomorrow evening sitting around the dining room table, filling the stockings and marking the different parcels."

Obviously a little homesick on this, her first Christmas at sea, and half a world away from her family, she reminisced about the previous Christmas: "I remember last Christmas Eve, Fletch [the family nickname for Grace's sister, Mary] and I went into town — coming back the bus broke down. We had to walk the remainder of the way through deep mud."

Christmas aboard a vessel at sea presented numerous challenges, and Grace often had to be creative in her preparations. In 1894, the Ladds were en route to Shanghai accompanied by "the most miserable crew a Ship ever left port with." Not only was the crew incompetent, the weather had been bad since they'd crossed the Gulf Stream. Grace wrote that the seas were so rough on Christmas Eve, "I thought I would have to give up making Doughnuts."

The tradition of making doughnuts and ginger beer to leave out as a treat for Santa on Christmas Eve had begun the year before, and Forrest had been eagerly anticipating the doughnut making for days. So when Grace told him she didn't think they would be able to make them that year, he was so disappointed by the news that she decided to make an effort despite the wild sea.

Santa was once again played by one of the sailors aboard ship, disguised in the manila wig and beard. This time, however, his arrival was marked by a fanfare of flares and foghorns. In spite of the fact that that Christmas was the "stormiest" the Ladds had ever encountered, Grace still managed to prepare the traditional turkey dinner with all the trimmings, including "Christmas pudding, German sauce, Nuts, Apples, Ginger Beer."

Although her letters indicate that she seemed to enjoy many of her Christmases at sea, like most Atlantic Canadians, Grace always longed to be home for the holidays. In her Christmas letter of 1893 she wrote, "I do wish we all could spend a Christmas at home. It is not the same anywhere else to me."

Quebec

ost of the land in Quebec is wilderness, so it is not surprising that there are many Quebec holiday stories about great adventures and survival in the bush. Dramatic tales abound, among them: 16th-century explorers coping with a mysterious illness, a natural catastrophe that interrupted a New Year's Eve party, and mayhem at a Laurentian ski resort.

Christmas 1535

Jacques Cartier's first Christmas in Canada was a nightmare. After exploring the St. Lawrence River and its shoreline, Cartier and his band of 110 men prepared to be the first European explorers to over-winter in Canada. These adventurers were brave, hardy souls with no fear of discomfort. They had experienced chilly weather before in France, but nothing prepared them for the hell they would experience during the winter of 1535.

In early September, Cartier and his crew reached Canada (the Native term for the area around present-day Quebec City), where they were greeted by Native people who were happy to trade eels and melons for glass rosary beads and little metal knives. The Native people were also overjoyed to see the return of Domagaya and Taignoagny, young men who had travelled to France with Cartier following his first voyage in 1534.

When Cartier and his crew reached Stadacona, the main settlement in Canada, they were greeted by chief Donnacona, Taignoagny and Domagaya's father. The explorers were not invited into the Native village right away, but they were welcomed with great enthusiasm and told many fascinating tales about other Native villages, including Hochelaga (site of present-day Montreal).

The French explorers' mandate was to find riches for France and, if possible, a route to Asia. Cartier believed that the St. Lawrence River was a possible conduit to the Kingdom of the Grand Khan, so he was determined to continue upstream towards Hochelaga. He moored the expedition's largest ships, the *Grande Hermine* and the *Petite Hermine*, in a nearby river, which he called the Ste. Croix (now the St. Charles River), and prepared the *Emérillon* to sail further upstream to Hochelaga.

The Iroquois villagers from Stadacona tried to dissuade

Cartier from taking this journey, claiming that the river was too dangerous upstream. Perhaps the Iroquois were also reluctant to share their generous guest, who was constantly handing out beads, trinkets, and other gifts. At any rate, just as Cartier and his men were setting out for Hochelaga, a group of Native people in frightening attire with blackened faces and horns on their heads approached Cartier's ship by canoe. They warned the explorers that their god, *Cudouagny*, had told them there would be so much ice and snow that all would perish on the journey.

Undaunted, Cartier took half of his crew and set off to visit Hochelaga anyway. Meanwhile, the rest of the crew set to work to prepare their lodging at the mouth of the Ste. Croix River. They constructed a simple wooden fort surrounded by a palisade — a fence made of stakes driven into the ground. Then the Frenchmen, who were obviously not completely at ease, inserted their ships' cannons into the palisade.

Upon his return from Hochelaga in mid-October, Cartier realized that it was too late in the year to pursue any more exploration, so the men settled into a wintertime routine at the fort. Snow began to fall, and soon the land was covered with a thick, white blanket. The north wind raced in through chinks between the logs of the walls and the men shivered in their light European clothing. The state of their larder was even more alarming — a few limp vegetables and salt meat were their sole provisions for the winter.

As the Canadian winter season began to enclose the

sailors in an icy prison, they must have begun to dream about Christmas merrymaking with their friends and family back home in France.

Some men probably reminisced about the way Christ's birth was celebrated in their hometowns. At Christmastime, they might have witnessed the performance of a liturgical drama in a cathedral square. The sailors probably also had fond memories of worshipping at a *crèche*. In 16th century France, most churches and many homes boasted beautiful handcrafted *crèches*.

In addition to the spiritual aspect of Christmas, some of the sailors surely recalled the sensory pleasures of the festive season, such as bustling Christmas markets, where fattened geese and other delicacies required for traditional meals could be purchased. Some may have remembered minstrels wandering from town to town, regaling people with stories and songs about the marvels of *la sainte nuit* (the holy night).

Cartier's crew hailed from very modest homes in Brittany, so the sailors' fantasies of Christmas dinner probably featured visions of buckwheat pancakes and sour cream. Nonetheless, a simple meal of buckwheat pancakes would have been a lot tastier than the stale biscuits and salt meat the men were eating in the Canadian wilderness.

Their ships were trapped in thick ice blocks and the snowdrifts grew higher than the ships' decks. The inner walls of the small fort were soon coated with frost. To add insult to injury, all of the crew's barrels of wine and cider were frozen onboard the ships.

But the worst was yet to come. In December, Cartier noticed that some of the Iroquois from Stadacona were affected by a mysterious illness that left them so weak they could hardly stand up. The most acutely ill had swollen limbs and rotting gums. Cartier forbade the Iroquois from approaching the fort for fear that they would bring the dread disease with them. However, despite Cartier's efforts, his own men were soon afflicted, moaning and groaning with pain as their bodies began to deteriorate due to internal bleeding.

According to Cartier's journal of the expedition, "some lost all of their strength, their legs became swollen and inflamed, while the sinews contracted and turned black as coal ... then the disease affected their hips, shoulders, arms and neck and their mouths became so diseased that the gums rotted away down to the roots of the teeth, which nearly all fell out."

The disease continued to take its toll on Cartier's men, until the sick and the dead began to outnumber the healthy ones. The fort had become a haven of misery and despair, and most of the men began to accept that they might never return to France.

At this point, superstitious members of the crew may well have remembered, with a shudder, the Natives' warning prior to their departure for Hochelaga that Cartier's men would perish in the snow and ice.

Cartier clearly knew how protect his men from military attack; at the beginning of the winter, the captain had ordered reinforcements to be added to the humble fort, including deep ditches all around the fort and a solid door with a drawbridge. He had also instituted a night watch. However, confronted with this dread sickness among his crew, Cartier was completely helpless. Finally, the captain decided to draw on the crew's religious convictions.

Cartier requested all of the men who could walk to participate in a special religious procession. The pathetic men hobbled through the snow and ice, reciting the Psalms of David with quiet desperation. The chaplain performed a mass by an image of the Virgin Mary that had been posted to a tree and asked Mary to have pity on the sufferers. While some sailors might have given a passing thought to the celebration of Christ's birth, most of the prayers that Christmas were probably to ask God to spare them death in a foreign land.

When religious entreaties failed to improve the situation, Cartier ordered that an autopsy be performed on one of the cadavers in a desperate attempt to discover the cause of the horrific disease. According to the journal of the expedition, "the corpse's heart was white and flaccid, lying in a reddish water. The liver was fine but the lung was black and degraded. When the body was opened, a large quantity of black and putrid blood came out ... then we cut open the leg which was black on the outside but the flesh was fine on the inside. He has been buried with the least harm possible. God of Holy grace, forgive his soul and all trespasses. Amen."

Today we know now that this man, and all of Cartier's other men who died, were afflicted with scurvy, a disease caused by a lack of vitamin C. The sailors' meagre winter diet of preserved meat and dry biscuits was virtually devoid of this vitamin. However, the primitive autopsy did not reveal the cause of the disease that was ravaging his crew, and Cartier was at a loss.

Cartier was determined to give a show of strength to the Natives, in case they should take advantage of the French crew's weakened state. When the Natives came near the fort, Cartier came out with a few healthy crew members. The captain pretended to get mad at his men and then ordered them to do certain chores, as if the men were being lazy. He also had these men make noise inside the ships so that the Natives would assume the reason they hadn't seen the sailors much was because they were all doing maintenance onboard.

Cartier had heard that Domagaya was deathly ill with the dread disease that was ravaging the French crew. But one day, Cartier was out for a walk and he met Domagaya, who was in perfect health. Cartier wanted to ask how Domagaya had been healed, but he did not want to reveal that almost his entire crew was bedridden. So the captain claimed that he wanted to know the remedy in order to treat a servant who was ill.

Domagaya immediately sent two women to gather branches from the annedda tree (white cedar). These Native women taught Cartier to grind up a few of the branches and then to boil this powder with the annedda leaves. The women told Cartier to give this potion to the sick man every two days and to rub the dregs of the potion on swollen parts of the body.

According to the journal of the expedition: "After the Captain made the medicinal beverage, none of the sailors wanted to try it. Finally one or two took a chance and tried this drink. Soon after they drank it, they started to see the result and it was like a miracle because after drinking this potion two or three times, they started to regain their health and their strength ... they used an entire tree, one of the largest I have ever seen, in less than eight days,"

Cartier and his surviving sailors returned to France in the summer of 1536.

Tragedy in Northern Quebec

As mayor of Kangiqsualujjuaq (an Inuit community near Ungava Bay in northern Quebec), Maggie Emudluk attended most of the traditional Christmas season festivities between December 23 and January 2. There were outdoor activities every day, like fishing contests and snow sculpting, and in the evenings there were indoor games and Christmas worship services in the arctic village's little Anglican church.

On December 31, 1998, Emudluk, along with about half

of the village's 650 inhabitants, were gearing up for the grand finale of the holiday season — the New Year's Eve celebration. This event was being held in the Satuumavik School gymnasium. The gym was a real focal point for the community — it was used for everything from bake sales to sporting events, and on this special night it would become a site of worship and a dance hall. Satuumavik School was the largest public building in Kangiqsualujjuaq.

The villagers started to gather in the gymnasium around 9 p.m. The gym was still decorated with children's artwork, which had been put up for the school Christmas concert a couple of weeks earlier. There were no glitzy banners or streamers festooning the gym. After all, this was not a chic urban bash. It was a low-key gathering for the entire community, from babies to elders, and they didn't need fancy decorations in order to feel festive. It was enough just to celebrate their togetherness.

There was a little canteen set up in the gym, selling pop and other snacks. Wine and beer were not available at the party because alcohol sales had been severely restricted by the town council since the mid-1990s.

The villagers slowly began to filter into the gym, joining their family and friends. "Then, at the stroke of midnight, the Canadian rangers [people trained by the Canadian armed forces to do search-and-rescue work] went outside to fire 60 or 70 shots in the air to mark the arrival of the New Year. Usually, we all went outside to see that, but that year we did not because there was such a bad snowstorm outside," Emudluk recalled.

Following the celebratory shots, there was a special Anglican worship led by one of the schoolteachers, who was also a lay preacher. The villagers celebrated an Inuktitut service, which included many rousing hymns and carols. There were also prayers for the coming year and prayers for the families of two local people who had drowned the previous fall.

Then it was time for the festivities to begin. Emudluk was eager to see what the recreation committee had organized that year. She knew there would be some form of community dance followed by games for all ages, including traditional Inuit games involving feats of strength and agility, and scavenger hunts adapted for different age groups. Dance contests, to see who could dance for the longest amount of time without tiring, were also very popular games.

But now, it was time for the traditional square dance. The accordion player was warming up, and everyone was looking for dance partners. Soon the dance was underway, and people were swinging every which way. The accordion player clearly knew which dances appealed to the crowd. Caught up in the rhythm of the music, small children darted between the adult dancers, until they were swept up into someone's arms.

The dance ended around 1:30 a.m., and it was time to award the door prizes. "I was sitting down like everyone else," said Emudluk. "We were very hot right after the dance."

Then the unthinkable happened. There was a terrific cracking sound and a mountain of snow exploded into the school gymnasium. Trucks and Ski-doos parked outside were tossed aside like playthings. An avalanche was plowing through the back wall of the gym!

The community had chosen to build the Satuumavik School very close to a small hill in order to protect the children from bitter winds. And yet, in a cruel irony, the school's proximity to the hill actually intensified the effect of the avalanche by enabling the snow to roar down into the gym at a furious speed.

The mayor was sitting with some friends about 10 feet away from the wall that came down. "Everybody did something," she said. "I do remember saving people, but there are some spots I can't remember."

Emudluk and other people who were not buried by the avalanche grabbed shovels, frying pans, and anything else they could find to dig with. Many people simply used their bare hands to rescue loved ones.

Mary Baron, the school director, was sitting with her three-year-old son after the dance. She was not completely covered by snow and was able to dig out her son in time to save his life.

Then a group of villagers ventured beyond the school to continue looking for friends and family members. For more than three hours, they battled 100-kilometre-per-hour winds and a raging snowstorm. It wasn't easy to see anything through the blizzard, but the rescuers were guided by calls of distress from people buried in the snow. The impromptu rescue team was freezing cold on that awful night in the Arctic, but they kept up the search effort. They knew they didn't have a lot of time to locate the victims before they suffocated in the snow.

The people of Kangiqsualujjuaq were used to being self-reliant. When you live 300 kilometres away from the closest hospital, you know that emergency workers can't arrive moments after an incident. So the brave villagers basically conducted their own search-and-rescue effort.

"More than 50 people were saved," said priest Benjamin Arreak, who ministers to five communities in northern Quebec. However, despite courageous rescue efforts, 25 people were injured in the avalanche crash and nine people died.

Nine hours after the avalanche, doctors and nurses arrived from the Ungava Tulattavik health centre in Kuujuuaq. Extreme weather conditions had prevented the medical personnel from arriving any earlier.

Following the incident, Emudluk explained that an outpouring of support from other villages and towns in northern Quebec helped to comfort the people of Kangiqsualujjuaq. The villagers also relied on the ancient Inuit tradition of *ayurnamat* (an Inuktitut term which means accepting things that you have no control over) in order to cope.

"That is our tradition to accept. That has helped people get past it," explained Emudluk.

The villagers of Kangiqsualujjuaq continue to celebrate New Year's with a worship service, traditional games, and dancing. However, these festivities are no longer held in the school gym; they are now held in Kangiqsualujjuaq's other new public building — a sophisticated and spacious community centre built with provincial and federal government assistance.

The New Year's Eve that Shook Saint-Sauveur

In the 1940s, the sleepy Laurentian village of Saint-Sauveur was gaining a reputation as a prime destination for downhill skiing. Hundreds of young men and women from Montreal rode up on the Canadian National and Canadian Pacific "ski trains" to try out their planks on the downhill slopes. It was an exciting way to escape Montreal during the long winter months. Debonair young men and comely girls wearing knickers and bright patterned sweaters had lots of fun on the trains, playing card games, reading, and flirting. The train cars were packed with skis and ski poles that poked out like saplings from between the short bench seats.

Naturally, the skiers frequented local restaurants and hotels for some *après-ski* fun, but for the most part the skiers and the townspeople of Saint-Sauveur were like ships passing in the night, each group minding their own business. Or at least that was the case until one wild New Year's Eve in

1948. "There had never been something like that before and never again, either!" remembered André Joncas, a native of Saint-Sauveur.

On the afternoon of December 31, the train platform at Saint-Sauveur was buzzing with skiers intent on having a good time. The young people headed straight for the hills to get in a few runs, then they looked around for some refreshments. There were many drinking establishments in Saint-Sauveur, but a hotel tavern nicknamed "the Pub" was the most popular one with the skiers.

The Pub was a vast drinking room downstairs from the hotel's few spartan lodgings. It was a rustic spot with long wooden tables and benches like those in European drinking halls. There was no décor to speak of, but the people who congregated there didn't seem to mind — they were there for the beer.

"It was New Year's Eve and the beer was flowing. The lads began buying each other round upon round," recalled Joncas.

Around 10 p.m., the drinking reached a fever pitch. Suddenly, one of the skiers made an inappropriate comment to another skier, which led to a hard punch in the face. As the rascal fell to the ground, his friends rallied round to take revenge. More fistfights started to break out around the room, and several patrons ended up on the floor with bloody noses and bruised egos. When a row of beer bottles went careening off the end of a table and crashed onto the wooden floor, the brawl was in full swing.

By this point, the manager of the pub was fuming; he called in the local police. Now this was the 1940s, so the policemen had no reservations about marching in and hitting the drinkers with their *garcettes* (small leather sacks filled with sand) to stop them from punching each other. Then the police chief called in reinforcements from local families, including the St. Denis, Lamoureux, Trottier, and Flynn families.

The local police were busy pushing some of the rowdy kids down the stairs of the side entrance to the pub when two provincial police officers (who were called in by the overwhelmed Saint-Sauveur police) arrived in riding outfits.

The shorter of the two provincial constables jumped up on one of the tables, ordered the revellers to be quiet, and threatened that he and his partner would be back to check on things around midnight. But the police were in over their heads. There were just too many drunkards out of control. There was no anti-riot squad in 1949, so the policemen did not have many resources at their command. One of the provincial constables was later found doubled over because he had been knocked out by one of the revellers on the Rue Principale.

André Joncas witnessed this disgraceful situation. Though he was shocked, he was also intrigued because he was an amateur photographer. Looking for some dramatic shots, Joncas decided to go to the police station to see who was there.

"The police station was really just a room with a desk and two cells. There were hardly ever any prisoners, so one of the cells was used as sleeping quarters for the policeman on night duty and the other cell was usually unoccupied," said Joncas.

But in the first hours of New Year's Day 1949, the simple police station was in an uproar. M. Chartier, an inexperienced officer who had been hired for that night only, had the radio blaring and he had put about 15 people into one of the cells.

"It was just wild. They were all still hitting each other and yelling. The cell was so crowded that they could barely stand up," recalled Joncas.

Then around 3 a.m., hundreds of young people who had not been locked up formed an impressive crowd and paraded down Lafleur Street towards the police station. The crowd marched boldly down the street before the break of dawn, loudly demanding their friends' release.

Finally, around 5 a.m., the jailed skiers were released; they had sobered up and there was really no reason to keep them in a cell. After all, the lads hadn't even broken anything. As the sun rose on the New Year, the noisy city kids went back to their hotels to catch up on their sleep. And the townspeople of Saint-Sauveur breathed a collective sigh of relief.

Ontario

n 1855, the editor of Brantford's *Expositor,
Railway Advocate and General Advertiser*
wrote, "Christmas is a season of festivity
and happiness. Many congregate together to spend the day
in the most hilarious manner, each striving to make the
other happy, and all contributing to throw such a fascinating spell around the scene as makes it highly congenial to
human nature."

Christmas is supposed to be a time for luxury and a
little indulgence. But not all Christmases can be described as
congenial, or even comfortable. When things don't turn out
the way they are supposed to, the only thing to do is make the
best out of a rather difficult situation, especially if circumstances are beyond one's control.

On December 24, 1986, the Ottawa Valley, parts of

eastern Ontario, and southwestern Quebec were hit with a severe ice storm. Freezing rain fell for nearly 14 hours, creating heavy accumulations that resulted in power outages. By Christmas Day, something like one in four residents of the area was without electricity. Determined to celebrate regardless of the power problems, many households cooked their holiday turkeys on the barbecue.

That was a minor inconvenience compared to those suffered by early Ontario residents. For some pioneers, Christmas 1837 was a difficult one. The holiday fell shortly after William Lyon Mackenzie led the rebellion in Upper Canada. Although government troops had quickly suppressed the uprising, rumours were still flying about the province in late December. The result in some communities, including Ancaster, west of Hamilton, was that people stayed away from services at the Anglican Church. According to Reverend John Miller, there were "only about 50 persons present at church" on Christmas Day 1837.

A few years later, Nathaniel Parker Willis (1806–1867) wrote about a particularly rough time experienced by two men shortly before Christmas. Willis, one of a myriad of writers who described the exotic wilderness of Canada in the 1800s, was in the Talbot settlement, near London and Nissouri Townships around 1840. Two weeks before Christmas, two hunters, Howay and Nowlan, went off in search of a bear. They stalked the beast for some 32 kilometres, but had not caught up to him as night fell. So they camped for the night, along with their dog. The next morning, they breakfasted on the crumbs left over from the meal they had brought with them, sharing part of it with their dog, then set off after the bear again.

By the end of the day, they realized they were lost and decided to head back towards the settlement. But they had become completely confused. Over the next several days, their situation went from bad to worse. Although they walked almost constantly all day long, they seemed to get no closer to any kind of settlement. They were out of food, frequently thirsty, usually cold, and one night, Nowlan's feet froze. Although they managed to shoot one partridge, it was hardly enough to satisfy them.

On the seventh day, their dog collapsed. The men were so hungry that they thought they were capable of eating anything, but they were reluctant to make a meal out of the dog that had stayed by them during their ordeal. Instead, they abandoned the animal and continued on their trek, convinced they could find their way out by following a stream. But poor visibility and a swampy area set them off course again. Soon they realized they were walking in circles.

Meanwhile, a search party had been organized; some of the "best dogs in the country" were rounded up, and several men of the Talbot District set off with compasses and trumpets, calling for the missing hunters as they scoured "thousands of acres of interminable forests and desolate swamps."

A light snow, which might have provided some help in tracking the missing pair, melted during a sudden thaw, making the search even more difficult. Finally, after two days, the search party gave up and returned to their homes, convinced the missing men were dead. The only consolation they had, Willis wrote, was that they were "men without families — they were strangers in America" and no one except some "unconnected neighbours" would be left to mourn them.

As far as Howay and Nowlan were concerned, they might as well have been dead. Panicked, starving, and completely despondent, the men were ready to give up all hope. But they headed once more for a river, and this time they heard what sounded like a cowbell. They followed it, discovered a log cabin, which, to their great surprise, turned out to be inhabited. They were 80 kilometres from home at this point, half-starved, and suffering from exposure, but a little food and some nursing put them in good enough condition to make the journey home. To the surprise of everyone in the settlement, including Nathaniel Willis, they returned on Christmas Day.

No Food for the Feast

The harrowing experience of the two hunters was not too far removed from that of many early Ontario pioneers. Although wild berries and game were plentiful in the Ontario backwoods, knowing which ones to gather or how to hunt successfully was a skill that many early settlers lacked. In addition, some of them, especially the more genteel settlers, preferred to eat familiar foods, even if they paid a high price for them. Writing anonymously around 1871, an "emigrant lady" described how her son provided a chicken and some mutton on Christmas Day. Although he paid a good price for it, the chicken was so thin that its bones were sticking out of its skin, and the women of the household were convinced that if it had not been butchered it would have soon died of consumption. In spite of the meagre size of the chicken, the emigrant lady added butter, onions, and spices, and "concocted a savoury stew which was much applauded." The woman also managed to produce a pudding, which was long on flour, short on currants and grease, and completely devoid of plums, sugar, spice, eggs, citron and brandy. The lady remarked, "the less said about that pudding the better."

Food was not the only difficulty. The emigrant lady, the widow of a British officer, had spent 15 years in Calais, France, until forced to leave in the aftermath of the Franco-German War. Although she was happy to be with the family in the Muskoka cabin, her thoughts naturally wandered back to happier, more prosperous times. She worried that all their efforts in the new land might never pay off, but, for the sake of the rest of the group, "I tried to simulate a cheerfulness I was far from feeling, and so we got over the evening. We had a good deal of general conversation, and some of our favourite songs were sung by the gentlemen."

Despite the brave face she put on things, the family's

situation in Canada did not improve. Christmas 1874 rolled around anyway. Very early that morning, the lady heard a cheerful shout and looked out to see her son Charles coming towards the cabin. With him he brought two very small salt herring and a large vegetable marrow. This was all he could contribute to the family's fourth Christmas dinner in Canada. Food shortages or not, the group prepared to celebrate. Charles was sent to retrieve his wife and two children, while someone else borrowed some butter from a neighbour, who was also invited for dinner. The feast that evening was mashed vegetable marrow, mashed potatoes, "well buttered, peppered, salted and baked in the oven," two herring, and plenty of tea. For dessert there were dampers — hot flour biscuits. And everyone dressed in their best for Christmas: "Cinderella transformations were not more complete. My daughter became the elegant young woman she has always been considered; my sons, in once more getting into their gentlemanly clothes, threw off the careworn look of working-day fatigue, and became once more distinguished and good-looking young men; and as to my pretty daughter-in-law, I have left her till the last to have the pleasure of saying that I never saw her look more lovely."

But even with the brave attempt, no one tried to sing that Christmas Day, not even the favourite hymns that had sustained the family in the past. The year had been far too difficult. The family had little food and less money. The wheat crop, which they hoped would partially alleviate their problems, was damaged by harsh weather. Although she had enjoyed some previous success, the emigrant lady's attempts to earn money through her writing met with rejection after rejection. Worried about the health of her eldest son, who seemed to be growing thinner each month, she made up her mind to find a way to return to England. Her first attempt failed because of lack of money. Hiding her disappointment as best she could, she settled in for another miserable winter in the bush. Fortunately, a glimmer of hope came with the New Year, when a kindly neighbour provided the family with a wild turkey. The situation continued to improve — friends in Britain loaned the family enough money to enable them to leave Muskoka. On March 2, 1875, with absolutely no regrets, the emigrant lady and her family left behind their wilderness home forever.

Wartime Christmas

For many Ontarians, the most difficult Christmases have been during wartime, especially during the First and Second World Wars. In both instances, food was rationed, making it difficult to obtain the sugar, butter, and other items essential to holiday goodies. More importantly, loved ones were often far away, so instead of joy and togetherness, Christmas was filled with longing and fear. Even after the soldiers came home there were difficulties, including housing shortages and problems adjusting to family members who were virtual strangers after years of separation.

All the same, just about everyone was smiling in 1945 as many soldiers returned from the war. Fairly typical was the arrival of the Queen's Own Rifles, who reached Toronto on December 17, 1945. Lieutenant-Colonel Stephen Lett, the commanding officer, was greeted by his English bride, who had already been in Canada for five months. Other soldiers were met by parents, siblings, wives, and children. For one soldier, the homecoming was extra special. Prior to the war, the parents of Regimental Sergeant Major Ted Hartnell had been living in western Canada and he had not seen them for nine years prior to joining up. After four years of wartime service that took him to the beaches of Normandy and made him a Member of the Order of the British Empire, Ted came home to find his parents had moved to Toronto. When his regiment was dismissed, he hurried to their Belgravia Avenue home, where he found his parents, his wife, and the young son he had never met. "Who says there's no Santa Claus?" he asked.

Yet amid the smiles and warm welcomes, there were problems. The same newspaper that carried the story of Ted Hartnell's return also reported that Torontonians should prepare for a temporary shortage of coal. At the time, most of the coal consumed in the city was shipped by rail from Buffalo, but a series of storms had delayed deliveries. They were also told to expect turkey shortages. With so many military personnel returning from overseas, the demand had increased to a point where suppliers were unable to keep up. Some measures were being taken to stretch the supply, however. Under regulations that stipulated prisoners of war could not receive goods that were being rationed for civilians, government authorities declared that Japanese and German prisoners of war still interned in Canada would not receive turkeys for their Christmas dinner. Meanwhile, authorities were also making arrangements for Canadian servicemen who were still stationed overseas to get turkey and all the trimmings for their holiday meals.

At least one returned serviceman had already feasted on turkey and was planning to do it again. In fact, he was determined to absolutely stuff himself over the holidays. William Kinmond, a reporter for the *Toronto Star*, had spent four years as a prisoner of war in Germany. Now safely back in Canada, he described Christmas meals that could hardly be thought of as festive. One year, the prison-camp cooks tried to make the usual fare of turnips look better by adding a broth made from bones and water. It still looked like bones and water, but a few of the bones had some marrow left in them. The lucky prisoners who found some of those bones in their bowls took them back to their bunks to suck on them as long as they could.

Christmas 1944 at the camp was better than most. Kinmond and his fellow prisoners were wakened by a newly arrived American captive who presented them each with a cigarette and a cup of ersatz coffee. Meanwhile, the cook had scrounged what supplies he could, and the meals served that day were better than the usual menu. Lunch was a soup made of peas and potatoes, although it was so thin that Kinmond commented, "without the peas we would have had three potatoes and a cup of hot water." Dinner was a stew made of some mysterious meat. There was even some dessert, thanks to the ingenuity of the men who hoarded supplies, including Red Cross rations of raisins, prunes, sugar, and biscuits. By combining these with water and whatever butter or milk they could find and cooking them in a powdered milk tin, the men were able to produce little cakes. Most were pitifully small, just a bite or two at best, but the more talented chefs made their cakes look very nice. Some even coloured the milk-powder icing with beet juice and used it to write Christmas messages across the top of their cakes.

By 1945, although he was still terribly thin, William Kinmond had put those lean days behind him and was looking forward to Christmas dinner. Lots of Christmas dinner. "There'll be no ersatz coffee or pea soup or mystery stew on the Christmas that is to come," he vowed. "The ghost of Christmas past can only spur me on to greater efforts and a stomach ache will only be an indication of successful eating."

The Prairies

hristmas in Canada's "Wild West" was not represented by a single set of traditions or predictable components. The experience of Christmas varied depending on the circumstances, place, and perhaps most of all, time. Europeans arrived on the Prairies in the 18th century. The world — and the Canadian Prairies — changed enormously between the 1700s and the late 1800s. The very earliest prairie Christmases were enjoyed, or simply endured, in Manitoba.

Fur Trade Festivities

Fur was king. In what we now call Canada, two fur-trading dynasties, the Hudson's Bay Company and the North-West Company, did the king's bidding, constantly seeking out new areas to bring under their commercial control.

The West beckoned.

Inside the forts, which had been fashioned out of timbers by small groups of adventurer-fur traders, Christmas was usually celebrated somehow, if only with a single special dinner. Conditions were primitive in the vast wilds of Rupert's Land, so the fellowship and feasting of Christmas was welcomed.

The first recorded prairie Christmas was described in a short journal entry in 1715. The unknown record-keeper lived in Manitoba's oldest settlement, York Fort (later York Factory), located on the shores of Hudson Bay. He wrote: "Had prayers twice today as usual, and the men did have plentiful good victuals."

According to another diarist, Christmas wasn't that much different half a century later. "Spent the day with sobriety making merry with innocent diversions ... Mr. LaTower gave us his company to prayers but we make a poor hand of it for want of prayer books."

By 1800, new forts had been built. One, Fort Wedderburn, on the southwest shore of Lake Athabasca, was the home of George Simpson, governor of HBC in North America. On December 25, the governor wrote, "... the people had a dram in the morning and were allowed to make holyday. The gentlemen sat down to the most sumptuous Dinner that Fort Wedderburn could afford, true English fare, Roast Beef and plum pudding and afterwards a temperature Kettle of punch ..." And, as an afterthought, the governor added, "The weather was bitterly cold." He didn't say how cold it was, but an earlier entry in his Athabasca journal gives a hint. He wrote that, "within 4 feet of a large fire the Ink actually freezes in my pen."

Within 10 years, the HBC had ceded a significant parcel of land, some 300,000 square kilometres, not for fur-trading endeavours, but "to establish agricultural settlers upon the lands." The recipient of the grant was Thomas Douglas, the fifth Earl of Selkirk. In 1812, Selkirk founded the Red River Colony. The grand gentleman did not lead the settlers himself, however. That task fell to his governor, Miles MacDonnell. It was no easy task in this wild country called Assiniboia, and, in the end, MacDonnell was replaced.

There was scarcely reason to celebrate Christmas during the first horrific years of the colony's life. Scurvy ravaged the men, and starvation threatened everyone. The first settlers were just glad to be alive. As conditions slowly improved, women and children joined the men. With their families in their midst, the men felt life was worth living again.

Inside the walls of stockaded communities, such as Fort Gibralter and Fort Daer, they celebrated Christmas with enthusiasm. In an 1812 journal entry, a gathering at the governor's residence at Daer is succinctly described: "We all dine at Mr. Hillier's. Dance to the Bag Pipe in the evening."

During the day, the men chose sides for Hurl, a game played by teams on the ice. The idea was to hit a ball with sticks and send it into the goal of the opposing team. Eighty years in the future, this primitive game played on a frozen river during the Christmas get-together at Fort Daer would be called hockey.

A few months after that Christmas, the colony was destroyed during a fur-trade war. Traders vied for land with farmers, and Nor'westers fought HBC personnel over trapping territory. By 1815, the first Red River Colony was a smouldering ruin.

The second colony fared much better. Five years later, the faithful were called to Christmas mass with church bells from two missions on either side of the river tolling out their message of peace and goodwill. Certainly, by this time, the colonists deserved a little of each. However, celebrations were premature. By the following Christmas, settlers were each rationed to a pint of wheat a day, which they boiled into a thin soup.

By 1830, after the amalgamation of the two huge fur empires, the lean, mean years were past, and Christmases were more bountiful. By the middle of the century, retired factors had made their home in Red River, now a settlement boasting 5000 souls.

More than 900 kilometres from any other settlement and 2400 kilometres from the nearest eastern city, the colonists were still isolated. Only the dog-trains provided a tenuous winter link with the outside world. However, Christmas was celebrated with tea-drinking, merry-making, and dancing to the lively sound of bows over fiddle-strings.

By the late 1840s, "civilization" had move west. At Fort Edmonton, artist and traveller Paul Kane sat down in the dining-hall to a 2 p.m. Christmas dinner with the others: the chief trader, clerks, and missionaries.

The artist wrote that the hall itself was a sight to behold, "painted in the style of the most startling barbaric gaudiness." There was a reason for the garishness. The dining room doubled as reception room for visiting chiefs, and the decoration was undertaken, Kane concluded, simply to "astonish the natives."

No tablecloths, no fine cutlery, silver candelabra, or china, but "bright tin plates" on hardwood tables. And on those plates were turnips, potatoes, portions of boiled buffalo hump and buffalo tongue, and a very tender boiled, unborn buffalo calf. The menu was surprisingly varied, and diners enjoyed beaver tail, wild goose, dried moose nose, and white fish browned in buffalo marrow, followed by something called "mouffle."

"Let us drink to absent friends," was the typical toast of men seated around the table, men celebrating far away from homes and families. Another toast might follow, "To the ladies!" As an HBC clerk was to remark, during Christmas at York Factory, the "ladies" were among the "absent friends." The chief trader's wife was the only European woman present. In fact, she was the only white woman to be found within 400 kilometres of the fort.

The high revelry of Christmas was carried out in the

same manner in virtually all the major forts, and the typical fur-trade yuletide celebration became a tradition unto itself. As the 20th century dawned, and the major forts — Garry, Calgary, and Edmonton — became cities, fur-trade Christmas traditions had all but passed into history.

Christmas During "The Troubles"

"The troubles." That's what people called the 1869 Riel Rebellion. Those particular troubles had been brewing for some time. There was fear and concern among the Métis people, the hardy prairie hunters of mixed French and Native blood. How could they safeguard their land? With the impending transfer of Rupert's Land, which included much of western Canada and the Red River Settlement to the Dominion of Canada, things started to happen fast.

First, the Métis leader, Louis Riel, formed a provisional government. Then the new government imprisoned 63 Canadians who, at the request of Governor Macdougall, had taken up arms as a show of strength against the Métis.

For those 63 men who were imprisoned, life was not so much nerve-wracking as boring. The meals were meagre: boilers full of hot tea and bread in the morning, and boiled beef and bread at noon. But now that Christmas was approaching, they hoped for a decent meal. However, food was not their main concern. They wanted to go home. The day before Christmas, one wrote, "Hoped to be released today, but were disappointed. One of the boys got hold of a violin and tonight there is music and dancing. Some of the guards came in and danced with us."

On Christmas Day, there was no breakfast. The prisoners were discouraged, then worried: what did this mean? What it meant was that women in the nearby village were trying to prepare Christmas dinner for them, but distance was making it difficult. The Fort Garry jail was more than a kilometre away from the housewives' homes. At last, as evening approached, a tasty meal was delivered to the jail. One prisoner wrote the following:

"Mr. Crowson brought in roast beef, plum pudding and tarts. We have few friends in town (as all who could do so have moved their families to remoter parts), but what we have are very mindful of us. I believe we are indebted for tonight's dinner to Miss Drever, Mrs. Crowson, and Mr. Alex McArthur. Long may they live! Music and dancing tonight."

The following year, General Garnet Wolseley led Canadian and British troops to the colony to put down the rebellion. Riel fled, and the rebellion was over. The next Christmas, Wolseley's forces were still in the Fort — much to their consternation. They had been unhappy since their arrival in Fort Garry; not only had Riel disappeared, so had the supplies. Naturally enough, the quartermaster sergeant took the brunt of their displeasure. Christmas dinner loomed. The quartermaster sergeant was in a quandary. What could he serve them for dinner? He came up with a plan.

When the soldiers trooped into the dining hall, they

were greeted by a wonderful sight. Beef boiled, beef soup, beef roasted and stewed! The laughing, joking men ate their fill. Eventually, the quartermaster sergeant got to his feet.

"Gentlemen, have I satisfied you at last?"

"You have!" they roared.

"Is there one man here present who is not perfectly, absolutely satisfied?"

"No, not one," came the cheers.

"The dinner was a great, a noble success?"

"It was!"

"Would you like it repeated tomorrow?"

As the rousing cheers died down, the smiling Quartermaster turned to his assistant and said, "The best thing we can do, Hank, is to go down and get the rest of that old horse."

There was a sudden stampede out the doors in the direction of the latrines.

The Other Men in Red

Beginning in 1874, a new kind of fort was being constructed on the Canadian Prairies: the North-West Mounted Police post. Once again, men were leaving family and friends behind and making the trip out west, which they called the North-west Territories. The "long march," which began in Dufferin, Manitoba, was gruelling enough, but once various troops reached their destination, their work began in earnest. There were forts to build, Native peoples to meet and impress, and whiskey traders to run to ground and arrest.

Much that we know of these days we owe to a handful of men who, either through their letters and diaries or through later reminiscences, related their experiences. One of those men was Richard Nevitt. He and his family had escaped the American Civil War by leaving Savannah, Georgia, when he was a small boy. They'd settled in Ontario, where Nevitt later entered the University of Toronto and obtained his Bachelor of Medicine.

He had to leave university before he became a qualified doctor, because his family could no longer support him. Nevitt knew he had to find a job, but his choices were few. Luckily, he was offered a position that would enable him to earn enough money to complete his education. It would also give him some unique experiences. He accepted a position as an assistant surgeon to the North-West Mounted Police, and joined them in Manitoba for the March West. Christmas found him at the newly constructed Fort Macleod, where Christmas Day was observed as a "Holyday." Nevitt watched policeman as they set to work creating festive mottos to be hung about the officers' mess: "Law and Order Is Peace And Prosperity" and "Nor'West Mounted Police, Pioneers of a Glorious Future."

It seems, in addition to other things, Christmas Day was an occasion to impress the area's Native people. That morning, the captain fired a few rounds from a howitzer, using a tree as a target. He was warming up for the big show to come.

At 2 p.m., the Blackfoot arrived at the fort and the police and Natives all went out onto the prairie so the Mounties could demonstrate the deadly accuracy of long-range artillery. With each roar of the howitzer, it was obvious that the "Pioneers of a Glorious Future" were going to ensure "Peace and Prosperity" through a strategy of persuasion by firepower.

After the demonstration, they rode back to the fort, where the Blackfoot enjoyed a "coffee break," with biscuits, rice, and molasses. After the Blackfoot left, it was time for the officers to enjoy Christmas dinner with their men.

On the menu that December 25, 1874 was roast hare, roast beef, and haunch of venison. After the plum pudding, out came the whiskey and talk of "Christmases gone by, of friends and home." At 11 p.m. the party moved to B Troop for dancing and a concert. An hour or so later, the officers visited the quarters of F Troop for a midnight supper of "oysters, canned fruit, pies, rice pudding, plum pudding and lots of it." The night was young! An interpreter was sent to bring local Natives in for more dancing and "we gave them some supper, and 4 o'clock saw the end of Christmas Day."

Everyone, Nevitt admitted, expected to have a gloomy time out on the primitive prairie, but the "united efforts of men and officers managed to dispel the gloom."

British Columbia

hough each is special in its own way, some Christmases are inevitably more memorable than others. Over the years, people throughout British Columbia have experienced Christmases filled with calamity and heartbreak, joy and excitement, action and adventure. Though they may have been heartrending or distressing at the time, these Christmases often turn out to be the ones we remember; the ones that we talk about — and maybe even laugh about — years later.

A Christmas Miracle

At the time the Puget's Sound Agricultural Company was establishing Craigflower, Hillside, and other farms, Victoria's Inner Harbour actually extended much farther inland than it does today. Long before the causeway in front of the

Fairmont Empress existed, there was a bridge that straddled the waters of the harbour, joining what is now Belville Street with the junction of Wharf Street and Government Street. In the 1850s, though, not even the bridge had been built. At the present site of the Royal BC Museum and legislative buildings, dark stands of fir and cedar stood, shrouded in the smoke from Native village fires. One Christmas Day, a mother tended one of those fires while her baby slept peacefully in her cradle-board nearby.

Suddenly, a giant bird swooped down, its talons extended, and the mother watched in horror as it snatched up the child. She screamed and her family raced to her side, only to see the gigantic bird wing its way across the harbour, in the direction of Fort Victoria. The men gave chase, but lost valuable time because there was no quick way across the harbour's water — they were forced to detour around the bay. HBC workers at the fort joined in the frantic search. Today, such a search would be easy: simply run up Yates or Fort Street. But where those streets are today, narrow muddy trails meandered through tangled rainforest.

Hope faded with the daylight. By nightfall, the rescuers were lighting torches, but soon, the search was called off; it was obvious that nothing could be seen. The next morning at daybreak, the search continued. Then, as the group was about to give up, they spotted the baby, miraculously unharmed, still strapped inside the cradle. The HBC called the site Lake Hill. Now, 150 years later, that area of the city of

Victoria is known as Christmas Hill, in remembrance of that long-ago Yuletide miracle.

Icy Terror

Wartime patriotic fervour called many pioneers away from their ranches, farms, and the lonely solitude of the northern wilderness to travel to "Blighty" and then to France to fight "The Boche." When war broke out, Cliff Harrison and his brother, Bill, were trappers operating south and west of what is now Burns Lake. Cliff left to join up. Miraculously, in 1919, he returned to his brother and the Lakes Country. Cliff Harrison had survived all the horrors of the "war to end all wars," but he was fated to have his closest brush with death his very first Christmas back in the pristine wilderness of British Columbia.

The two brothers looked at their piles of furs and decided they had enough to justify the trip to buyers at Burns Lake. Besides, it was Christmas Day, a day to shake off the isolation and spend some time with other people. They poled up the White Sail River to the foot of White Sail Lake. The lake — at least at that end — was frozen solid.

"We put our boat on the sleigh with all our supplies and our equipment," Cliff remembered, "and then we proceeded on up the lake, and the ice didn't appear to be too sound or too safe, so I kept testing it. I'd go ahead possibly 50 or 60 yards and I'd take the axe to get the thickness of the ice. We were doing quite well. We got up about a mile, possibly a mile and a half and the ice appeared to me to be getting very, very clear."

Without warning, catastrophe struck.

"Everything just exploded," Cliff recalled. "Great sheets of ice broke up in front of me and in I went."

It was about 30 below zero when Cliff went through the ice and into the numbing water. As the ice fractured around him, he glanced back and saw his brother frantically scrambling toward him with the sleigh. Using his upper body as a lever, Cliff managed to roll onto a larger cake of broken ice where he lay panting for breath. The ice held him above water until Bill drew up as close as he dared with the sleigh. Cliff pushed himself to the edge of the hole, and as carefully as possible, Bill pulled him onto the sleigh.

"We've got to get to shore as quickly as we can," Cliff gasped to his brother, "because I can't live very long under these conditions, and I know that I'm going."

Bill began pushing the sleigh as hard and as fast as he could toward the shore, three-quarters of a kilometre away. Shivering inside his sodden clothing, each second seemed an eternity for Cliff. By the time the sleigh nudged the gently sloping shoreline, what little body heat Cliff had left was dissipating quickly.

"We've got to get a fire going," Bill gasped frantically.

Encased in stiffening, icy clothes, Cliff blinked and looked around. Four feet of snow hid whatever firewood might have been lying about. With the spectre of death staring into his frost-encrusted face, Cliff made a desperate decision. In front of his uncomprehending brother, he threw off the furs that covered him and began to struggle to his feet.

"I gotta keep moving!" he grunted. "Bill, if you can strap the snowshoes on me, I'm gonna try it. Before you could get a fire going, I'd be frozen to death." He swung hard and thumped his fist against his thigh. "There's no feeling in my legs! We've got to work fast."

Bill didn't argue. Shoving aside the furs in the sleigh, he extricated Cliff's snowshoes. As Cliff leaned his shuddering body against a nearby tree, Bill knelt down and began wedging his brother's feet through the straps.

The moment his brother was finished, Cliff turned and began to lurch away, ploughing through the snow between the trees. After a moment's hesitation, Bill grabbed at his own snow-shoes and quickly followed.

Breaking snowshoe trail is arduous work, even for someone in peak condition. Just a few minutes later, the half-frozen trapper was stumbling and gasping for breath. The temptation to give up, to simply relax and drift away in welcome, painless slumber was overwhelming.

A few steps behind, Bill watched his brother fearfully and shook his head. "Let me go ahead and break," he offered.

"No, no!" Cliff shouted, shrugging off his brother's hand. "I've got to do it. I've got to get this circulation coming back!"

After a quarter of an hour, Cliff could feel a telltale tingling around his knees. A few minutes later, the uncomfortable tingle had turned to searing, burning pain. Cliff winced in agony, and then began to smile through his tears. The pain was good! It meant the circulation was coming back. Yes, he thought, he just might make it.

Cliff and Bill Harrison made their way six kilometres through the snow. Their destination was the cabin of two fellow trappers, Al Price and Tom Crawford. Bill didn't wait to knock. He simply ran past his brother to the door and threw himself inside. Stunned, Al and Tom rose from the table and dashed across the room to the open door. Tom caught the stumbling form of Cliff Harrison in his arms and knew immediately what had happened.

"My heaven, you've gone through the lake!" he shouted.

"Yes," Cliff mumbled, trying desperately to hold on to a vestige of his composure. "We've had quite a bad experience down there..."

Together, Al and Tom led Cliff to the front of an old box heater. The men attempted to remove Cliff's stiff, unyielding clothing, but gave up. Cliff stood wreathed in a fog of vapour while his clothes thawed, clutching a mug of hot coffee in his shaking hands.

Al and Tom had just finished their Christmas dinner. Pots and pans rattled as Al busied himself gathering together and reheating leftovers for their two unexpected visitors. Tom, who was the same size as Cliff, brought out a suit of clean, dry Stanfield underwear and a pair of mackinaw pants. Before long, Cliff's own clothes lay steaming in a puddle of water on the rough-hewn flooring in front of the heater, and all four men were sitting around the table.

"It was," Cliff recalled half a century later, "the most memorable feed I ever had. They had killed some wild mallards early that fall, going in, and somehow or other they kept them and they had wild cranberries and they had fruit and they had potatoes, and it was just one of those feeds out of this world."

Cliff Harrison lived to see many, many more Christmases, but Christmas 1919 was one he would never forget. "I just say that the Lord wasn't ready for me yet and didn't have room for me and so I survived it."

What Day Is It?

Cathy English, manager of the Revelstoke Museum and Archives, remembers her father, Charles, telling a sad story that took place on Christmas Day 1920, when he was still kid.

Life was difficult for the Harrison family, who, like thousands of other English families, journeyed to Canada just after World War I to start a new life. After a few months in Calgary, the Harrisons made a deal on a "country cottage" and an "orchard" somewhere in the Slocan Valley. The property was called Appledale, and it sounded idyllic. Of course, none of the family had ever seen it. In the late fall, father and son packed up and headed west to their new land — the rest of the family would come later.

Sadly, the country cottage turned out to be a cow shed, and the orchard, nothing more than a swamp. Nevertheless, the work began, from sun-up to long past sundown. Charles Harrison, a boy at the time, remembered being cold almost all the time. He and his father, Campbell, were not prepared for a Kootenay winter.

One day, Campbell asked his son to go to the store to buy some supplies. It was a long and difficult walk from the homestead. Then, to make matters worse, when Charles reached the store, much to his dismay, he found it was locked up tight. On his long walk back, he met a man and asked him why the store was closed.

"Why, it's Christmas Day!" the man exclaimed.

Charles was stunned. He'd had no idea. As he walked on his despondency turned to frustration, then to anger.

"Where's all the supplies?" his father asked when he saw him walk up empty-handed.

"It's Christmas Day!" the boy shot back.

"Oh, well," his father shrugged, turning back to yet another chore. "Happy Christmas, then."

"Yeah, some Christmas!" Charles shouted, and ran, crying, into the nearby woods. He stayed out there all day, in the cold, then came back to the house that night. To keep warm, he heated up some rocks to put into his bed and tried to get some sleep.

Those looking for a happy ending to this story won't be disappointed, although it came many years later. Cathy recalls that the young boy — now her father — would tell this story on Christmas Day, finishing off with, "and now, I have a warm, comfortable house, a delicious dinner on the table and my family all around me. What more could anyone want?"

Chapter 7
Inspirational Tales

Atlantic Canada

hen it comes right down to it, Christmas is not about how many presents we receive, how perfect the tree looks, or even how tender the turkey is. It's really about compassion and goodwill towards our fellow human beings. This was the principle that the miserly Ebenezer Scrooge found so difficult to comprehend prior to his enlightening tour of Christmases Past, Present, and Future. But for many, displaying the true spirit of Christmas just seems to come naturally.

The Greatest Gift of All
In the fall of 1996, Scott Crocker was desperately struggling to maintain a normal life. The 40-year-old junior high school principal had been diagnosed with kidney disease over a decade earlier, and by 1996 he had been on haemodialysis

for more than two years. His condition, Polycystic Kidney Disease, was genetic. Both Scott and his sister had inherited the disease, which had claimed the lives of both their aunt, and their father, who had died at age 45, just five years older than Scott was then.

Haemodialysis meant three, four-hour visits to the hospital each week. So, three times a week after work, Scott made the 20-minute drive from the school in Mount Pearl, Newfoundland, to the Grace Hospital. There, he spent the next four hours hooked up to the dialysis machine, arriving home around 9:30 p.m. Between dialysis and work, Scott had little time left over for his family or anything else. Once heavily involved in sports and numerous outdoor pursuits, Scott now had no energy or enthusiasm left for such activities. Fatigue, dizziness, and a general feeling of unwellness constantly plagued him. Just getting through the day was a slog, and sheer force of will was all that kept him going. Although the fall semester was only half over, Scott could hardly wait for the Christmas holidays so he could have a few days off.

Then, at 3 a.m. on Monday, October 6, 1996, Scott received a phone call that changed his life. It was the General Hospital in St. John's calling. They had a kidney match for him. The person on the other end of the line asked if he was prepared to accept the kidney and go ahead with the transplant. It was the most terrifying yet exhilarating moment of Scott's life. Time was a critical factor. His decision to accept or refuse the donor kidney had to be made immediately. If he refused, there were many others waiting in line for it. He took a deep breath and said, "Yes!" After hanging up, he sat on the edge of the bed and shook uncontrollably for close to an hour.

The rest of the day was a blur. Scott was flown to Halifax, where he was admitted to the Victoria General Hospital and prepped for surgery. And late that night, Scott underwent the transplant.

After convalescing in Halifax for a while, Scott arrived back home in time for Christmas. It was an extraordinary Christmas for the transplant recipient. Although he was still recuperating from the operation, he felt as though he'd been given a second chance in life. While in Halifax, he'd discovered that the kidney he had received was from a child who had died in a tragic house fire. Throughout the Christmas holiday, Scott's thoughts kept returning to the parents of that child. It astonished and moved him deeply to think that in the midst of their "terrible suffering and grief," they had been selfless enough to think of others and donate their child's organs for transplant. Although he had no idea who the couple were, he felt they had given him the single most precious gift he would ever receive.

Mission to Seafarers
Being home, surrounded by family and loved ones, is something we all desire at Christmas. As the song goes, "there's no place like home for the holidays." But for many, getting

home for Christmas isn't always possible. Seafarers in particular often find themselves thousands of miles from home in foreign ports, or out at sea over the holidays. With no gifts, no contact with family, and often no Christmas dinner, December 25 can be the most miserable day of the year for these people.

Maggie Whittingham-Lamont knows all about the feelings of desolation that seafarers experience during the holidays. Prior to the death in 2003 of Maggie's husband, Ned, he had spent many of their 21 Christmases at sea. With her husband away and no relatives in the region, Maggie would gather up her two daughters and they'd spend the day down at the Mission to Seafarers, a non-profit organization dedicated to both the material and spiritual needs of seafarers around the world. There, they helped brighten the day for lonely mariners from other countries. When Ned finally arrived home on leave, no matter what month it was, the Whittingham-Lamonts would have their family Christmas, tree and all. This occurred so frequently over the years that one Christmas, when the girls were young, they asked if they could please have "Christmas *at* Christmas" for once.

Although Maggie knew that spending Christmas at sea or in a foreign port was often lonely, she had no idea just how miserable it could be until one year when Ned called home and mentioned that all he'd had for Christmas dinner was a tin of tuna. Having just become the manager of the Halifax branch of Mission to Seafarers, Maggie decided that from then on, the mission would put on a *real* Christmas dinner, with all the trimmings, for every sailor in port over the holiday.

Preparing dinner for 60 or 70 people is no simple task. It requires a great deal of organization and a cool head. One of Maggie's most vivid memories is that of Christmas 1997. It was one of the first years the Christmas dinner was being put on at the mission and she was really looking forward to the event. The food had been purchased, the room had been decorated, and the seafarers had been invited. Bright and early on Christmas morning, Maggie went in and started preparing the dinner. After peeling, dicing, and chopping all morning, she and her team of volunteers had the turkey all stuffed and ready to go in the oven when she realized something was wrong. The oven wasn't heating up. They changed the fuses and checked all the connections to no avail. The oven was simply out of commission. As the guests began arriving, Maggie tried to remain calm. Determined not to disappoint anyone, despite the fact that she had no oven, she soldiered on. Amazingly enough, using only the top of the stove, she and her helpers managed to put together an entire Christmas dinner for 60 people that day.

Mission to Seafarers tries to fill the void that most mariners experience over the Christmas holidays. In addition to the Christmas dinner at the mission, volunteers arrange for the seafaring men and women to get access to a phone so they can make their Christmas calls home. They also deliver

Christmas boxes filled with goodies to every person onboard every vessel in port, a task that Maggie and the other volunteers enjoy tremendously. As she says, "It's nice to play Santa Claus."

In her 10 years at the mission, Maggie has had some pretty colourful experiences during the Christmas season. Among the most memorable was the time that Willy, an Indonesian engineer aboard a gypsum carrier in port, called her up a few days before Christmas and asked her to help him obtain a pig. It turned out the gypsum carrier was heading back out to sea for Christmas, and Willy had decided that for Christmas dinner he was going to prepare barbequed pig — he'd even built a makeshift barbeque on the deck of the ship. Maggie called around and finally found a place in Dartmouth where they could purchase a whole pig. Once they got to the butcher shop, they realized there was no parking anywhere nearby and had to park several blocks away. After making their purchase, she and Willy ended up wandering through the streets of Dartmouth lugging a frozen pig, which was about 30 centimetres taller than the engineer.

Although every Christmas morning she and her daughters have to rush to open their presents in order to get to the mission in time to start dinner, Maggie wouldn't trade her Christmas tradition for any other. Bringing some joy into the lives of seafarers who are lonely and far from home during the holiday is, she feels, one of the most uplifting experiences imaginable.

Santa Claus Ltd.

On December 6, 1917, the largest man-made explosion prior to Hiroshima shattered the city of Halifax. The entire north end of the city was levelled in the blast. At least 2000 people were killed. Nine thousand were injured and hundreds blinded by the explosion. To make matters worse, a major blizzard slammed into the city late that night, hampering search and rescue efforts and intensifying the suffering of the thousands of victims who were trapped in the ruins. It was a tragedy of overwhelming proportions.

At the worst possible time of year, 20,000 people found themselves homeless and destitute. Many had lost everything in the blast. There was hardly a family in the city that wasn't affected in one way or another by the disaster. But those who suffered most, perhaps, were the children. Many children lost one or both parents in the explosion. Hundreds of others were separated from their parents in the chaos following the blast, some never to be reunited. Still others were wounded and convalescing in hospitals. All in all, it was estimated that 10,000 children were left homeless that December.

As Christmas approached, a cloud of melancholy hung over the city. Normal life, as Haligonians knew it, had ceased to exist. The usual hustle and bustle of Christmas shopping, concerts, sleigh rides, and skating parties had vanished. The festive lighting and window displays of years gone by were also non-existent. Almost every window in the area had been shattered in the explosion. And with an extreme glass shortage in the region, the windows of the buildings that were still standing had been boarded up in an effort to keep out the cold, snow, and looters. The boarded up windows only added to the unsightly appearance of the beleaguered city that Christmas.

In the weeks leading up to Christmas, just about everyone in the area was busy with the relief effort, or struggling to cope with losses. Hundreds of people were still searching for missing family members. Each day, the newspapers were filled with long columns listing missing persons, those in hospitals, and the dead. Parents made desperate pleas for information regarding their missing children, and search parties continued to sift through the ruins searching for bodies. Hospitals and makeshift infirmaries all over the city were filled to capacity, and doctors, nurses, and volunteers worked around the clock to save lives and make patients as comfortable as possible. The shelters were also overflowing, and many people were forced to sleep out in the cold. Shortages of everything, including coal, only added to the misery and hardship. People lined up for hours to receive food, clothing, and necessities from depots set up at various locations around the city. With everyone frantically trying to deal with the aftermath of the catastrophe, Christmas was all but forgotten until it was almost too late.

On December 20, however, a group of merchants and concerned citizens got together and hastily formed an organization called Santa Claus Limited. Their mandate, they declared, was to collect and distribute "Christmas cheer" to the 10,000 homeless children in the city. On December 22 the organization placed an appeal for donations in the *Halifax Herald*. The verse accompanying the appeal imaginatively summed up the situation in the city:

OLD SANTA CLAUS was sailing his aeroplane
    so swift,
When, poof! There happened something that
    gave him quite a lift;
He was passing over Halifax with Yankee
    children's toys,
And it clean upset his balance with its rattle and
    its noise.
Down, down, he tumbled madly till those
    presents out he tossed;
And they'll need them, laughed old Santa, to
    replace the ones they've lost.
And so that good old Merryman can always see
    a way
To make a
MERRY CHRISTMAS
    out of the darkest day.

The bleak mood in the city was also reflected in the wording of an ad placed by Mahons Limited, a downtown merchant. "We're Nearing the Edge of Christmas. Let us face it bravely, even cheerfully," the ad began. After an appeal for donations for Santa Claus Limited, it continued, "And, no matter how much you are opposed to a 'celebration,' let there be something of Christmas in your own home ..."

Despite the fact that Santa Claus Limited was formed at such a late date, the organization managed to bring a little Christmas cheer to the children who had been so adversely affected by the disaster. Christmas trees were hastily erected in all of the shelters and many hospitals throughout the city. Decorations were also strung up in an attempt to add a festive appearance to the dismal surroundings of the makeshift infirmaries and shelters. And doctors and others were pressed into service to play Santa. On December 25 the shelters all served Christmas dinner to their patrons, and the relief committee distributed food to victims who weren't staying in shelters. That day, Santa visited each and every shelter and hospital to distribute gifts to the children. One reporter for the *Halifax Herald* wrote, "At some of the shelters there was much merriment among the little folk. Added to the attractions of the tree there were games, music, songs and the children will never forget the first Christmas after the great explosion."

For many it was a bittersweet Christmas. The outpouring of generosity from all around the world in the wake of the disaster was inspiring. In a letter to Father Thomas P. McManmon, a Sister of Charity in Halifax described the city's overwhelming gratitude at the kindness shown by the United

States in particular following the explosion: "The sisters in these institutions were assisted by the Rhode Island Unit [the medical unit of doctors and nurses from Rhode Island] during the two weeks following the explosion. I wish you could hear the blessings which the poor and suffering invoke on the Americans. Surely the United States is the great, warm heart of the world."

It was true that the Americans were unstinting in their generosity. As soon as word of the explosion reached Boston, relief trains loaded with doctors, nurses, supplies, and equipment were dispatched. Medical units from Maine, Massachusetts, and Rhode Island flocked to the city in the days following the explosion. And ships and trains loaded with food, bedding, clothing, and medicine continued to bring much-needed relief to Halifax.

In addition, countless charitable gestures were made by Canadian corporations, governments, and individuals alike. Ordinary Canadians donated every penny they could spare. Children from all across the country donated their allowances. Glee clubs, Girl Guides, and Boy Scouts organized funding drives to raise money for the children of Halifax. The cities and towns of Moncton, Amherst, New Glasgow, Kentville, Truro, Charlottetown, Montreal, and Toronto all sent aid in the days and weeks following the explosion. And Sir John Eaton, president of T. Eaton Company, arrived in town with a train loaded with everything from medical supplies to household goods.

On Christmas Day, a commercial traveller from Truro was seen passing out "crisp bank notes" to survivors staying in the temporary shelter at the Acadian Hotel. When questioned about his generosity, the man said that the money had come from a charitable group of people in Truro. He had been around to several shelters visiting homeless adults and children that day, an experience that moved him deeply. "This has been the saddest and yet the happiest Christmas I have ever spent," he said.

Quebec

hristmastime is not a joyous event for all Quebecers. Some people are more melancholic than usual during the holidays because they feel like they are the only ones in the world who are not joining in the festivities. But then there are those Christmas angels, Quebecers who make an extra effort during this season to help both loved ones and complete strangers to enjoy a Christmas filled with love and caring.

Fleurette's Christmas Party

In November 1970, Fleurette Bilodeau went looking for elderly people in Longueuil, a Montreal suburb on the south shore of the St. Lawrence River. "I went through the streets in my car and when I saw houses that were in rough shape, I would knock on the door. Then, when the occupant answered, I would pretend that I had the wrong address as an excuse, so that they would open the door. Of course, I did not want to say that I knocked on your door because your house is decrepit," she explained.

Fleurette's intentions were entirely honourable. She wanted to find elderly people who were poverty stricken or lonely, and then throw a Christmas party for them. By December 24, Fleurette had located 27 people — including a couple who had barely left the house in 11 years — and invited them all to her apartment for a traditional Christmas Eve celebration. There was a midnight mass, followed by a *réveillon* meal in the wee hours of the morning. Volunteers helped to make the turkey dinner and decorate the apartment, a Montreal religious order loaned the necessary dishes, and a child Fleurette knew provided the musical entertainment. Fleurette selected presents for each of the guests and financed the whole operation.

"I grew up in the Lac St. Jean region, one of 19 children, and as we were growing up we were taught to value older people," explained Fleurette.

Thirty-four years later, Fleurette Bilodeau, (now a senior citizen herself at 74 years old) is still organizing an annual Christmas party in Longueuil. The guest list has broadened somewhat to include other people in need, including disabled people, cancer patients, teenage mothers, and people in drug rehabilitation. However, the original mandate — to provide a Christmas celebration for people who would otherwise have a lonely time at Christmas — has not changed.

Fleurette's first experience working with elderly people was in the late 1960s, when she joined the *Petits Frères des Pauvres*, a religious community in Montreal that she'd heard about from a family member. As a member of this community, she was fed, lodged, and paid five dollars a day in exchange for promises (not vows) that she would do her best to help underprivileged people. For two and a half years, Fleurette visited shut-ins and helped elderly people with domestic tasks. Then the philosophy of the *Petits Frères* changed in 1969 — members were given working hours (8 a.m. to 4 p.m.) and a salary, and they needed permission to leave the building. Fleurette resisted these restrictions.

"People can need you at any time, at eight o'clock at night or even at midnight. I could not stay there (at the *Petits Frères des Pauvres*) any more because it had changed too much," she said.

The next year, Bilodeau took a job in student services at Collège Marguerite-Bourgeoys in Westmount, and it was then that she organized her first Christmas party. By the time of the second Christmas party, in 1971, the guest list had more than doubled as information about the party spread throughout the community. Elderly people started calling Fleurette to ask if they could attend.

Meanwhile, Fleurette continued to seek out elderly people who were alone in the world. One such case was

Eugénie Vallée, a woman in her 60s who was bedridden due to a severe case of arthritis. Mme Vallée was barely able to walk, let alone take care of herself.

Fleurette began to visit Eugénie on a regular basis, and she added Eugénie's name to the growing list of Christmas party guests. Eugénie attended every Christmas celebration until she died. Every year, two students from College Marguerite-Bourgeoys would bathe her, dress her, and bring her to the party.

Fleurette realized early on that there was a ready-made team of volunteers at the college. Dozens of Marguerite-Bourgeoys students threw themselves into Fleurette's project with gusto. Not only did the students organize fundraising activities at the college, they also volunteered to perform a multitude of tasks, including helping to buy presents, wrapping presents, driving the guests to the party, decorating the hall, assisting with the entertainment, setting the tables, decorating the Christmas tree, greeting the guests, buying groceries, preparing the traditional turkey dinner, serving the dinner, singing in the improvised midnight mass choir, and helping to clean up at the end of the party.

Jean-Pierre Lapointe was a student volunteer more than 25 years ago. "I first helped out with the Christmas party when I was 17 years old," recalled Lapointe. "I wanted to do it because it felt good to deliver a service to the community and to help people during a period when it is very hard to be alone ... I wanted to find the real meaning of Christmas."

The first year that Jean-Pierre was involved, his mother was very proud that her son was going off to do volunteer work, and the Lapointe family simply celebrated Christmas the following day. But the second year, his parents decided that if Jean-Pierre was really moved by Fleurette's Christmas celebration, then the whole family ought to join him. So Jean-Pierre's parents, sister, and brother all volunteered to help.

"It became a family tradition," remarked Jean-Pierre.

Jean-Pierre and fellow volunteers got to know many of the Christmas party guests during the course of the year as they visited elderly people and brought hot meals. Some of the shut-ins whom the volunteers called on had not received visitors for weeks or even months.

In the months leading up to Christmas, Jean-Pierre and a dozen other students would begin to prepare for the Christmas party. Jean-Pierre became a proficient multi-tasker. "I approached businesses for donations, picked up food, wrapped presents, peeled potatoes, and blew up balloons. By the time the Christmas party ended in the wee hours of the morning, I had been standing up for about 30 hours in a row."

Jean-Pierre has not missed a Christmas party in 25 years. These days, he attends the parties with his wife and his teenage children. "I also think that it is important for my children to see something other than the happiness which they see at home. They are lucky to have parents who are in good shape and to not lack for anything, but they must also see that there are other things in the world, too. They are always happy to come help out," he said.

Jean-Pierre was one of 150 volunteers who helped to organize the 2003 Christmas party, which was held in the basement of the Saint-Charles-Borromée church in Longueuil. There were 400 guests at the event and Fleurette was quick to point out that during the week before the party, her volunteers also made 527 visits to people who were invited to the party but who were unable to come.

The Christmas party has been celebrated at lunchtime since 1996, because some of the elderly people were finding it too difficult to stay up late for the traditional midnight mass and *réveillon*. Yet the mass still begins with *"Minuit, Chrétiens!"* and the worship still follows the order of service of a traditional midnight mass.

Another aspect of the celebration that has changed over the years is that volunteers are no longer expected to sing in an improvised midnight mass choir. These days, Fleurette hires a professional musician who plays an electronic piano and sings the special Christmas hymns and carols.

At a recent Christmas party, Fleurette's guests were treated to a delicious *réveillon* meal with turkey, *tourtière*, cranberry sauce, mashed potatoes, cooked vegetables, and dessert. Then the singers who performed during the mass became the afternoon's entertainment. One of the musicians brought out a saxophone, another became the master of ceremonies, and the guests settled into the party atmosphere. Volunteers who had sat with the guests while they finished up their dinner joined them for some old-fashioned dancing.

Finally, the Christmas presents were distributed. Fleurette keeps a file for each guest with their age, sex, clothing size, and a record of past gifts. Every year, her guests receive two presents — one practical and one for pleasure. Presents for male guests typically include shirts, pyjamas, knitted socks, shaving lotion, or a deck of cards.

"It's more difficult to choose presents for women, because their dress size can change a lot. We start to buy the presents in September, so it is not possible to return anything," said Fleurette. Female guests generally receive slippers, scarves, household items like tablecloths and dishtowels, as well as some kind of beauty care product.

Remarkably, every year, Fleurette has been able to raise sufficient funds to cover all of her costs. In the fall, she sends out letters to friends and family in the Lac St. Jean region. Monies received from them, as well as the Club Optimiste in Longueuil, Club Richelieu de St. Lambert, and donations from old students cover the costs of hall rental, food, entertainment, and the Christmas presents.

Agathe Landry-Bouchard has been invited to the Christmas parties for 26 years in a row. Though Agathe has enough to eat and is not in a desperate situation, she is alone because she has no children and few friends.

"The beauty of Fleurette's event is that she does not

exclude anyone. Some people come with beautiful jewellery and others practically have rags on their backs. The main criterion for Fleurette is loneliness. She does not want people to feel lonely at Christmas," explained Jean-Pierre Lapointe.

For more than 30 years, Fleurette Bilodeau has helped thousands of people to enjoy the religious and secular aspects of a traditional Christmas party. If not for Fleurette's concern, most of these people would have spent Christmastime in misery.

One Last Christmas Wish

In Christmas 2003, the Tremblay family learned first-hand about the power of love. The patriarch of the family, Édouard, was extremely ill, so his children Suzanne, Josée, and Marc — along with their spouses and children — joined their mother, Mathilde, at the family home in Chicoutimi.

Édouard had been diagnosed with lung cancer more than a year before, and the Tremblay family were reluctant witnesses to his slow and painful deterioration. He was clearly having more and more trouble breathing, and he was so weak that he had a difficult time walking across the room. Yet, somehow, Édouard mustered enough strength to celebrate one last Christmas with his family.

The holiday passed slowly, with Édouard spending most of his time sitting in his armchair in the living room. He watched his children and grandchildren passing through on their way to and from tobogganing and skating expeditions.

From time to time, Mathilde would bring him a cup of tea and one of her famous Christmas cookies, and his children would poke in their heads to tell him their latest news and ask whether he needed anything. And that was just about right for Édouard. He was included in the family bustle, yet he wasn't required to spend a long time talking.

Sometimes Édouard would sit back in his armchair and close his eyes, exhausted by his efforts to breathe. He appeared to be in a deep, deep sleep. But when the grandchildren chased each other around the house, yelling and squealing, a broad smile of joy flashed across his face.

On Christmas night, Édouard pulled himself into the kitchen to help peel potatoes for dinner. He diligently prepared each potato, as he had done for decades of family gatherings. Unfortunately, when everyone sat down to dinner, Édouard was too ill to join them.

One afternoon, Édouard asked his six-year-old granddaughter, Sara, what she was learning at her new school. She mentioned a Christmas song called *Petit Papa Noël*, but when prompted by Édouard to sing the traditional children's song about Santa Claus, Sara feigned shyness. So Édouard began, "*Petit papa noël, quand tu descendras du ciel...*" and then he paused as if he could not remember the words. Sara joined in with the next line, and then grandfather and granddaughter sang the rest of the song as a duet. Édouard was so entranced that he almost seemed to be reliving his own childhood.

The next day, Édouard's brother René was invited for

lunch. Édouard proudly dressed for the occasion, discarding his faded housecoat and putting on a crisp striped shirt, black pants, and an elegant velour vest. He was in an uncharacteristically jocular mood, reminiscing with his brother and gently teasing Mathilde for not having lunch ready on time.

On December 28, Édouard's children and grandchildren began to leave Chicoutimi and go back to their respective homes. Christmas was over. That afternoon, Édouard suffered a respiratory attack, which led to his death two days later.

The Tremblay family was in shock as they turned their focus from celebrating Christmas to planning a funeral. However, beneath the despair and the grief, there was a real sense of gratitude that the family had had one last Christmas season with Édouard — somehow, he had postponed his death until after Christmas.

Doctors and nurses who work in palliative care settings are quite familiar with the concept of death postponement. According to Dr. Balfour Mount, co-founder of Montreal Royal Victoria Hospital's palliative care centre: "Some people appear to be able to wait until after a special occasion. We have had many cases of people who were extremely ill who seemed to hold on in order to see someone or to be part of a special event and then they died after that event had happened."

Édouard must have had a very strong desire to celebrate one last Christmas with his children and grandchildren. His love for his family and his ardent desire to share Christmas with them may have even enabled him to delay natural physical processes. Édouard's death immediately following Christmas supports the conclusions of research conducted by Dr. David P. Phillips, a sociologist with the University of California at San Diego.

Dr. Phillips has been studying the relationship between death rates and important social occasions in California for more than a decade. According to his research reports, the imminence of a social occasion to which a dying patient has strong emotional ties can affect the patient's date of death.

In one study, Dr. Phillips examined the death records of Chinese Californians over a 25-year period and discovered that there was a lower-than-average number of deaths among Chinese-Californians right before the Harvest Moon Festival, and a higher-than-average number of deaths immediately following the holiday. Dr. Phillips has also observed a similar mortality pattern among Jewish men immediately before and after Passover.

Édouard was mourned for the rest of the holiday season. Naturally, the months following his death were extremely difficult for family members — but his family never forgot how fortunate they were to have had one last Christmas with him.

Although the religious aspect of Christmas is of decreasing significance for many modern Quebecers, this holiday remains an extremely important time for everyone to visit with friends and family. In fact, spending *Les Fêtes* with loved ones is so meaningful that Quebecers are willing to travel great distances, overcome logistical hurdles, and, if need be, even postpone their own deaths in order to achieve that goal.

Ontario

hristmas brings out the best in people. For at least one day of the year, almost everyone makes the effort to get along. The idea of peace on earth and good will towards all prevails, and it can make a huge difference in how individuals treat one another.

Christmas Miracles

When a child is sick, hope and faith is often all parents have to rely on. When a child dies, it is a tragedy, especially if the death occurs close to Christmas. But sometimes miracles of hope and faith bring a measure of peace.

Shortly before Christmas 1984, three-year-old Gordie Lock of Hamilton was riding in his father's cab. When the taxi turned a corner, the door suddenly flew open. Gordie flew out, fell to the curb, and was struck by another car. He was rushed to McMaster University Medical Centre, where doctors told Paul and Dianne Lock that their son was brain dead. Struggling through their grief, the couple decided to donate Gordie's organs.

Meanwhile, in Louisville, Kentucky, five-year-old Amie Garrison was slowly dying of liver disease. Biliary atresia, a birth defect, prevented her liver from functioning properly, and her body was slowly shutting down. Her parents had been trying for years to find a liver for her and, to increase the chances of locating one, had publicized her plight. Just a week before Gordie's accident, Amie had been invited to the White House to place a star atop a Christmas tree, an event that was televised nationally.

The donation of Gordie's organs made Amie's survival possible. In a lengthy operation, the Ontario boy's liver was transplanted into the body of the American girl. Amie responded well to the surgery. Two days later, the families were in touch. Although donors are usually anonymous, as soon as they made the decision to donate their son's organs, Paul and Dianne Lock contacted the media. They wanted to focus attention on the need for transplant organs. The ensuing publicity made it easy for Teresa Garrison, Amie's mother, to reach the Hamilton couple after the girl's operation. The long distance chats resulted in a meeting a few weeks later and a friendship developed between the families of the two children.

Knowing that part of their son survived in Amie helped the Locks come to terms with Gordie's death. For Amie and her family, the new organ was the best Christmas gift of all. As a result of the operation, Amie grew into adulthood and eventually had a little boy of her own.

Peaceful Wishes in Wartime

For A.F. Kemble of Toronto, evidence of the spirit of Christmas was clearly demonstrated in a German prisoner of war camp during the First World War. In 1917, the Toronto man's third Christmas in prison was approaching. The first two holidays had been no different from any other days in the camp. But the third was special because of the efforts of one man, a German officer.

Shortly before Christmas, the prisoners received an invitation to a Christmas party. At the time they were skeptical — after three years surrounded by barbed war and bayonets, they had little reason to trust their captors. But, more from curiosity than anything else, they accepted the invitation.

When they awoke on Christmas morning, two surprises greeted them. First, all the guards were unarmed. And secondly, right in front of the guardhouse was a huge Christmas tree, dripping with tinsel and dozens of presents. The prisoners were asked to gather round the tree. Then the camp commandant spoke, telling the men how much he regretted that the war had taken them so far from home and family at

Christmas, and how he hoped that the gulf between the two warring nations would eventually disappear after peace. He also asked that the men say nothing about the Christmas party in their letters home as he was acting without the permission of his superior officers.

For the rest of the day, he told the men, discipline would be relaxed. He trusted they would not attempt to escape. He also informed them that they could buy as much wine from the canteen as they wanted. As he finished his speech, a small gramophone started to play "Silent Night" and the commandant began to remove small presents from the tree, passing them out to each man.

The prisoners responded with three cheers and a rousing rendition of "For he's a jolly good fellow." Then, taking their gifts with them, they went back to their barracks. Most were convinced the commandant's conciliatory gesture meant the war must be winding down.

As it was, the war dragged on for another 10 months, until November 1918. And, just a month after the Christmas party, the camp commandant was suddenly replaced by "a hard-boiled scoundrel." But, 20 years later, Kemble vividly remembered the other commandant and the Christmas of 1917: "I for one will always have a kindly feeling for this German officer who was not afraid to step from behind the great false face of hate that nation presents to nation in time of war and show his true features to us in recognition of the all-embracing kinship of Christmas Day."

How can you celebrate when loved ones are so far from home and in grave danger? How do you deal with Christmas carols and cards wishing "peace on earth" when war is raging? In December 1939, shortly after the start of the Second World War, the wife of Canada's governor-general addressed those questions. In an article for *Saturday Night*, Lady Tweedsmuir urged Canadian parents to celebrate Christmas in as normal a fashion as possible for the sake of their children. Speaking of the "awful feeling of insecurity" that war created, she pointed out that despite their parents' best efforts, children would hear about the horrors of war and worry about it. "They feel that nothing is safe, everything is rocking round them. At any moment their father, brother or schoolmaster may be taken by this monster whose fiery breath fans their cheek," she wrote. But Christmas, she continued, provided the security of familiar and cherished traditions, "a festival of the church, spiritual and joyous, something warm and human and generous, a light which nothing can put out!"

As for "peace on earth, goodwill to men," Lady Tweedsmuir suggested the historic lines be taken as a challenge, an impetus for parents to spend the rest of their lives fighting the causes of war, poverty, and racism. The present might have seemed gloomy and threatening, but she maintained it could also encourage people to "put our hopes for the future into our singing, and pray fervently that our children may live in an age in which peace and goodwill reign on earth."

Operation Santa Claus

In effect, Lady Tweedsmuir was trying to persuade Canadians to carry the Christmas spirit through the rest of the year. That's a difficult undertaking for many, but there are some people who make the attempt. One of the most celebrated is Jimmy Lomax of Hamilton.

As a young child, Jimmy developed a serious lung disease and spent many months in hospital. Doctors predicted the ailment would kill him before he was out of his teens. But they were wrong. An encounter with Santa Claus changed his life.

When Jimmy realized that Santa was just an ordinary man dressed up in costume, he was amazed. He vowed that if he lived he would put on a Santa costume himself and do whatever he could to make sick children happy at Christmastime.

To the surprise of medical experts, Jimmy recovered. And he kept his promise. At 15, he persuaded a gas station owner to give him five dollars to buy candy for sick and needy kids at Christmas. To stretch the money, he bought leftover Halloween goodies. Then he put on a Santa Claus suit made by a local schoolteacher and went door to door, giving candy to children who were facing the prospect of a less than wonderful Christmas.

That was in 1958. Jimmy grew up and went to work at Stelco, the steel mill that is one of Hamilton's major employers. The money was good, but the job was not particularly prestigious — at one time Jimmy described himself as a "flunky from the steel industry." The position really did not matter that much because by this time Jimmy Lomax had found his true vocation.

Every year, he put on the red Santa suit. Every year, there were more sick and needy children to attend to. And every year, as word of his activity spread, Jimmy collected more money and gifts to distribute.

By 1980, he was delivering more than $50,000 worth of gifts to more than 3000 people. Eventually, he was collecting more than a quarter-million dollars in donations. Much of the money came from others, but Jimmy regularly added some of his personal savings. He also took his annual vacation in the weeks leading up to Christmas so he would have time to distribute gifts to sick children, physically and mentally handicapped youngsters, and the elderly.

Operation Santa Claus became a registered charity, well known throughout the city of Hamilton. Preparing for the Christmas distribution of gifts was a year-round effort. It included a summertime garage sale, with donated items being sold to raise money for Christmas. Closer to the holiday, a Christmas gift shower was held. Anyone could attend the party, providing they brought along something to donate to Hamilton's needy and a can of food for the Hamilton food bank.

When he started out, Jimmy Lomax operated pretty much alone. Over the years, a corps of regular volunteers came to his assistance. One of the busiest was his wife Susan, a school friend and neighbour who knew Jimmy was already deeply involved in his Christmas work when they started dating. Before they were married, he made it clear that, at Christmastime, his charity work took precedence over everything. So Susan became almost as deeply involved as her husband, packaging gifts, organizing his schedule, soliciting donations, and writing thank-you notes.

The couple had one child, Ryan, born a short time before Christmas 1972. As soon as he was able, Ryan starting helping out at Christmas. For several years, he marched side by side with his father in the annual Santa Claus parade.

By the early 1980s, Jimmy Lomax was a Hamilton institution. His work brought him numerous honours. He was named Hamilton Citizen of the Year in 1981. He also received the Ontario Medal for Good Citizenship and was named to the Order of Canada. He was so well known he could not even go out drinking with a friend. In bars, people recognized him and insisted on giving him something for Operation Santa Claus.

It was difficult to mistake Jimmy Lomax for anyone else. Like Santa, he was a very large man who weighed more than 300 pounds at one point. Most years, he did not need any padding for his Santa suit. Getting the requisite long white hair and beard was a little more difficult. Some years, Jimmy grew his beard and hair and bleached them. He used correction fluid to colour his eyelashes white because it was the only thing that didn't run when he cried.

And he cried frequently. An emotional man, he was often moved to tears when encountering sick children, the handicapped, or the elderly. Usually he controlled himself by leaving the room for a few moments to regain his composure. It hurt him to see suffering, but he faced it because he understood the effect Santa has on people.

At one hospital, he brought presents to a three-year-old boy who had burns on his legs, arms, and face. At first, the child wasn't sure how to react to the big man in the red suit. Santa laughed and jingled the sleigh bells on his wrists. He sang Christmas carols to the boy and handed him several gifts. The boy was quiet, hesitant. Then Santa went down the hall to make another visit. On his way, he encountered an elderly woman sitting in a wheelchair. She was staring vacantly, but when he stopped and talked to her she smiled in recognition. Meanwhile, the little boy, with the help of his physiotherapist, had followed Santa down the corridor.

Today, Jimmy Lomax has dozens more stories about the reaction of patients to Santa's visits. One old man, bedridden for weeks, got up and danced. Jimmy frequently shares the stories with reporters, along with various opinions, some of which are unpopular. His outspokenness has offended some people, and there have been accusations of glory seeking. But, after more than 40 years of playing Santa Claus, it seems evident that Jimmy Lomax is deeply dedicated to his chosen work. "Christmas is my whole life," he once told a reporter. "I live for it from year to year."

Personal problems have not stopped him from keeping his promise to be Santa Claus. He has suffered heart attacks, serious illnesses, and has undergone hip surgery. When his father died suddenly a couple of days before the annual fundraising garage sale, Jimmy decided it should go on as usual.

Most heart wrenching of all was the loss of his only son. Ryan was diagnosed with a rare form of lung cancer while in his early teens. Everyone rallied behind the Lomax family, praying for the boy's recovery, sending cards and gifts. Although Ryan improved briefly, he died in May 1987. There was not much Christmas joy in the Lomax household that year, but Operation Santa Claus went ahead anyway. Sadly, there was more heartbreak ahead. On the anniversary of his son's death, Jimmy got drunk and decided to commit suicide by driving into a bridge abutment. He hit another car instead, sending several people to the hospital, and was later convicted of drunk driving. Still, in view of his charitable work and the tragic loss of his son, many people forgave him.

The degree of respect for Jimmy and his work was further demonstrated in 1992. For several years, Operation Santa Claus raised funds with a one-day drive at the Stelco plant. But that year, the union asked that the drive be postponed. A day earlier, the company had announced that 800 jobs would be cut. Many of the workers were facing an uncertain future and the prospect of a Christmas without any income. Jimmy went ahead with the drive anyway, fully expecting to get less money than in the previous year. Instead, the steelworkers donated $9000, considerably more than the year before.

In recent years, Jimmy's health has deteriorated. But Operation Santa continues, proof that one inspired, determined man can spread the Christmas spirit through an entire city and beyond.

The Prairies

gaily decorated tree, the familiar strains of festive songs, and the mouth-watering aroma of baking are all part of Christmas. But the holiday season is frequently made special by something else — something that we can't see, hear, or smell. It is the special word or deed shared, either unexpectedly or spontaneously, with friends, family, or strangers. These acts of warm-hearted generosity embody what we call the Sprit of Christmas. That spirit lives on in our hearts long after the material trappings of Christmas have been put away for another year.

A Hold-up, High jinks, and Humanity

The spirit of Christmas means, among other things, joy. There was plenty of joy within Calgary's large King family.

In her evocative book, *The House With The Light On*, Horace King's daughter, Eleanor King Byers, shares many whimsical and touching Christmas stories that tell us much about the Christmas spirit.

Say the words, "Tea Kettle Inn" to long-time Calgary residents over the age of 50 and watch their eyes light up. Run by Horace King and his sister, Millie Snowden, the 7th Avenue restaurant was, during the 1930s, 40s, and 50s, one of the city's finest dining spots. The inn, located next door to the Kings' House of Antiques, boasted "Delicious Meals of Quality prepared by expert Lady Cooks." It was no idle boast. A bevy of uniformed waitresses served prime rib, chicken pot-pie, and real tea made from real tea leaves, poured from real china teapots.

One Saturday evening in December, business, as usual, was brisk at the Tea Kettle. Horace and Millie had already gone home to their families, leaving their staff to look after the last diners and close the restaurant. Near closing time, a solitary man walked in. The silent stranger didn't pull up a chair and sit down at a table. Instead, he walked right up to the cashier and pulled out a gun.

The terrified cashier didn't hesitate. She emptied the till and handed over the cash. The robber grabbed the bank notes and simply walked quickly out of the restaurant. Once the door closed behind him, pandemonium reigned. It took only a few seconds for one plucky waitress to jump over the counter and give chase. A short time later, she staggered into the restaurant, gasping for breath. She was empty-handed. After pursuing the thief for blocks, she had finally given up.

Horace was upset about the incident, but in the swirl of pre-Christmas activity, he didn't waste too much time thinking about it. However, two days before Christmas, someone jogged his memory.

On returning home from shopping, the Kings found a large cardboard box on the front porch. From the top of the box, a wooden pole pointed skywards. Perplexed, they climbed the steps to take a closer look. Attached to the box was a note that read: THIS IS A STICK-UP. It was a pre-Christmas "present" from Eleanor's cousins.

This kind of joke was typical of the King family. They enjoyed high jinks and imaginative shenanigans, especially at Christmas. One year, Eleanor's uncle, Harry, mischievously invited his kids and their cousins to "go fishing" for Christmas presents. He led them to the kitchen, where a bed sheet concealed a corner of the room, and ducked behind the sheet. Meanwhile, Eleanor's aunt, Lil, handed out "fishin' poles" (sticks tied with string "line" and safety-pin "hooks"). When the fishing lines sailed across the top of the sheet, Harry put little presents onto the hooks for each of the yuletide anglers, announcing each "catch" with a sharp tug.

At one of the Tea Kettle's staff Christmas parties, it was the same Uncle Harry who announced a "Guess the Baby's Weight" contest. He collected all the guesses, then, not content to simply tell the party-goers the correct weight, he carefully lifted real, live, four-month-old Audrey King onto the restaurant's big butcher scales.

For other parties, Horace King wrote inspirational plays that cast waitresses, cooks, and others in such roles as Humility, Forgiveness, and Charity. There were lessons, as well as laughter, to share.

Horace King was a generous man who actively sought out and helped needy people. Eleanor remembers delivering food, clothing, and toys to families who had fallen on hard times. One repeat recipient of Horace's charity was the reclusive Miss Moss, a lady who lived in a weather-beaten, dilapidated house across from what is now Memorial Park. She rarely ventured out of her house, even to go shopping. Instead, she hired neighbours to get her groceries and do the outside chores. Her instructions were always the same: take the groceries around the back, please. Nobody — except Horace — had ever seen the inside of her house.

Horace called on Miss Moss every Christmas Eve to deliver a turkey dinner with all the trimmings, compliments of the Kings and the folks at the Tea Kettle. Significantly, Horace was granted a front-door entrance. All he asked in return was that she leave the empty tray on the porch for Boxing Day pick-up. Naturally, Horace's kids were curious about the old woman's house. Eleanor and her brother Don begged repeatedly to be taken along when he took the dinner tray.

One Christmas Eve, Horace relented. He warned the

two that they might be left standing out on the porch, and to "accept her choice graciously." Wonder of wonders, Miss Moss let them all in. Once inside, the brother and sister stared at "a lifetime of newspapers, periodicals and nondescript collectibles stockpiled from floor to ceiling."

Eleanor remembers that Horace urged the old lady to get outside more often. She also remembers Miss Moss telling Horace that she had taken a walk in the park the previous July, "veiled, of course."

On Boxing Day, when the Kings' car pulled up in front of the old house, the Tea Kettle tray was waiting on Miss Moss's front porch, as usual. There was no note of thanks or belated Christmas card. None was expected. The tray was empty, and that was reward enough for Horace King.

The Extra Hamper

It was 1935 and, according to the calendar, Christmas was just around the corner. Yet, for many Depression-era households, Christmas might never have come at all if it hadn't been for the generosity of others. For thousands of families, Christmas actually arrived with an unexpected knock at the door. The door would open to reveal a smiling stranger standing on the porch with a shopping bag in his hand, or with arms wrapped around a large cardboard box.

"Merry Christmas," he would say. "Merry Christmas from Rotary." Or the Lions. Or the Legion. Then, gesturing at the bag, "Here's something for the kids ..." or, "Christmas dinner, Ma'am."

Calgary's Archdeacon Cecil Swanson, or "Swanny" as he was known, told many touching tales of Christmas generosity. One particular story concerned two men who somehow found themselves with an extra Christmas hamper.

As they had before, Harry and his friend Pete were bringing a little Christmas to needy folks living in the small wooden houses not far from downtown Calgary. That December in 1935, hefting the Club Christmas hampers into and out of the car, climbing flights of stairs, and standing on tiny porches was cold, hard work. But the two men didn't mind. Their shivering stopped when they felt the warmth of abashed smiles and choked murmurs of thanks from grateful men and women.

Harry and Pete were just saying goodbye to the lady at the last home on their list when they remembered the last hamper, an extra hamper, sitting on the floor behind the front seat of the car. They asked the woman if there was another family nearby that might appreciate a little "Christmas," too. She pointed up the street, in the direction of a home of new neighbours. Three or four children, she thought.

The pair thanked her for the tip and went to the house. Harry and Pete took one look inside the home, at the bare wooden floors, the shabby furniture, and the hollow-eyed youngsters, and instantly knew their extra hamper was going to make a big difference.

How many kids? they asked. The mother held up four

fingers. Harry looked around. There was dad, and three youngsters. "Okay, where's number four?" he laughed.

"Oh, he's in the shed," the father replied nonchalantly.

"In the shed? Harry exclaimed in surprise. There was something about the furtive, hesitant look in the father's eyes. "Where's the shed?" Harry asked.

"I'll show you."

While Pete helped the mother empty the hamper, the father led Harry through the kitchen. There, attached crudely to the back of the house itself, was a small plank lean-to, scarcely bigger than a bathroom. Inside the lean-to was a narrow bed. And there, nestled beneath the old blankets, white and wan, lay a little boy.

Harry swallowed hard and approached the bed. He had seen that look before. He knew what it meant: tuberculosis. A terrible life-threatening illness for anyone who contracted it, TB also instilled a terrible fear in those close to the afflicted. Harry knew that fear all too well; he remembered the strict instructions, the boiling, bubbling water in which bed sheets were washed, and the warnings not to share drinking glasses, cutlery, or even a kiss. Harry had been a TB victim, too. He gave the boy a warm smile and then led his father aside.

"I'll be back Wednesday morning," he said quietly. The father looked up and nodded wordlessly.

As Harry turned the ignition in the car, he told Pete what he had seen. He had an idea, he said, and then, before he pulled out onto the silent, snow-covered street, he told

Pete not to tell a soul. But sometime later, Pete told "Swanny" because the story was too wonderful not to share.

The following Wednesday, as promised, Harry arrived back at the house. He had a carpenter with him. Two days later, a new, bigger, brighter lean-to had been built, one with a large glass window. Also, Harry had furnished it with a new bed and new warm, colourful blankets. Later, a doctor arrived to check the boy. It was the first of many visits.

Generosity comes in many forms. In this case, it was a food hamper and $1800 worth of labour, materials, and medical care. But the "gift" was a gift of hope to a sick boy and his frightened family.

Ridin' the Rods

They called it "ridin' the rods." The "rods" might be those tracks that snaked away from Banff, or led into Edmonton, cut through Regina, or ran in and out of the huge CPR marshalling yards in the centre of Winnipeg. It could have been 1930, or '33, or '36. Whatever the place, whatever the year, there was no Merry Christmas for these men; bitter, destitute men on their way to ... anywhere.

They were the hobos, the vagrants, the tramps and troublemakers, the unemployed thousands without homes, the kind of homes they watched speed by as the long freights sped away from 'the peg' on the CPR main line. Homes of ordinary families — homes like that of the Payjacks'...

Just a few blocks away from "CPR town," close enough

that you could hear the long, low mournful sound of the train whistle, the family was gathering inside the Payjack house. It was Christmas Day and aunts, uncles, and cousins were at the table eating dinner. They were happy. They knew how fortunate they were. They had a warm, roomy house — not like those mean-looking shacks closer to the yards. There was a wage earner in this house, so in spite of hardship all around, there was plenty to celebrate.

Because this was a family gathering, they were surprised to hear a knock at the door. Mr. Payjack answered the knock, wondering who could possibly be calling on this day of days. There, on the veranda, stood a teenager. Collar turned up against the cold, face and hands streaked with grime, he looked a sad sight. Shivering, the boy asked if he could have something to eat — or maybe a little something so he could buy a bite somewhere.

Mr. Payjack immediately invited him in. Living so close to the rail yards and depot, he could guess the boy's story; he had seen others like him before. First the boy was led to the bathroom. A few minutes later, he emerged with a clean face and hands, and wearing a clean shirt. An extra place was set at the table, and he was asked to join them for dinner.

After the last relative had left, Mrs. Payjack made up a bed on the chesterfield. It must have felt like a cloud under the young vagabond's bruised and weary body. In the morning, the Payjacks gave him some warm clothing, a lunch of Christmas leftovers, and a gift of folding money. There were handshakes and good luck wishes, and the boy disappeared around the house and out of their lives.

Many years later, Mrs. Payjack answered the door to find another stranger standing on the veranda. The smiling man greeted her and asked to see her husband. The middle-aged woman shook her head sadly and told him that her husband had passed away some years ago. To her surprise, the man began to weep. Regaining his composure, the caller reminded her of a Christmas Day many years before, and of her husband's generosity towards a hungry, homeless young hobo who had been riding the rods.

During the years he had spent struggling up from poverty, the boy had never forgotten that unhesitating gesture of goodwill on that long-ago Christmas Day. Now, he had returned to say thank you. Not knowing what else to do, he pulled some money from his wallet and offered it to Mrs. Payjack. She thanked him for the offer but refused to accept it.

"That's the way my husband would want it to be," she explained.

Nodding, the young man thanked her and said a final goodbye. The Payjacks never saw him again. Except, of course, in their memories when they thought about that Christmas when a homeless young man shared their Christmas dinner.

British Columbia

C hristmas is a time for decorating trees, singing carols, enjoying feasts, and exchanging gifts. But more important, it's a time to cherish our loved ones and express good will towards others. It is a time for generosity and thankfulness. Over the years, countless British Columbians at home and overseas have done what they can to spread the spirit of the season — even during times of poverty and war.

The Worthless Mine

Newspaperman David W. Higgins knew well the symptoms of gold fever. The Halifax native had lived in San Francisco during the California rush and came north with the first prospectors in 1858. He ran a store and express office at Yale, where, at the head of the Fraser River, steamboats disgorged thousands of hopeful prospectors. By 1860, he was back in Victoria and working for Amor de Cosmos at the *Colonist* newspaper.

On Christmas Eve day, working frantically on the next edition of the paper, Higgins was interrupted by a visitor to the office. It was obvious the attractive young woman was in desperate straits. She was from California and things had not gone well. The woman — Miss Forbes — had written a poem. Could the *Colonist* publish it? One look told Higgins that it wasn't worth inserting into the newspaper, but he didn't have the heart to tell her so.

The next day, Christmas Day, while walking back to his office with an acquaintance by the name of George Barclay (who, like Higgins, was living at the Hotel de France), the newspaperman saw Miss Forbes lingering at the office. She asked if he had decided to publish her poem. He had not and would not, and so he put her off again. As she walked away, Barclay confided to Higgins that he loved the woman and had actually proposed marriage to her when they lived in Grass Valley, California. Things had gone badly; their mine had proved worthless. Recently, Barclay had visited her at the cottage where she lived with her parents and brother and had kindly offered her money. The offer failed to impress either father or daughter, and she had dismissed him.

Barclay reached into his pocket, handed Higgins a $20 gold piece, and asked him to tell her it was in payment for her poem. Higgins did so, and Miss Forbes almost fainted at the sight of it. She would use it to buy Christmas dinner for her poverty-stricken family. Higgins offered to order dinner for her at the hotel and bring it to the cottage. Then he went further: he and Barclay were without family themselves, so he asked if they might join in the dinner. Miss Forbes consented, but, worried perhaps by her father's attitude, requested that Barclay arrive a little later, as if by accident.

Everything went as planned, and, as Higgins later wrote, a "real live, polite little Frenchman" from the hotel served a sumptuous meal, complete with claret and champagne. All in all, it was to be one of the most memorable Christmases in the lives of both men. Higgins and Barclay didn't get back to the hotel until midnight.

The very next day, Boxing Day, Barclay returned to the Forbes's squalid little cottage with a Christmas present none of the family expected. He had news from California: that worthless mine, it turned out, wasn't as barren as everyone had thought. The family was rich!

Soon after this discovery, Barclay proposed to Miss Forbes again. This time, the woman's answer, and her father's attitude, were different. Barclay returned to California with the Forbes family to start his life anew.

Comrades-In-Arms

Patriotic fervour was high at the start of World War I, and it got to Victoria newspaperman Archie Wills. An "energetic young buck," as he later described himself, Archie quit his job as marine editor at the *Times* and joined about 500 other "nice fellows" who were forming a battery in the Parliament buildings.

In May 1916, Archie and the other nice fellows of the 62nd Battery, including friend Percy Gilson, marched down through the crowds to Victoria's Inner Harbour, climbed up the gangway of the *Princess Charlotte* troopship, and sailed off to war.

In a scenario that would be repeated in the first years of World War II, the men were stationed in England for training, then more training, and still more training. "We were the best trained outfit you ever saw!" Wills laughed. For most of these men — some barely out of their teens — these were the first Christmases away from home.

As Christmas neared, mail was the tie that bound these homesick men to families and friends back home. Given wartime conditions, it was a tenuous tie at best.

"We had a lot of letters and the parcels came through pretty good, so we were pleased about that," Archie Wills recalled. "It was a question of when the mail would arrive, you know, shipping losses and all that, and I think there was some pilfering and some fellows would get them [the parcels] all bashed up, but I was very lucky. My wife sent me a two-pound box of Laura Secord chocolates ... every Saturday!" Thoughtfully, Mrs. Wills had chosen hard-centered chocolates to avoid mushing in the mail. Food, candy, and, of course, cigarettes were the most appreciated gifts from home.

"We used to smoke the darndest stuff over there," Wills remembered. "I think they swept it up off the floors of factories, so my parents used to send me a tin of Old Chum tobacco. You were thankful when the mail came. I was always receiving a great deal of stuff, but other fellows wouldn't get anything, so we'd split it up."

Aside from taking care of the horses — artillery batteries were horse-drawn — Christmas Day in England's Witley Camp was a pretty easy-going occasion. Upwards of 500 men sat down to a special Christmas dinner in the mess hall. On the printed menu, items were given their own military "flavour."

"We had all these different names for them; peas were 'shrapnel.' We started out with 'cordite,' which was celery; 'lyddite grenades,' that would be olives; 'limbergunner cheese'; well, the 'limbergunner' was the fellow that kept the gun in shape; 'number nine,' well, number nine was the 'opening medicine' they used to give you."

A Christmas Promise
The next year, Christmas was a far, far different affair for Wills, Gilson, and the others in the 62nd Battery of the Canadian Field Artillery. By December 1917, they and thousands of other Canadians were weary, battle-hardened veterans "somewhere in France."

"My gun crew ... we didn't have a very happy Christmas,"

Percy Gilson remembered. "Christmas morning, we were detailed to go up and take over a position." The position only had one gun, and so only Gilson's crew was ordered to the front. "It was bad timing," the veteran remembered sadly. There would be no Christmas dinner for Gilson, Wills, and the rest of the crew. The men were certainly ready to celebrate, and Percy remembered that Wills and others had done a little "Christmas shopping."

"I think — if I recall — Archie Wills and a few more went scavenging around and they were able to get a couple of pigs and a few bottles of wine."

"We were gonna lay one on," Wills said, smiling at the memory of it. "Old Wills had detailed a little raiding party... and we bought two pigs from some farmer. I took a wagon and two horses and a couple of men, and we scouted around the back areas. We bought some red wine and provisions ... special, so that it'd be a little different. We expected that since we were in a cushy spot that we'd be all right."

No such luck.

"I was a bit cheesed off because all the food is back there," Archie recalled. "They're going to have a party that night; Christmas dinner and it would be fairly good, and here we are, he [Percy Gilson] and I were walking down the road together."

"It was a very, very cold day," Gilson recalled, "and we had no more or less than just our little morning rations with us, which was a piece of bread and perhaps a tin of bully beef ... and we stopped on the road for a rest and I turned to Archie and I said, 'Archie, if we ever live through this, I will always phone you on Christmas Day and jack up your memory on it."

That promise, made that Christmas Day between two mud-splattered soldiers on the road to the front line, was kept faithfully every Christmas morning for over half a century. Unfortunately, neither one of the men needed to have their memories refreshed. The day was, sadly, memorable enough.

"Some say that Christmas Day was quiet and that all guns ceased," Percy Gilson said, shaking his head. "But that is not right."

Not then. During the very first Christmas on the front, three years before, there had been an informal camaraderie between opposing forces with scarcely a shot fired on Christmas Eve. Christmas Day, mud-splattered Germans and Canadians had lifted themselves out of their trenches and stood shaking hands and exchanging season's greetings in the middle of no-man's land.

But by 1917, things had changed. As Christmas neared, Canadians were recovering from the death and destruction of Passchendaele, an objective the British failed to take and then insisted the Canadians try, although there was no strategic advantage to be gained. The Canadians succeeded, but at a cost of 16,000 casualties. That Christmas the mood was much different than it had been in 1914.

"That day we got strafed very bad," Gilson recalled as he shook his head sadly. "We took over the gun position and started in right away in retaliation." Somewhere in the world during that winter of 1917, there was a feeling of peace and good will towards men, but not in Flander's fields.

A New Start

As many reminiscences make clear, Christmases were not always "merry and bright." For newcomers to Canada, for those returning home from war, and for those who were suffering economic deprivation, the emotionally charged and expectation-laden Christmas season was always an especially challenging time. However, resourceful, determined, and imaginative people rose to the challenge, over and over again.

Having survived World War I as a member of the Fifth Western Cavalry, Henry Copeland sat on the train and contemplated his future. What future? Henry had sold his farm in Paton, Saskatchewan, before he left Canada to go overseas.

"I didn't know whether I was coming back or not," he later joked.

Well, now he was back. In October 1919, he and his wife stepped off the train in Manitoba to visit his sister. The visit was a great excuse, and the couple had a place to stay for free, but the real reason for the trip was to allow Henry to assess prospects for starting over again. But timing, they say, is everything. Farms were already in the grip of winter.

The memories came flooding back, and not all of them were pleasant. Henry shook his head.

"I'm not staying down here," he told the women. "I'm getting the heck out of this country. I'm going up to Vancouver."

Once in Vancouver, Henry thought his luck had turned. Just by chance, he ran into an officer he had known in France. When Henry mentioned he was a man searching for a new start and a new place, his wartime acquaintance mentioned that he knew of a farm that had just foreclosed. That was interesting news, but the former army officer also had a tip: Henry could probably buy it under the federal government's new "Returned Soldiers" program. The farm was located near Notch Hill, east of Kamloops.

"It was 20 acres cleared and there was a house on it. And the house was what I was after. Some place to live."

The deal was made and the Copelands moved in just before Christmas. Before long, they had a visitor. A representative of the Soldiers' Settlement Board paid a call. It wasn't a benevolent gesture. The government man's mission was to assess the Copelands' financial situation. Under the scheme, the Board could claim 50 percent of the farm's profit. Henry knew why the man was there, and he simply told him that he would just stop earning any money altogether.

The representative nodded. He was a veteran, too, like Henry. He was sympathetic. "And he says, 'I haven't seen anything, I don't know anything', and that was that." The man's understanding was probably the best Christmas present the Copelands could have asked for.

"We just celebrated ourselves," he recalled. "We didn't know anybody." The present was bleak, but it was the future they concentrated on. "We were looking forward to spring, you know, and getting something going. And we did. I got some cows and chickens," Henry reminisced years later.

Over time, Henry and his wife made friends with others in the area, including World War I veterans like himself. A few years after they first settled in Notch Hill, when they got together with neighbours for Christmas, one of the dinner guests was an old Scotsman who made smooth, potent cider, and sold it for a dollar a gallon. After Christmas dinner, out came the cards — and the Scotsman's jug. As the night progressed the jug became lighter and lighter.

"Well, there's not much left, we might as well finish it," the Scotsman said. Henry remembered well what happened next.

"So, when he tilted the jug, out fell a mouse. No hair on it! All raw," Henry laughed many years later. "We'd been drinking that all the way through Christmas ... but nobody got sick." Still, Henry added, "I never drank cider out of a brown jug again."

A Christmas lesson learned and never forgotten!

Select Bibiliography

Atlantic Canada

Campbell, Sabine, ed. *Home for Christmas: Stories from the Maritimes & Newfoundland.* Fredericton: Goose Lane Editions, 1999.

Galgay, Frank and Michael McCarthy, eds. *A Christmas Box.* St. John's: Harry Cuff Publications Ltd., 1998.

McCarthy, Mike and Alice Lannon, eds. *Yuletide Yarns: Stories of Newfoundland and Labrador Christmases Gone By.* St. John's: Creative Press, 2002.

Weale, David. *An Island Christmas Reader.* Charlottetown: Acorn Press, 1994.

Quebec

Aubry, Claude. *The Magic Fiddler and Other Legends of French Canada.* Toronto: Peter Martin Associates Ltd., 1968.

Lamothe, Jacques. *Le Folklore du Temps des Fêtes.* Montréal: Guérin, 1982.

Select Bibliography

Lemay, L.P. *Fêtes et Corvées*. Lévis: Pierre-Georges Roy, 1898.

Provencher, Jean. *Les Quatres Saisons dans la Vallée du Saint-Laurent*. Montréal: Éditions Boréal, 1988.

Ontario

Christmas in Upper Canada and Canada West: Customs and Practices (typescript). The Ted Brown Room, Niagara South Board of Education, St. Johns Outdoor Studies Centre, c. 1976. Located at Niagara Falls Public Library.

Coffin, Tristram Potter. *The Book of Christmas Folklore*. New York: Seabury Press, 1973

Crean, Patrick, editor. *The Fitzhenry & Whiteside Fireside Book of Canadian Christmas*. Toronto: Fitzhenry & Whiteside, 1986.

Knowles, Kathleen M. *To Honour the Holiday: Canadian Christmases Past*. St. John's: Creative Publishers, 1988.

The Prairies

Charyk, John C. *The Biggest Day Of The Year*. Saskatoon: Western Producer Prairie Books, 1985.

Dempsey, Hugh. A. *Christmas In The West*. Saskatoon: Western Producer Prairie Books, 1982.

Hayter, Ron. "Cornerstones of Christmas." *Saskatoon Star Phoenix*, Dec. 23, 1972.

British Columbia

Adams, John. "Christmas In Old Victoria." *Discover The Past,* 2003.

Mole, Richard. *Seasons Greetings From British Columbia's Past.* Victoria: Provincial Archives of British Columbia, 1980.